PIERS PLOWMAN

LONGMAN MEDIEVAL AND RENAISSANCE LIBRARY

General Editors:
CHARLOTTE BREWER, All Souls College, Oxford
N. H. KEEBLE, University of Stirling

Published Titles:
Piers Plowman: An Introduction to the B-Text
James Simpson

James Simpson

PIERS PLOWMAN
An Introduction to the
B-text

LONGMAN
LONDON AND NEW YORK

Longman Group UK Limited,
Longman House, Burnt Mill, Harlow,
Essex CM20 2JE, England
and Associated Companies throughout the world.

Published in the United States of America
by Longman Inc., New York

© Longman Group UK Limited 1990

First published 1990

British Library Cataloguing in Publication Data
Simpson, James, 1954–
   Piers Plowman: an introduction to the B-text. –
   (Longman medieval and renaissance library).
   1. Poetry in English. Langland, William. Piers
   Plowman. Critical studies
   I. Title
   821'.1

ISBN 0-582-01392-5 CSD
ISBN 0-582-01391-7 PPR

Library of Congress Cataloging in Publication Data
Simpson, James, 1954–
   Piers Plowman: an introduction to the B-text / James Simpson.
      p.   cm. – (Longman medieval and Renaissance library)
   Bibliography: p.
   Includes index.
   ISBN 0-582-01392-5. – ISBN 0-582-01391-7 (pbk.)
   1. Langland, William, 1330?–1400? Piers the Plowman. 2. Justice
in literature. 3. Mercy in literature. I. Title. II. Series.
PR2017.L38S56   1990   89–34272
821'.1 – dc20   CIP

Set in Linotron 202 10/12 pt Bambo

Produced by Longman Singapore Publishers (Pte) Ltd.
Printed in Singapore

Contents

Preface

The main aim of this book is to convince undergraduate readers of *Piers Plowman*'s centrality in any account of the literary and cultural history of the later English Middle Ages. I seek to do this by trying to demonstrate how the poem, despite being deeply anchored in a conservative literary, ecclesiastical and social culture, in fact questions that culture in moving towards positions of doubt and dissent, and in reimagining social and religious institutions.

I argue that Langland consistently develops one theme throughout the poem, that of the relations between justice and mercy. In following this theme, certain psychological, institutional, and literary changes become necessary: broadly speaking, the poem moves away from a rational to an affective approach to problems; from a hierarchical to a more horizontal sense of ecclesiastical and social institutions; and from authoritarian, 'closed' literary forms to more exploratory and open-ended procedures.

I seek meaning in the poem less out of the development of 'character', than out of the relationship of different genres of writing which constitute the poem. I do this not because the notions of 'character' and personhood are irrelevant in this work; on the contrary, I will argue that the narrative structure of the poem is shaped out of Langland's conception of what it is to be a person. But exclusive focus on the personal development of Will seems to me to eclipse Langland's interest in corporate institutions, and in the ways in which individuals and institutions intersect. In trying to encompass both Langland's sense of the self, and his sense of institutions, my approach has been to begin with the formal, textual choices Langland has made, and to work out from there to his sense both of institutions and the self.

The argument will take into serious account Langland's theology, his idea of the Church as an institution, and, in a broad sense, his politics. But I will also try to make sense of the formal qualities of the work, by showing how ecclesiastical and political attachments are written into the formal choices Langland makes – how, that is, the formal characteristics of the poem have historical significance. The questions I will consistently ask of the poem (though in no consistent order) are these: What genre is being practised here? What claims to authority does such a genre make? What aspect of the self does it appeal to? What social or ecclesiastical institution is it produced by and does it support? And, finally, in what ways are authoritative genres (what I call 'discourses') found by Langland to be inadequate?

I aim to address the argument of the book to readers who might have no previous experience of medieval culture; a secondary function of the book is, therefore, to provide brief expositions of any relevant backgrounds which need to be understood before an understanding of Langland's enterprise is possible.

In writing a book of this kind, I have quite deliberately tried to incorporate what strikes me as the best scholarly work on different areas of the poem, both in terms of my argument and the expository background necessary for its comprehension. To the very many scholars whose work I use in this way, I am much indebted, and I shall try to register each of these debts in the footnotes. My indebtedness to my former teachers, George Russell in Melbourne and Carl Schmidt in Oxford, is of a different magnitude, and one that I warmly acknowledge here. I should also like to mention the inspiration of my friend Steven Clingman, who, while working in an entirely different field, provided me with a model of sorts. I am indebted to the General Editor, Charlotte Brewer, and to my colleague Julia Boffey for many helpful suggestions; all my former colleagues in the English Department at Westfield College, University of London, deserve many thanks for providing a co-operative environment under the sometimes difficult institutional conditions of the University of London.

The bibliographical policy of the book is designed largely with an undergraduate or college student readership in mind: in the footnotes and references running through each chapter I cite the relevant sources (primary or secondary) upon which my own argument may be based, or, in the case of secondary material, which have treated a given problem authoritatively (though I do not try to incorporate the scholarly history of particular issues). I hope the necessity of acknowledging indebtedness will not daunt the undergraduate reader with the impression of many more secondary works which must be read: of course I would like to stimulate students to read more about the poem, but I also hope to provide an introduction to the work which is self-contained.

Each chapter is introduced with a sketch of the 'argument' of the poem; these are intended merely as memory refreshers for the reader coping with a poem whose 'plot' is not always easy to keep clear in the mind. Inevitably much is sacrificed in such bare accounts. I italicise the names of main actants on their first appearance.

Many of the glosses provided are reproduced from Schmidt (1987a). The square brackets used in the citations are reproduced from Schmidt, and indicate 'readings adopted from the A and C versions of the poem, and for reconstructed or conjectural readings' (Schmidt 1987a, p. xl).

The Publishers are grateful to J. M. Dent & Sons Ltd for permission to quote extensively from *The Vision of Piers Plowman: A Complete Edition of the B-Text* (1987), edited by A. V. C. Schmidt.

This little book is dedicated with affection and gratitude to my parents

Introduction

THE POEM AND ITS AUTHOR

Pier Plowman was one of the most widely read medieval poems from the time of its composition until at least the early Elizabethan period. Fifty-two manuscripts of the poem survive (excluding fragments), which compares well with the number of surviving manuscripts of, say, *The Canterbury Tales* (eighty-two), and Gower's *Confessio Amantis* (forty-nine), and suggests a much wider audience than existed for texts which stand high in modern estimation, like *Sir Gawain and the Green Knight*, of which a single manuscript survives. The early establishment of the manuscript tradition of the poem (fifteen manuscript survive from before *c.* 1400) attests to its wide and immediate currency in the late fourteenth century (Fisher 1988, 269; Kane 1988b, 186); most of the surviving manuscripts derive from the fifteenth century; and three manuscripts survive from the first half of the sixteenth century. In 1550 the London printer Robert Crowley printed the poem, reprinting it twice in the same year, and it was reprinted again by Owen Rogers in 1561.[1]

A very early fifteenth-century note in a manuscript of the C-Text, Trinity College, Dublin MS D. 4.1, ascribes the poem to 'Willielm[us] de Langlond', and there is no necessary reason to doubt the veracity of this ascription. The Christian name 'William' is corroborated by the references within the text to the narrator (who is represented as a poet) as 'Will'; and there is possible corroboration for the whole name in the line at B. XV. 152, "'I have lyved in londe,'" quod I, "my name is Longe Wille'",

---

1. For a full list of manuscripts and printed editions, see Middleton (1986, 2420–3).

if we read it as a cryptogram (for which there is conventional support from the practice of other poets).[2]

Unlike Chaucer, independently known as a court official in his own right, very little is known of Langland. The early manuscript ascription of the poem to him tells us that his father was 'Stacy de Rokayle', that he (the father) was both 'of gentle birth' (*generosus*), and that he 'lived in Shypton-under-Wychwood, a tenant of the Lord Spenser in the County of Oxfordshire' (Kane 1965, 26). This information, if correct, tells us more about the father than the son. The most extended knowledge we have of Langland the man comes from passages in the poem itself which can be called 'biographical'. Of course such passages must be treated with caution as direct evidence for biography, for they are not unmediated by convention or theme; there is no necessary reason, however, why conventional and thematic presentations of the self should not at the same time be genuinely biographical in some respects.

In all the 'biograpical' passages the narrator presents himself as a marginal and self-doubting figure: he is represented as a false hermit (B. I. 1–4); a lazy, poor and time-wasting cleric in minor orders (C. V. 1–108); a time-wasting poet (B. XII. 1–28), and as a marginal figure without resources (B. XX. 1–50). All these images are related to important themes in *Piers Plowman* (e.g. mendicancy and the role of poetry), and it could be argued that Langland uses his own *persona* as a negative example of these themes; but it is at least possible that these representations are at the same time historically accurate in some respects.

The most extended biographical passage of the poem in particular (C. V. 1–108),[3] is at once a partly conventional (based as it is on both legislative and literary conventions), and a plausible account of Langland's biography. The figure Reason accosts the narrator in harvest time, as he lives in Cornhill with his wife among idlers; he asks Will whether he can do agricultural work, or whether he has lands and noble lineage which provide him with sustenance, or whether he is physically maimed in such a way as to excuse him from work (C. V. 1–35). These categories

---

2. The points made here are drawn from the argument of Kane (1965, Chs 3 and 4).

3. All citations from, and references to, the C version of the poem are to the edition of Pearsall (1978). Letter forms have been modernised.

are modelled on legislative topoi, drawn as they are from the Statutes of Labourers of 1349 and 1351. The first of these statutes,
for example, says that because of the shortage of labour caused
by the plague, there are some who will not work unless they
receive excessive wages, and 'some rather willing to beg in Idle-
ness, than by Labour to get their Living'. It ordains that every
man and women, 'of what condition he be, free or bond, able in
body . . . not living in Merchandize, nor exercising any Craft,
nor having of his own whereof he may live, nor proper Land
. . . be required to serve'.[4]

If these statutes provide the legislative conventions by which
Langland represents himself, Will's self-defence which follows is
indebted to certain satirical literary traditions: he says that he was
put to 'scole' by his father and relations ('My fader and my
frendes'), and that since his benefactors died he has practised the
trade of living by the 'tools' of his prayer book, saying prayers
for the souls of those who feed him; this description is not unlike
that of Chaucer's portrait of the poor, unbeneficed Clerk:

> But al that he myghte of his freendes hente,
> On bookes and on lernynge he it spente,
> And bisily gan for the soules preye
> Of hem that yaf hym wherwith to scoleye.
> (Canterbury Tales, Gen. Prol. 299–302)[5]
> hente: get; scoleye: to attend school.

The reference to living in London also recalls satirical traditions
against provincial clerics moving to London for financial gain,
found in both the portrait of the Parson in the General Prologue
(ll. 507–11), and in Langland's own Prologue (B-Text, ll. 83–6).[6]

But however much the passage is framed within certain legislative and literary conventions, it remains possible to read it as
an account of Langland's own life. If we were to take this as a
portrait of Langland, nothing the poem implies about its author
contradicts what is said here, and much supports it: the author
was clearly a provincial man – his dialect can be localised to South
West Worcestershire (squaring with Malvern referred to in the

4. Anno 23 Edw. III AD 1349 (Statutes of the Realm I. 307).
5. All citations from, and references to, the works of Chaucer are from The
   Riverside Chaucer (Benson 1988).
6. All citations from the B version of the poem are from the edition of Schmidt
   (1987a).

poem) (Samuels 1985), familiar with life in London; the poem is clearly written by someone with an academic training, and with a deep familiarity with both the Bible and the liturgy. And from outside the poem, literary practice of the period provides other examples of satirical portraits of poet figures, who are, nevertheless, unmistakably modelled on what can be verified as the poet's historical person. This is true of Chaucer's portrait of the poet 'Geffrey' in *The House of Fame*, for example, and of Hoccleve's portraits of his narrator as an impecunious, mentally disturbed clerk at the office of the Privy Seal. Langland, then, seems to have been educated near Malvern (named in l. 5 of the Prologue), come to London as a married cleric in minor orders, and lived in the London district of Cornhill where he gained a meagre sustenance by singing for the souls of his benefactors.[7] It seems probable, from the dialectal evidence of the C manuscripts, that he moved back to Malvern in later life (Samuels 1985, 56). Approximate dates for his birth and death are 1330 and 1387.

If Langland's delicate self-portrait is that of an idler, another quasi-biographical passage in Passus XII of the B-Text tells us how he spends his time; the figure Imaginatif accuses Will of wasting his time by 'meddling' with his 'makynges' (i.e. his poetry), while he should be praying for the souls of those who provide him with food. The hint here that Langland was completely immersed in his poetry, and his one poem, is overwhelmingly supported by the evidence of the manuscripts, which attest to the existence of at least three, possibly four, separate versions of the poem, each with its own identity. These are now known as the A-Text (approx. 2500 lines), the B-Text (approx. 7200 lines), and the C-Text (just slightly longer than the B version, with some major structural changes, and hundreds of minor revisions). Recent scholarship has argued for the existence of a fourth version, prior to A, B, and C, which has been called the Z-Text, after the manuscript siglum by which it has been known (Rigg and Brewer 1983). If we accept Professor Kane's powerful argument for the identity of authorship of the A, B, and C versions (Kane 1965), then it seems that Langland spent at least

---

7. The best account of Langland's profession remains that of Donaldson (1949, Ch. 7). See also Bowers (1986, Ch. 7) and Courtenay (1987, 91–106) for intellectual life in fourteenth-century London. This reference has potential relevance to Langland's biography.

twenty years, between *c.* 1367 and *c.* 1385 (the putative dates of the
A- and C-Texts respectively) constantly revising his single poem,
his 'werkes . . . Of peres the plowman and mechel puple also'
(A. XII. 101–2).[8]

The date of the B-Text is between 1377 and 1379. This is the
text which will be discussed in this book, mainly because it is,
in the view of most scholars, the most imaginatively powerful
version. It is also available in an accessible edition of the poem,
that of A. V. C. Schmidt (1987a).

LANGLAND'S IMMEDIATE POETIC CONTEXT

Piers Plowman is written in an alliterative metre, and a few intro-
ductory words should be said about the literary context – that of
the so-called 'Alliterative Revival' – in which we might think of
placing the poem. In the brief discussion of this context which
follows, however, I should also like to sketch the ways in which
Langland's poem is unable to be categorised within the literary
frame of the alliterative tradition (or, incidentally, within the
frame of much contemporary poetry outside the alliterative
tradition). Langland seems to me to observe neither the social nor
the literary decorum which pertains in most other poems of the
revival; given this we are obliged to borrow or devise some terms
of textual analysis which are not specific to the analysis of literary
texts. It is for this reason I introduce the term 'discourse' in the
next section of this chapter.

From the middle of the fourteenth century in England, a wide
range of poetry was produced in an alliterative metre. There
survive, for example, the historical narratives *The Gests of Alexander, Alexander and Dindimus, The Wars of Alexander, The
Destruction of Troy, The Siege of Jerusalem,* and the *Alliterative Morte
Arthure*; the recastings of biblical narrative *Patience* and *Cleaness*;
the works of spiritual and moral instruction *Pearl, The Parlement
of the Three Ages, St Erkenwald* and *Death and Life*; the romance
Sir Gawain and the Green Knight; and a series of satirical works,
Winner and Waster (probably written before the first version of Langland's poem), *Richard the Redeless, Mum and the Sothsegger,* and

8. All citations from and references to the A version of the poem will be from
   the edition of Kane (1988a). For discussion of the text of all three versions,
   see Kane (1988b).

Pierce Plowman's Crede (all three of which are clearly indebted to *Piers Plowman*).[9]

Leaving aside the works which might be said to belong to the '*Piers Plowman* tradition' (*Richard the Redeless, Mum and the Sothsegger*, and *Pierce Plowman's Crede*), we can see how all these other works, despite their many differences of genre, clearly accept a kind of contract with their audience to satisfy expectations of a specifically literary kind. They imply an audience's shared expectations and assumptions both by working securely within a given genre, and by drawing upon the resources of a relatively closed poetic diction (Turville-Petre 1977, Ch. 4). The Prologue to one of these Western, alliterative poems, *The Wars of Alexander*, reveals the kind of intimate literary and social world implied by many alliterative texts:[10]

> When folk ere festid and fed . fayn wald thai here
> Sum farand thing efter fode . to fayn thare hert,
> Or thai ware fourmed on fold . or thaire fadirs other.
> Sum is leue to lythe . the lesing of Sayntis,
> That lete ther lifis be lorne . for oure lordis sake;
> And sum has langing of lufe . lays to herken,
> How ledis for thaire lemmans . has langor endured.
> Sum couettis & has comforth . to carpe & to lestyn
> Of curtaissy of knyghthode . of craftis of armys,
> Of kyngis at has conquirid . & over-comyn landis.
> Sum of wirschip I-wis . slike as tham wyse lattis,
> And sum of wanton werkis . tha that ere wild-hedid
> . . .
> And I forthwith yow all . ettillis to schewe
> Of ane Emperoure the aghefullest . that ever armys hauntid,
> That was the athill Alexsandire . as the buke tellis
> . . .
> I sall rehers, & ye will, renkis . rekyn your tongis,
> A remnant of his rialte . & rist quen vs likis.
>
> *farand*: suitable; *fayn*: please; *fold*: earth; *lythe*: listen; *lesing*: (?)legends; *lorne*: lost; *lemmans*: lovers; *carpe*: speak; *slike*: such; *lattis*: consider; *ettillis*: intend; *aghefullest*: most terrible; *hauntid*: practised; *athill*: noble.

Whether or not this five-and-a-half-thousand-line text was in fact performed as after-dinner entertainment, the poet in any case

---

9. For an account of the revival, see Turville-Petre (1977), and Lawton (1982).
10. Ed. Skeat (1886). Letter forms have been modernised.

evokes a world to which minstrel and audience both belong, and signals to his audience that what they are about to read to hear is designed for entertainment. The minstrel clearly sees his own role as one of satisfying an audience's demand, rather than forcing them in any way to listen to matter which he decides they *should* hear; or at least that is what the poet encourages his audience to believe in this opening move to capture their goodwill: he repeatedly stresses that an audience is 'leue' to listen, or, more emphatically, that in some cases it 'has langing' to hear entertainment of certain kinds. The address of the minstrel to his audience is a courteous one: he gestures towards his listeners' generosity in allowing him to speak in the first place, and in being able to decide, with the minstrel, when they want to pause:

> I sall rehers, and ye will, renkis . reykn your tongis,
> A remnant of his rialte . & rist quen vs likis.

If the narrator of *The Wars of Alexander* implies a social decorum pertaining to himself and his audience, it is also clear that there exists a literary decorum which is shared by both minstrel and audience, at least in the matter of genre: here in this secular context (apparently a lord's hall), there is clearly a wide range of genres from which a poet can choose; the matter is on the whole secular, but also religious, and it offers a fair, if not a complete summary of the range of literary types we find represented individually by many of the alliterative works mentioned earlier, and, one might add, of the range of genres we find represented in the *Canterbury Tales:* he mentions what we might call the saint's life, courtly romance (of different kinds), historical romance, and fabliau.

This intimacy of relation between minstrel and audience, defined by both a social and a literary decorum, is altogether missing from the Prologue to *Piers Plowman*. At the very beginning of his poem, Langland deflates the 'literariness' of the conventions he gestures at adopting; the opening sequence promises the marvellous staple of romance literature: the narrator says he went wide in the world to hear 'wondres'; before he sleeps he says that a 'ferly' befell him, which seemed to come from 'Fairye', or the land of enchantment; and in his sleep, he says that he dreamed a 'merveillous swevene'. Many other alliterative poems lay stress on the marvellousness of the events they describe: the poet of *Sir Gawain and the Green Knight*, for example, introduces his marvellous matter by saying about Britain that

> Mo ferlyes on this folde han fallen here oft
> Then in any other that I wot, syn that ilk tyme,
>
> (ll. 23–4)[11]
>
> *ferlynes*: marvels; *folde*: land; *ilk*: very.

and he says that Arthur will not sit down at Christmas until he has heard 'sum mayn meruayle' (l. 94); and in *Pearl* the narrator says about his dream that he is transported through God's grace 'In auenture ther meruayles meuen' (l. 64).[12]) In both these instances the poet devotes the full resources of his rich and specialised alliterative vocabulary to describing what are indeed 'meruayles', and, in the case of *Gawain* at least, a convincing 'ferlye'. But the promise of such a world in *Piers Plowman* is quickly undermined: the world with which we are presented here is far from being any 'ferly', or other world; it is neither marvellous in the sense that the events of both *Sir Gawain and the Green Knight* and *Pearl* are, nor is it concerned with events that happened before the audience were 'fourmed on fold. or thaire fadirs other', as the minstrel of *The Wars of Alexander* says; instead, it treats the energetic, teeming world of contemporary life:

> Some putten hem to the plough, pleiden ful selde,
> In settynge and sowynge swonken ful harde,
> And wonnen that thise wastours with glotonye destruyeth.
>
> (Prol. 20–2)

This sobering deflation of specifically literary expectations suggests a distance between Langland and the kind of relaxed minstrel voice of the Prologue to *The Wars of Alexander*. In Langland's poem there is no apparent entry into the walled, enclosed space of literary play, with its attendant, if provisional, immunities.

Langland not only detaches himself from more specifically literary traditions in his initial marking of genre; his detachment is also apparent in his stylistic decisions, in matters of both diction and versification. It is not possible to characterise the style of the whole poem with a single description – part of the enterprise of this book will be, indeed, to account for the many changes of

---

11. Ed. Davis (1967). Letter forms have been modernised.
12. Ed. Gordon (1953). Letter forms have been modernised.

style which occur in the poem. We are, nevertheless, able to say that in matters of diction and versification *Piers Plowman* is markedly different from the bulk of surviving alliterative verse. The formally elaborate group of alliterative texts, known as the 'formal group' (Lawton 1982), draw on a relatively closed vocabulary, specific to alliterative poetry; metrically they observe a basic pattern of alliteration aa/ax, where 'a' represents an alliterated, stressed syllable (a 'full stave'), '/' represents a caesura, and 'x' represents a stressed, but unalliterated syllable (a 'blank stave'). Within each half line ('verse'), the unstressed syllables ('dips') can stand in different relations to the stressed, and thus create different rhythms within each verse, but in the formal corpus, rhythm serves to highlight the metre (i.e. there is minimum competition between stress and alliteration); finally, each verse normally contains a clear syntactic unit. The passage cited from the *Wars of Alexander* above may serve as an example of the formal corpus on each one of these counts (diction, metre, rhythm, syntax), with two examples of an extended metre, aaa/ax; we can see this by citing a few lines, where the italicised words are found only in the alliterative corpus:

> And sum has lánging of lúfe . láys to hérken,   (aa/ax)
> How *lédis* for thaire lémmans . has lángor endúred.   (aa/ax)
> Sum cóuettis & has cómforth to *cárpe* and to léstyn. . .   (aa/as)

Langland differs from the practice of poets in the formal corpus on each of these points: he hardly draws at all on the vocabulary specific to alliterative poetry; he offers a much wider range of metrical possibilities than the the aa/ax group – even taking into account variations on the aa/ax pattern in the formal corpus (Duggan 1987, 43); in Langland's poetry there is a much higher frequency of lines in which rhythm (the pattern of stresses within each half line) competes with metre (the pattern of alliteration), producing 'modulation' (Kane 1981; Lawton 1988); and in *Piers Plowman* there is a higher incidence of enjambement, or lines in which the pressure of the syntax overbears the boundary of metre and carries the rhythm of one line into the next.[13] The net effect

---

13. For technical discussions of Langland's metre especially, see Lawton (1988), Schmidt (1987b, Ch. 2), and Duggan (1987), the last two of whom are divided as to the rules which govern Langland's metre. Much more attention needs to be paid to Langland's diction, but such work is hampered without a concordance.

of these differences is to create a more flexible, informal medium, which is at the same time consistently patterned, and by no means prohibited from the great expressive power of the more formal corpus.

There are various possible explanations for the differences in Langland's style: (i) Langland came from the South West Midlands, whereas the more mannered texts have their provenance in the North West Midlands and the North; (ii) perhaps Langland's text was written before the development of a fully fledged alliterative style; (iii) Langland was writing in London, and writing for a national audience, unlike other alliterative poets who were writing for a more localised audience; (iv) the sheer scope and variety of subject matter of the poem demanded a more flexible medium; and finally (v), it could be argued that Langland chose not to adopt the mannered style because he felt distanced from the courtly and leisured assumptions behind such a style.

These arguments are not all each exclusive of the other, and the third, that Langland was writing in London for a national audience, seems to me the most important factor in any account of his diction. Southerners certainly did register the strangeness of alliterative poetry: the reason Chaucer's Parson gives for being unable to alliterate (to '"rum, ram, ruf", by lettre', as he says (X. 43) is that he is 'a Southren man'; and Chaucer himself draws upon the mannered, expressionistic alliterative style only on exceptional occasions. Langland's poetry is less regionally restricted than much alliterative poetry. And point (iv), regarding the scope of his matter, must also be an important factor in the deliberate fashioning of a style capable of sustaining it. These points having been made, point (v) also merits consideration: whenever Langland aims at an imitation of the formal style, it is in contexts where he is clearly sceptical about its ideological assumptions. In Passus III, for example, the narrator describes the welcome Mede receives at the court of Westminster. The King orders a cleric to act as Mede's host:

> Curteisly the clerk thanne, as the Kyng highte,
> Took Mede by the myddel and [mente] hire into chambre.
> Ac ther was murthe and mynstralcie Mede to plese;
> That wonyeth at Westmynstre worshipeth hire alle.

Gentilliche with joye the justices somme
Busked hem to the bour ther the burde dwellede,
Conforted hyre kyndely by Clergies leve . . .

$$\text{(III. 9–15)}^{14}$$

highte: commanded; *mente*: led; *wonyeth*: dwell; *busked hem*: took
themselves quickly; *bour*: chamber; *burde*: damsel.

The diction especially of these lines creates their courtly effect: the
opening 'curteisly' marks the lexical set from which the words are
chosen: 'chambre', 'murthe and mynstralcie', 'worshipeth',
'gentilliche' and so on all reinforce each other as designating a
courtly ambience. The word 'burde' is largely restricted to alliterative texts in the late Middle English period, and Langland uses
it here presumably to evoke the courtly atmostphere characteristic
of many alliterative poems (Burrow 1957). The metre of the lines
conforms in each instance (with the emendation of l. 10) the aa/ax
pattern of the formal corpus, and in no case do the patterns of
rhythm interfere with the metrical pattern; the one instance of
enjambement (l. 13) serves to evoke the swiftness of the justices
to receive Mede, but this effect is quickly reined in by the end
stopping of l. 14. The syntax serves the formality of metre and
diction; the use of adverbs in prominent positions in particular
serves to create the courtly emphasis on manner ('curteisly',
'gentilliche', 'kyndely').
There is a comparable scene in *The Destruction of Troy*, where
Helen is welcomed into Troy by Priam:

And er thai comyn to courte this cumpany faire,
Priam full prudly with mony pert knightes,
To welcom to that worthy went on there gate,
And fonget full feire all hir fre buernes.
To the lady, that lege kyng, with a light wille,
Past full pertly all with prise wordys;

14. I have emended the line 'Took Mede by the myddel and broughte hire into
    chambre', as it reads in both Schmidt (1987a) and Kane and Donaldson (1975).
    As it stands in the two editions just mentioned (aa/xy), the line conforms to no
    metrical pattern. MS F reads 'mente' at this point, which makes sense (from
    'menen', MED v. (4), 'to direct (one's horse), guide', from OF *mener*, 'to lead,
    guide'), Langland would be unlikely to write the line as it stands, particularly
    so in this formal context. 'Mente' is certainly a harder reading. Kane (1988a)
    remarks that he would definitely amend this line thus (461).

Obeit that bright all with blithe chere;
With worship & wyn welcomyt the grete;
And somyn to the Cite softly thai rode.

(ll. 3423–31)[15]

pert: valiant; gate: way; fonget: received; buernes: men; pertly: quickly; prise: choice; obeit: obeyed; bright: beautiful woman; wyn: joy; somyn: together.

Like the passage describing Mede's welcome to Westminster, this passage evokes a courtly world through its style: the vocabulary itself consists of 'prise wordys'; metre, rhythm and syntax all conspire to create a stately effect; in particular the density of adverbs and adverbial phrases creates the same emphasis on manner in this courtly ambience as the adverbs in the Langland passage. And a few lines further on the people of Troy are said to welcome Helen 'with myrthes of mynstralsy' (l. 3436), the tag characteristic of alliterative verse which we also find in the welcome of Mede (l. 11). But if this poet evokes a courtly ambience through his style, he does so without any satiric purpose towards the style itself. In the Langland passage, on the other hand, the style is subverted by the sense of the action: it is the allegorical figure Mede, representing reward beyond desert, who is being welcomed here; the action of courteously 'receiving' her resolves neatly and surgically into an image of clerics and judges receiving bribes. But the satire of these lines is directed not only at the social phenomenon they represent: the passage also satirises the bland, unquestioning courtly style characteristic of so much alliterative verse, since that style here is the polite cover for corruption. The institutional bases of the style, that is, are brought to the surface of the narrative, and because they are corrupt, seem to prohibit any extended use of the style.

And if Langland detaches himself from the literary decorum of the alliterative tradition in matters of both genre and style, so too does he fail to create any sense of a social decorum which pertains between himself and his audience. The speaker is pictured not as a member of a community with shared assumptions, but rather as an ambiguous and alienated figure, dressed in disguise and wandering:

15. Ed. Panton and Donaldson (1869). Letter forms have been modernised.

I shoop me into shroudes as I a sheep were,
In habite as an heremite unholy of werkes,
Wente wide in this world wondres to here.
                                    (Prol. 2–4)
  shroudes: garments; *sheep*: shepherd.

And unlike the many alliterative and non- alliterative poems
which signal themselves specifically as entertainment for the
amusement of an audience, and unlike Chaucer's *Canterbury Tales*,
which are spoken as entertainment, 'to shorte with oure weye'
(Gen. Prol. 791), Langland's verse is projected from a position of
moral urgency which precludes amusement, or which precludes
amusement of the standard literary kind, at any rate. It is true that
in the course of the poem Langland does seek to transform literary
entertainment into an extremely playful, intellectually stimulating,
spiritual 'solace', or entertainment; but he makes this transformation in the light of his awareness that most literary entertainment
is, in his view, a waste of time (it is characteristically figures like
Sloth who are pictured as being occupied by idle tales (V. 396.
407)). Unlike many poets of the period, who propose their work
as a way of passing time, Langland associates his kind of poetry
with the exploitation of time for spiritual purposes. This is
what is said about the best kind of activity in Passus IX, where
Langland possibly has in mind his own, personal ideal as a
poet:

[Tyn]ynge of tyme, Truthe woot the sooth,
Is moost yhated upon erthe of hem that ben in hevene;
And siththe to spille speche, that spire is of grace,
And Goddes gleman and a game of hevene.
Wolde nevere the feithful fader his fithele were untempred,
Ne his gleman a gedelyng, a goere to tavernes.
                                    (B. IX. 99–104)

  tynynge: wasting; *woot*: knows; *spille*: waste; *spire*: shoot, sprout/breath, *gleman*: minstrel; *fithele*: fiddle; *gedelyng*: wastrel.

And in the Prologue itself, this urgency is registered by the
historical frame in which Langland sees the field; the friars, for
example, are seen to be precipitating a state of crisis:

Sith charite hath ben chapman and chief to shryve lordes
Manye ferlies han fallen in a fewe yeres.

But Holy Chirche and hii holde bettre togidres
The mooste meschief on molde is mountynge up faste.
(Prol. 64–7)

sith: since; *chapman*: merchant; *ferlies*: marvels; *hii*: they; *molde*: earth.

This is the kind of 'ferly' which concerns Langland; it is not of a kind which occasions any familiar type of literary entertainment, as does the marvellous in many of the alliterative texts. Instead, the 'marvel' here is of an institutional kind, produced by disorder within the Church, and the discourses it provokes are, initially at any rate, those of the moralist and reformer.

'DISCOURSE'

It will be clear from the foregoing sketch of Langland's poetic context that *Piers Plowman* is projected from the margins of the literary world implied by the corpus of formally elaborate alliterative poems (and, it should be added, of many contemporary poems outside the alliterative tradition). Langland's poetry might be projected from the margins of literary discourses, but it is projected from the theoretical centre of different institutional discourses: where certain institutional ideologies might be *implied* by the setting of works of literature (e.g. the lord's hall evoked in the Prologue to the *Wars of Alexander*). Langland brings ideological, institutional attachments to the surface of his narrative, and explores the theoretical bases of those institutions: thus the main actants in the first vision, for example, are Holy Church and the King, representing the two fundamental institutions of Langland's age.[16] This is not to say that Langland is unconcerned either with poetry as a craft, or with the status of specifically poetic modes of apprehension; in fact he is deeply concerned both with the craft (Schmidt 1987b) and with the status of poetry. But this commitment to specifically poetic modes of apprehension is not a given in the poem; instead it becomes part of the poem's own subject, as other, institutional ways of saying things fail. For Langland's initial commitment in the poem is not to poetry as a self-justifying art; on the contrary, his commitment is rather to

16. I use the word 'actant' in this book simply to designate the generators of action in any given narrative; I use this neutral word to avoid the complications of personhood involved with words like 'actor', 'character', which may not be relevant to personification allegory.

the reformation of both social and ecclesiastical institutions, and his initial reliance is on genres of writing and speaking which ideally sustain these institutions.

A working assumption of this book, then, will be that Langland's poem cannot be understood within standard literary categories;[17] Langland is essentially concerned to transform institutions, and as such he often adopts the textual (or oral) forms of those institutions. These forms cannot readily be called 'literary' forms, since their presuppositions are distinct from those of a body of writing which may be described as 'literary' in Langland's England. The word 'genre' will serve to designate the formal characteristics of these textual forms, and I will continue to use it throughout this book. But in adopting such genres, Langland is exploiting or questioning the authority of those genres, and, thereby, exploiting or questioning the authority of the institution from which the genre derives. It is for this reason that I use the word 'discourse', since while denoting the formal characteristics of a way of writing or speaking in the way 'genre' does, the word 'discourse' also denotes (in a branch of contemporary theory, at least) the claims to power made by a given genre.[18] So the word 'discourse', as used in this book, will never denote anything less than the word 'genre' (i.e. the stylistic and structural characteristics of a given way of writing), but it will denote something more – the authoritative claims made by a given way of writing or speaking.

A word of caution should be added about the terms 'genre' and 'discourse' as applied to Langland's poem: Langland often merges recognisable genres in the one sequence of his poem (e.g. dream-vision and sermon in Passus I), often with the effect of creating poetry which is distinctively Langlandian, and beyond the reach of traditional generic categories. It remains true that the poem

17. For the problems of reading much medieval writing 'as literature', see Burrow (1982, 12–23).

18. The branch of 'contemporary' theory which defines the notion of 'discourse' and points to the claims to power made by different discourses, is that derived from the writing of Michel Foucault. Foucault's notion of discourse is more far reaching than the one I propose here, since he is concerned to define the underlying conceptual rules which govern 'forms of co-existence between statements' (Foucault 1972, 73). But this does involve questions of style (Foucault 1972, 33–4), and it certainly involves questions of power (particularly institutional power) which the use of a particular way of speaking raises (Foucault 1972, 50–2). See Lawton (1987) for a discussion of how the notion of discourse affects subjectivity in *Piers Plowman*.

is constituted by distinct blocks of kinds of writing, discussion of which requires formal analysis.[19]

SCHEMATIC STRUCTURE OF POEM

The poem has two structuring principles which are certainly authorial, that of the passus (from Latin *passus*, 'step', plural *passus*), and that of the vision. These two principles are related: on the whole, passus markers either coincide with the boundaries of visions, or else mark smaller thematic or narrative boundaries within larger visions. As my discussion of the poem is largely determined by the structure of the poem's visions, I offer here a schema of the eight visions of the B-Text (lines not indicated represent waking moments):

First Vision: Prologue 11 to Passus V. 3

Second Vision: Passus V. 8 to Passus VII. 140

Third Vision: Passus VIII. 68 to Passus XIII. 1
                  (including an inner-dream,
                  Passus XI. 5 to XI. 404

Fourth Vision: Passus XIII. 21 to Passus XIV. 332

Fifth Vision: Passus XV. 11 to Passus XVII. 353
                  (including an inner-dream,
                  Passus XVI. 20 to Passus XVI. 167)

Sixth Vision: Passus XVIII. 5 to Passus XVIII. 428

Seventh Vision: Passus XIX. 5 to Passus XIX. 485

Eighth Vision: Passus XX. 51 to Passus XX. 387.

19. See Bloomfield (1962, Ch. 1) for an account of the genres of *Piers Plowman*. The best overall attempt to read formal categories into the central meaning of *Piers Plowman* is Carruthers (1973); see also the interesting article by Justice (1988), where it is said that 'Langland's shifting generic commitments form the real plot of the *Visio*' (p. 292). This article was read after the completion of the present book.

Chapter 1

The First Vision:
Prologue and Passus I

PROLOGUE: the narrator recounts that he wandered in the world before falling asleep (ll. 1–10); he has a vision of a field, bounded by a castle and a 'dungeon' (ll. 11–19). On the field the dreamer sees a conspectus of occupational and moral types: ploughmen, wasters, contemplatives, merchants, minstrels, beggars, pilgrims, false hermits, friars, etc. (ll. 20–111). A king enters, led by Knighthood; a realm is established (ll. 112–22), followed by a short debate about the place of the king in relation to the law (ll. 123–45). The questions of kingship raised in this debate are played out in a fable of rats (ll. 146–210), before the vision returns to occupational types: lawyers, barons, burgesses, serfs, bakers, etc. (ll. 211–31).

PASSUS I: the narrator promises an explication of the previous vision (ll. 1–2); an authoritative figure descends from the castle, and declares that the castle is the locus of Truthe; she goes on to affirm the temperance required by Truthe, and to define the proper use of earthly wealth (ll. 3–57); she interprets the 'dongeon' (ll. 58–70), before declaring herself to be *Holy Church* (ll. 71–8). *Will* asks how he might save his soul, to which Holy Church replies by defining Truthe (ll. 79–137). Will asks about the source of truth in his own soul; Holy Church answers by affirming the soul's inherent knowledge of truth, and the complex relations of truth and love (ll. 138–209).

INTRODUCTION

The theme of Holy Church's sermon in Passus I centres on the word 'truthe': 'Whan alle tresors arn tried . . . Treuthe is the beste' (l. 85) is the theme which she reiterates at strategic moments (ll. 135, 206). In Middle English the word 'truthe' has a wide range of meaning, but three senses in particular help us to understand the position of both Holy Church and the narratorial voice in the Prologue and Passus I. One sense of 'truthe' given by the OED concerns truthfulness in speech: 'truthe' is a 'disposition to speak or act truly or without deceit; truthfulness, veracity, sincerity' (sense I. 4). This definition will be useful in understanding the particular discourses adopted by Langland as a truth-telling poet in the Prologue and Passus I. Another sense given by the OED concerns a deeper, existential concept of the word: 'that which is true, real, or actual; reality; spec[ifically] in religious use, spiritual reality as the subject of revelation or object of faith' (sense 10). Holy Church clearly has this sense in mind in her personification 'Truthe', and we will look to this sense in considering how Holy Church presents and elaborates her concept of theological 'truthe'. And lastly, we will look to what the OED gives as the first sense of the word: 'the character of being, or disposition to be, true to a person, principle, cause, etc.; faithfulness, fidelity, loyalty, constancy, steadfast allegiance. (See also TROTH) . . .' In looking at this last sense of the word, we will be able to understand the central idea in Holy Church's conception of society.

Throughout the chapter as a whole, I want to argue that Langland's commitment to 'truthe', in the three senses of the word outlined above, leads him into what can be described as conservative and authoritarian literary, theological, and political positions.

LITERARY 'TRUTHE'

At the very end of Chaucer's *Canterbury Tales*, Chaucer's Host asks the Parson to 'tell a fable anon, for cokes bones'. Unlike every other figure who has been asked to tell a story, the Parson refuses in this way:

> Thou getest fable noon ytoold for me,
> For Paul, that writeth unto Thymothee,
> Repreveth hem that weyven soothfastnesse
> And tellen fables and swich wrechednesse.
> ...

For which I seye, if that yow list to heere
Moralitee and vertuous mateere,
And thanne that ye wol yeve me audience,
I wol ful fayn, at Cristes reverence,
Do you plesaunce leefful, as I kan.

(X. 31–41)

for: by; *weyven*: depart from; *yow list*: it pleases you; *fayn*: willingly; *leefful*: legitimate.

So here, at the end of a series of tales, or fables, which have ranged from the high style, philosophical *Knight's Tale* to the scurrilous and neatly bawdy *Shipman's Tale*, the closing 'tale' dismisses the rest of the entire series as mendacious 'wrecched-nesse', and insists on other discourses, those of 'moralitee and vertuous mateere'. And the particular objection made by the Parson to the rest of the tales is that they are fictive – they diverge from 'sothfastnesse'.

In one sense, the Parson's rejection of fiction is marginal, coming as it does at the margin of Chaucer's work. But this is not to say that it is without force; on the contrary, the Parson (who is, after all, one of the very few unequivocally ideal figures among the pilgrims) rejects fiction as the pilgrims approach very near to Canterbury. As they approach the physical institution which is the ostensible goal of their pilgrimage, then, the ideal representative of that institution insists on a different, non-fictional discourse which focuses what should be the central interests of the pilgrims; in this sense it is the body of fictional tales which constitutes the marginal matter, rather than the *Parson's Tale*, which is central. Chaucer himself seems to accept the marginal status of his tales, since they are spoken, revealingly, as a diversion for the pilgrims as they move towards their real, and ostensibly more important spiritual goal at the shrine of St Thomas à Beckett. However much such tales clearly interest Chaucer, the fact that they are delivered on the road to Canterbury may serve as an emblem for the status of 'fiction' in a society where powerful cultural, and especially textual models are controlled by the Church: even for Chaucer, fiction takes place in the shadow of larger, spiritual truths, 'by the weye'. Whereas the *Parson's Tale* has the authority of the Church behind it, the immediate institution behind the pilgrims' tales is a casual and 'service' business of guided tours. The prize held out by the

Parson's Tale is salvation, whereas the prize for the literary contest is a free meal.

Langland, unlike his more secular contemporary Chaucer (who is at least prepared to countenance such a diversion), begins his poem from a position more explicitly committed to 'telling the truth'. Far from entering into the fictive tales of pilgrims who 'weyven sothfastnesse', Langland dismisses such tales in his Prologue. His description of pilgrims recalls the terms of Chaucer's Parson:

> Pilgrymes and palmeres plighten hem togidere
> For to seken Seint Jame and seintes at Rome;
> Wenten forth in hire wey with many wise tales,
> And hadden leve to lyen al hire lif after.
> I seigh somme that seiden thei hadde ysought seintes:
> To ech a tale that thei tolde hire tonge was tempred to lye
> Moore than to seye sooth, it semed bi hire speche.
>
> (Prol. 46–52)

palmeres: pilgrims to the Holy Land; *plighten*: pledged; *tempred*: tuned.

Whereas Chaucer's Parson speaks at the end of the *Tales*, Langland, at the very beginning of·his poem, apparently dismisses a whole range of fictional possibilities exploited by Chaucer.

But if Langland does reject fiction in favour of a poetry which is 'truthful', then what are the discursive possibilities open to him? Here I should like to describe Langland's particular use of three genres not mentioned in the Prologue to *The Wars of Alexander*, those of estates satire, dream vision, and sermon. I shall briefly consider Langland's use of these genres in the Prologue and Passus I, arguing in each case that he exploits their moral and moralising potential, and that in each case Langland's disposition may be characterised by the definition of 'truth' given by the OED as 'a disposition to speak or act truly or without deceit; truthfulness, veracity, sincerity'.

Estates Satire

The 'fair feeld ful of folk' Will sees in the Prologue of the poem is peopled by different groups seen in their characteristic activity. The literary tradition upon which Langland draws here is the estates satire form, a form exercised by medieval satirists in their conspectus and criticism of society as a whole (Miller 1983; Yunck 1988). Langland's satire is only loosely within the genre, since he includes groups like pilgrims and beggars, who do not formally constitute an estate or an occupation. But he does, nevertheless, represent the three basic orders of society as conceived by this genre: peasants, priests, and knights; and, in keeping with the premise of this satiric tradition, he does take his vision of society as the occasion for both moral correction, and the application of remedies.

When we look across to the example of this genre in Chaucer's work, the General Prologue to *The Canterbury Tales*, we can see how, within the given bounds of the genre, Chaucer minimises its moralising potential.[1] He sets the pilgrims in a context not of work, but of play and diversion; he does not pretend to see them from any absolute perspective, but insists instead that his knowledge is his own, and open to doubt (the text is interspersed with unobtrusive comments like 'I gesse' (l. 82), or 'for aught I woot' (l. 389)); and the descriptive element of the genre takes precedence over the normative: Chaucer in fact creates a courteous, subtle relationship with his reader by inviting him to see possible, oblique ironies which emerge in the description itself, and there are no direct, exclamative comments made by the narrator in what is distinctly his own voice. In each one of these respects, Langland's Prologue provides a polar opposite: (i) he sets his society on a space reserved for work, a field. Whereas Chaucer's pilgrims are first seen in the quotidian world of a tavern, Langland's world is set between the austere frame of Heaven and Hell – the 'tour on a toft' (l. 14) and 'a deep dale bynethe – a dongeon therinne' (l. 16). (ii) Within this absolute frame, the dreamer's own perspective is absolute: he attacks almost every class of people he sees without hesitation. And (iii) the normative, or critical attention takes precedence over the descriptive attention of the satirist. In the descriptions themselves, that is, Langland implies criticism:

Somme putten hem to the plough, pleiden ful selde,
In settynge and sowynge swonken ful harde,
And wonnen that thise wastours with glotonye destruyeth.

---

1. The best account of Chaucer's use of estates satire is Mann (1973).

And somme putten hem to pride, apparailed hem therafter,
In contenaunce of clothynge comen disgised.

(Prol. 20–4)

swonken: worked; contenaunce: outward show.

Here the verb to 'put oneself', meaning 'to set oneself to' (MED sense 22(c)), has a descriptive force in the first line, but this descriptive verb becomes moral in force in the 'observation' that other people 'putten hem to pride' – which is not so much an observation as a moral judgement.[2] The normative predisposition of Langland's satire is so strong, in fact, that normative models invade the narrative action itself: at l. 112 a king enters; he is clearly not of the same narrative status as the classes of people described by Will as failing in their duties, since he comes as a remedy and an ideal of justice by which other estates might be judged and constrained:

The Kyng and the Commune and Kynde Wit the thridde
Shopen lawe and leaute – ech lif to knowe his owene.

(Prol. 121–2)

shopen: formed; leaute: justice/fidelity.

This precipitation from description towards judgement and remedy creates a relationship of subservience between poet and reader: whereas Chaucer's reader is brought into play by the narrator's irony, here the reader is not invited to participate in the process of judgement – he is simply presented with a judgement completed.

The only exception to this closure of judgement is in the fable of the rats and mice, which follows the entry of the ideal King (ll. 146–210). The burden of this fable is a practical, worldly-wise recognition that the King (or his guardian) is not to be constrained or even criticised, even though there is an implicit criticism of the King made in the biblical reference to the woes of a country whose king is a boy (l. 194–195a). After the fable, the narrator addresses his audience:

(What this metels bymeneth, ye men that ben murye,
Devyne ye – for I ne dar, by deere God in hevene)!

(Prol. 209–10)

metels: dream; murye: cheerful; devyne: interpret.

2. For an account of larger similarities between the two prologues, see Cooper
   (1987).

Here the reader *is* invited to interpret the dream, but Langland's motive is not to create the intimate but intriguing relation between reader and narrator which we find in the *Canterbury Tales*; instead, his motive is political wariness: he does not *dare* to interpret the fable, in which he has simultaneously argued that the King (or his guardian) is not to be toyed with ('defame we hym nevere', as the cautious rat says (l. 190)), *and* implied that the King is not sufficiently mature (Richard was ten years old at his coronation in 1377).

Dream Vision

In Langland's adoption of the estates satire, then, he exploits it, where possible, for its most aggressively critical and forthrightly normative potential. When we look to his adoption of the dream vision and the sermon, we find them being exploited in the same way. In adopting the dream vision as the 'envelope', as it were, for his use of other genres, Langland is adopting a genre with extensive literary possibilities;[3] we need only think of the prologue to Chaucer's *House of Fame* for the plethora of dream kinds available to a literary artist – there the dreamer is confused by this range, and wonders

> Why that is an avision
> And why this a revelacion,
> Why this a drem, why that a sweven,
> And noght to every man lyche even;
> Why this a fantome, why these oracles . . .
>
> (ll. 7–11)

This list is difficult to analyse in its entirety, but some of the terms clearly fall within the general categories of dreams offered by Macrobius (early fifth century) in his influential commentary on Book VI of Cicero's *De Republica*: the 'avision', the 'revelacion', and the 'oracle' fall generally within Macrobius's category of truth-bearing dreams (Macrobius uses the term *'visio'* for a prophetic vision which comes true, and the term *'oraculum'* for a dream in which the dreamer is instructed by 'a parent, or a pious or revered man, or a priest, or even a god'); and the term 'fantome'

---

3. For a conspectus of medieval English and Scottish dream poetry, see Spearing (1976).

is clearly related to the insignificant, deceptive category of dreams (for one of which Macrobius uses the term *'phantasmata'*) (Macrobius, trans. Stahl 1952, 87–92). In his dream-poems, Chaucer capitalises on the different interpretative requirements of these different categories of dream to establish a playful relationship between poet and audience, by allowing the dreams to be categorised in different ways, and thereby allowing the reader different interpretative choices. Langland, on the other hand, presents us with a dream which we can in no way dismiss as 'fantome' in the seriousness and explicitness of its moral attention; even within the Prologue we have already noticed how interpretation is preempted by explicit moralising. And in Passus I we move to the firm authoritative and interpretative base of an *oraculum*. The passus begins by promising the reader exactly this kind of stability:

> What this mountaigne bymeneth and the merke dale
> And the feld ful of folk, I shal yow faire shewe.
>
> (I. 1–2)
>
> *merke*: dark.

And the figure who appears is characteristic of the *oraculum* tradition – Holy Church descends from the castle of Truthe, and in response to Will's question 'Mercy, madame, what [may] this [be] to mene?' (l. 11), Holy Church (who addresses Will as 'Sone' (l. 5)) proceeds to explicate the meaning of the 'tour upon the toft'. So when Will says that *he* will explicate the vision of the Prologue, he is in fact identifying his own perspective entirely with that of the institution of the Church itself, since it is Holy Church who offers unhesitating interpretations of the field. And Will's own reśponse to Holy Church here is one of complete moral and intellectual obedience, unlike, say, the dreamer in the *oraculum Pearl*, who questions the dream-guide: Will falls on his knees, and

> . . . cried hire of grace,
> And preide hire pitously to preye for my synnes,
> And also kenne me kyndely on Crist to bileve . . .
>
> (I. 79–81)
>
> *kenne*: teach; *kyndely*: properly.

Will, that is, once he knows that his interlocutor is Holy Church, immediately concedes Holy Church's power to intercede for his sins, and to instruct him in orthodox faith. And this little scene seems to me not only to represent a moral and spiritual choice on Will's part to accept unquestioningly the authority of the Church, but it is also a *literary* choice, in so far as the institution of the Church will adopt, as in fact Holy Church does, the discursive modes appropriate to the interests of that institution. In the *Divine Comedy* Dante's choice of a guide also presupposes profound literary choices, since in accepting Virgil's guidance Dante is accepting the full force of the classical poetic and philosophic tradition. Langland's initial choice, on the other hand, seems unpromising for an engagement with specifically literary traditions (of any open-ended kind, at any rate), since the institution of the Church might reasonably be expected to adopt discourses which unequivocally promote 'moralitee and vertuous mateere'.

Sermon

When Holy Church does speak, she uses the homiletic, didactic style we might expect of the authority figure in an *oraculum*. Having interpreted the 'tour upon the toft' as the dwelling place of Truthe, her speech leaves us in no doubt that she herself has access to the 'truthe', both in the confidence and in the didactic style of her speech: in naming the three things which are necessary to man's physical survival, she asks Will to repeat them after her – 'reherce thow hem after' she says (l. 22). And in response to Will's specifically spiritual question, about the salvation of his soul, she adopts something approaching the sermon form proper. She begins with a statement of her theme (where 'theme' is used technically, meaning the 'text' of a sermon (l. 85)):

> 'Whan alle tresors arn tried,' quod she, 'Treuthe is the beste.
> I do it on *Deus caritas* to deme the sothe.'
>
> (I. 85–6)
>
> *do it on*: appeal to; *Deus caritas*: God [is] love.

She repeats this theme at strategic points within the sermon; at l. 134, for example, she recapitulates in this way:

> Forthi I seye, as I seyde er, by sighte of thise textes –
> Whan alle tresors arn tried, Truthe is the beste,
>
> (I. 134–5)

and at l. 206 she concludes with the same words. It is true that
Holy Church does not follow the strict pattern of 'ancient' or
'modern' ('university') types of sermons (Spearing 1972, 114;
Wenzel 1988, 160), and that her speech is interrupted by Will. She
does, nevertheless, structure her speech around a theme, and
supply many examples to sustain this theme, in the manner of
sermons (Wenzel 1988).

In a way characteristic of *oraculum* figures, Holy Church marks
her dependence on authoritative texts behind her instruction, and
the text to which she refers is consistently the Bible. Her examples
are drawn from biblical or apocryphal sources (e.g. Lot, David,
Lucifer), and her speech is always within 'sighte of thise textes':
'by the Gospel' (l. 90), 'by Seint Lukes wordes' (l. 91) are the kinds
of phrase by which Holy Church signals her reliance, in the
texture of her speech, on the Bible as the unimpeachable source
of her authority.

So in the discourses which Langland adopts – estates satire, the
oraculum dream form, and the sermon – we can see that his
commitment is to 'truthe' in the first sense I defined, the 'disposition to speak or act truly or without deceit; truthfulness,
veracity, sincerity', and that this commitment, for Langland,
seems to disallow any possibilities for the literary play of fiction,
of the kind we find in Chaucer. Instead, this commitment to
'truthe' predisposes Langland to exploit the genres he adopts to
make them 'closed' and authoritative: however lively it might be,
the text presents itself as unquestionable; the reader is not allowed
much room for movement in the face of the textual and institutional authorities from which the poetry is projected. However
much the opening of the poem might invite us to be wary about
the voice of the narrator, who is 'unholy of werkes' (l. 3), the
actual practice of the Prologue and Passus I seems to offer no
space for the play of ironies which result from an untrustworthy
voice.

THEOLOGICAL 'TRUTHE'

Having outlined Langland's initially conservative position through
the form of the Prologue and Passus I, I would now like to
consider the content of these opening sequences from a theological
perspective.

In specific theological questions, Will defers entirely to the authority of Holy Church. The period in which Langland wrote witnessed the growth of a literate, lay public interested in theological questions. The proto-protestant Lollard movement, which developed in England from the 1380s, is itself in part a manifestation of this phenomenon. The reaction of the established Church was to try and stifle lay interest (and the use of English) in any sort of sophisticated theological discussion. The Constitutions of Archbishop Arundel, published in 1409, for example, attempt to constrain lay interest of this kind. Thus Constitution V forbids any master of arts, or grammar master, to treat of 'the sacraments of the church, or any other theological matter against what has been determined by the church', when instructing boys in the arts, or in grammar (Wilkins, III, 317). Although this constitution is clearly directed at the Lollards, who had developed as a popular movement just after the period of *Piers Plowman*'s composition, there is clear evidence of lay interest in theological matters in the pre-Lollard period (Coleman 1981; Courtenay 1987, Ch. 1; 368–74). In *Piers Plowman* itself, it is interestingly the figure Study, who is responsible for the teaching of grammar to boys, who condemns the idle and ill-informed speculation of lay people in theological matters. She says she has heard

> . . . heighe men etyng at the table
> Carpen as thei clerkes were of Crist and of hise myghtes,
> And leyden fautes upon the fader that formede us alle,
> And carpen ayein clerkes crabbede wordes:
> 'Why wolde Oure Saveour suffre swich a worm in his blisse,
> That bi[w]iled the womman and the [wye] after . . .'
>
> (X. 103–8)
>
> *carpen*: speak; *myghtes*: powers; *fautes*: faults; *biwiled*: deceived; *wye*: man.

If this represents part of the theological climate in which Langland is writing, where lay people are appropriating the function of 'clerkes' themselves, then the relation of Passus I to the Prologue implies an initial readiness on Langland's part to concede to the Church an unquestioned right to stand in judgement over the field.

Holy Church's sermon, however, cannot be characterised as simple instruction in matters of the faith, in the manner of many manuals of orthodox spiritual instruction designed for lay people, written in English, in the fourteenth century. A good example of such a manual is the text of John Gaytryge, known as 'Gaytryge's Sermon'. This text was a translation of the instructions of John Thoresby, Archbishop of York (issued in 1357, and themselves modelled on the Lambeth Constitutions of 1281). The text is directed to parish priests, but for the instruction of the laity, 'opynly, one ynglysche, apon sonnondayes' in 'the lawe and the lare [doctrine] to knawe God Almyghty' (ed. Perry 1867, 2). The prologue to the work specifies that parish priests should teach their parishioners to know by heart, in English: the creed; the Ten Commandments; the seven sacraments; the seven works of mercy; the seven virtues, and the seven deadly sins. Holy Church's responses to Will's questions certainly address the problems of lay society – her discussion of measure in the basic necessities of life, and the ownership of worldly money are not directed to those 'ancres and heremites that holden hem in hire selles' whom Will sees in the fair field (l. 28). But her response to Will's question about the salvation of his soul, which is Holy Church's domain proper, is not constituted by the formulae of dogma; instead, it presents in a direct but theoretical way the two foundation stones of the Christian religion, justice and love, with the emphasis on justice.

The theme of her sermon, as I have already mentioned, concerns the preciousness of 'truthe':

> 'Whan alle tresors arn tried,' quod she, 'Treuthe is the beste'.
> I do it on *Deus caritas* to deme the sothe'.
>
> (l. 85–6)

In considering the word 'truthe', we have already seen the relevance the sense 'disposition to speak or act truly or without deceit' might have to Langland's enterprise as a poet; but what does Holy Church mean by the word? She equates God, or the 'fader of feith' with Truthe at I. 14; this implies the sense recorded by OED as 'that which is true, real, or actual; reality; spec[ifically] in religious use, spiritual reality as the subject of revelation or object of faith' (sense 10). This sense, of the most profound existential reality, is closely related to another, which implies conformity with the standards of that reality; thus when Holy Church first explains the 'tour on the toft', she invokes not only the existence of Truthe, but also its force as a model:

> . . . Truthe is therinne,
> And wolde that ye wroughte as his word techeth.
>
> (I. 12–13)

wroughte: acted.

The action designated here points to another sense of 'truthe', defined by OED as 'conduct in accordance with the divine standard' (sense 9(b)), which makes intelligible the specific force of the adjective 'true' as used by Holy Church; after the statement of her theme about the preciousness of Truthe as a treasure, she goes on immediately to insist on its force as model of behaviour:

> Who is trewe of his tonge and telleth noon oother,
> And dooth the werkes therwith and wilneth no man ille,
> He is a god by the Gospel . . .
>
> (I. 88–90)

This sense, of acting according to the dictates of existential, or divine 'truthe', implies a concept of justice – whoever acts truly, that is, will of necessity be acting justly. Holy Church places the strongest emphasis on the justice which 'truthe' both personifies and demands. In the earthly sphere, she sees the defence of 'truthe' as essentially the enactment of justice – 'truthe' is both the model and the essence of justice:

> Kynges and knyghtes sholde kepen it by reson –
> Riden and rappen doun in reaumes aboute,
> And taken *transgressores* and tyen hem faste
> Til treuthe hadde ytermyned hire trespas to the ende.
>
> (I. 94–7)

rappen doun: suppress; *trangressores*: lawbreakers *ytermyned*: judged.

And in the divine sphere, God, too, is represented as essentially a judgemental figure in His aspect as Truthe. The presence of Hell, pictured as a 'dongeon',[4] underlines Truthe's quality as

---

4. MED defines 'dongeon' as (a) 'A fortress, citadel, castle', and (b) 'the most strongly fortified central part of a citadel or castle, donjon, keep'. It cites Prol. 15 under (a), which is supported by the apparent identification of 'dongeon' and 'castel' in I. 59–61. Theological issues are involved, since in Passus XVIII, it is an essential legal point that the devil be judged to be a mere gaoler of mankind, rather than having legal possession of them. In summary, we can say that 'dongeon' in Prologue and Passus I does seem to mean 'castle', but that it is the penal aspect of the castle which is stressed (Prol. 15–16; I. 59); it is for this reason that I refer to it as a 'dongeon', acknowledging the ME meaning, but stressing the penal aspect.

judge. And the standards of divine judgement are presented as uncompromising:

> And alle that werchen with wrong wende thei shulle
> After hir deth day and dwelle with that sherewe;
> Ac tho that werche wel as Holy Writ telleth,
> And enden as I er seide in truthe, that is the beste,
> Mowe be siker that hire soules shul wende to hevene,
> Ther Treuthe is in Trinitee and troneth hem alle.
>
> (I. 128–33)
>
> *wende*: go; *sherewe*: evil one; *siker*: sure; *troneth*: enthrones.

Holy Church does not present God as singularly judgemental: in the very statement of her theme about 'truthe' being the best treasure, she appeals to a scriptural authority '*Deus caritas* to deme the sothe' (l. 86). Embedded in these lines is the central paradox of the Christian religion, that the God who is the essence and model of justice, should also mercifully release man from the unremitting but deserved punishment for original sin; what credentials can Love (*caritas*) have for '*judging* the truthe' (to 'deme the sothe'), when Love's predisposition will be to ignore the demands of justice? Mercy and justice can, in short, be contradictory.

Holy Church does not resolve the paradox in response to Will's question about how he might know Truthe in himself. She says that it is by natural understanding that Will knows the 'truthe', which is to love God and to do no mortal sin (ll. 142–5); she goes on from here to say that Truthe tells that love is

> . . . the plante of pees, moost precious of vertues:
> For hevene myghte nat holden it, so was it hevy of hymself,
> Til it hadde of the erthe eten his fille.
> And whan it hadde of this fold flessh and blood taken,
> Was nevere leef upon lynde lighter therafter,
> And portatif and persaunt as the point of a nedle,
> That myghte noon armure it lette ne none heighe walles.
>
> (I. 152–8)
>
> *fold*: earth; *lynde*: linden tree; *portatif*: portable; *persaunt*: piercing; *lette*: obstruct.

This mysterious passage suggests the radical potency of love by describing Christ's incarnation in unfamiliar, paradoxical poetic images: the word 'vertues' suggests immediately the natural 'vertue', or life-giving force, of a plant (OED sense 9(b)); but the paradoxical development of the plant imagery, according to which the heavy plant becomes light by taking on flesh and blood, and according to which the plant becomes as sharp as a needle, a lance and a battering ram, activates a different sense of 'vertue', according to which it means 'power', and especially 'divine power' (OED sense 1). This is a powerful and suggestive passage, but if this is what Truthe can tell about love, then its metaphorical density suggests that Truthe, or justice, contains meanings which are not open to rational analysis.

So Holy Church does broach the other foundation stone of the Christian religion, which is love, and she devotes the second half of her sermon to a discussion of how human charity should be exercised on the model of Christ's charity (I. 159–205). But her initial emphasis falls clearly on the idea of God as Truthe, or justice. Even in her exhortations to earthly judges to be merciful in their judgements, she insists, by reference to Christ's words (cf. Luke 6.38), on the strictness of God's own judgements:

> For the same mesure that ye mete, amys outher ellis,
> Ye shulle ben weyen therwith whan ye wenden hennes.
>
> (I. 177–8)
>
> *mete*: measure out; *amys*: wrongly; *wenden*: go.

And from this standpoint, we can see that Holy Church's theological emphasis on the justice of God corresponds with the secular remedy posed in the Prologue for the corrupt state of the world. The King, along with the 'commune' and 'Kynde Wit', are said to devise 'Iawe and leaute – ech lif to knowe his owene' (l. 122), where 'leaute' denotes the essence of the law (deriving from Latin *legalitas* through Old French *lealté*), and includes senses of both 'lawfulness' and 'faith-keeping' (MED sense (a), (b), (c); Alford *GLD*).

There is nothing original in this presentation of God as a personifed Justice; the very concept of the Christian era, or the 'New Law', is defined as a liberation from the strict, unremitting justice of the pre-Christian period, or the 'Old Law'. The Old Testament furnishes us with many narrative examples of God as vengeful judge, and many statements are made expressing this idea: 'Lord . . . thou turnest myn enemy abac; thei schulen be maad feble . . . For thou hast maad [maintained] my doom [judgement] and my cause [legal case]; thou, that demest [judge] rightfulnesse, hast set on the trone [throne] . . . The Lord made redi his trone in doom; and he schal deme the world in equite [equity/strict justice], he schal deme puplis [peoples] in rightfulnesse'.[5] The idea of God as judge is so deeply embedded in the Christian tradition that it remains in constant dialectic with the idea of God as Love throughout Christian history. In the fourteenth century, however, for reasons that will be explained later in this book, there were strong currents of theological, scholastic writing which laid particular emphasis on the idea of God as all-powerful judge. Much popular devotional literature of the late Middle Ages tends to ignore these more learned traditions, and focuses instead on the loving, wounded humanity of Christ. But in the works of writers who do register the more learned theological currents, we can see a marked interest in the image of God as justice, as 'resoun of right that con not raue' (*Pearl* 665). God is not only presented as just, but as inscrutable, since He decides what the standards of justice are. This image of God is one we find in both *Pearl* and *Cleaness*, and, for example, in Chaucer's *Clerk's Tale*, if we read it as an allegory, in the way the Clerk suggests we should. It is this image of a judgemental God we find stressed, then, in Holy Church's sermon, and it is an image which will have compelling force for Langland throughout *Piers Plowman*.

SOCIAL 'TRUTHE'

If Holy Church's theological position evokes an Old Testament idea of God as personification of justice, that view is given an anchor in the social forms of Langland's England. For Langland the biblical and the contemporary are not easily distinguishable; even in the opening vision we can see how the representation of God is at once biblical and contemporary: the 'tour' on the hill

5. Psalm 9.3–8 (Vulgate). Cited, as all citations from the Wycliffite Bible in this book, from *The Holy Bible . . . made from the Latin Vulgate by John Wycliffe and his Followers*, 4 vols., edited by J. Forshall and F. Madden (Oxford: OUP, 1850) (later version). Letter forms have been modernised. All citations from the Latin Vulgate are from *Biblia Sacra iuxta Vulgatam Clementinam*, fifth edition, edited by Alberto Collunga and Lorentio Turrado (Madrid: Biblioteca de Autores Cristianos, 1977). All other biblical citations in English are from the Authorized Version (1611).

in which Truthe lives has biblical resonance (in the Psalms, for example, God is often associated with hills and with places of defence (e.g. Ps. 47. 12–14)). But if the image is biblical in origin, its force is specifically social in its context: the castle ('tour', OED sense 2) is part of a spatial set, overlooking an agricultural space, and a 'dongeon'. The kind of society implied by this cluster is a feudal society, localised in its manorial form.

On the field itself, however, we can see deviations from the social model implicit in the space castle/field/'dongeon': Will sees merchants, for example (l. 31), who have no formal place in a feudal ideology, according to which society was constituted by knights, priests, and peasants. Will disparages merchants only lightly, but what provokes his sharpest satire is the 'trading' of those whose responsibility is spiritual. Of the friars, for example, it is said that

> . . . hire moneie and hire marchaundise marchen togideres.
> Sith charite hath ben chapman and chief to shryve lordes
> Manye ferlies han fallen in a fewe yeres.
>
> (Prol. 63–5)
>
> *sith*: since; *chapman*: merchant; *ferlies*: marvels.

The friars have made their confessional activity a function of their economic interests, in such a way as to extinguish charity altogether. And many other groups belong to a mercantile and/or bourgeois (by which I mean 'urban') rather than a feudal, manorial context: this is true of the lawyers who 'pleteden for penyes and pounded the lawe' (l. 213), as it is of the

> Baksteres and brewesteres and bochiers manye,
> Wollen webbesters and weveres of lynnen,
> Taillours and tynkers and tollers in markettes . . .
>
> (Prol. 219–21)
>
> *baksteres*: bakers; *webbesters*: wool-weavers; *tollers*: toll collectors.

The space in which this society is set, then, is at odds with, and serves to criticise the actual practices of many groups within that society; equally, it could be argued, the complexity of the mercantile and bourgeois world represented by the Prologue cannot be constrained by the very simplicity of the space in which it is set.

The society represented by Langland on the 'fair feeld ful of folk' clearly registers some of the changes occurring within fourteenth-century English society. I will discuss these in more detail at different points in this book, but for the moment we could simply say that different strata of society in the fourteenth century, for different reasons, experienced a shift from a feudal and/or a standard manorial economy to a cash-based economy. This is true both of the king's army and of baronial households in the period. England was engaged in extremely costly wars with both Scotland and France periodically throughout the entire fourteenth century. To wage these wars, kings required much greater sources of manpower than could be raised through their traditional feudal resources of their fiefs, which were estates 'in land (in England always a heritable estate) held on condition of homage and service to a superior lord' (McFarlane 1944, 162). To make up for this deficiency, a system of contracts, or indentures was developed, whereby soldiers would agree to fight for a fixed period in return for an annual fee. This form of service also served to furnish baronial households with a stock of retainers who would not only serve the lord in times of war, but also attend him in the normal course of public life, by accompanying the lord at tournaments, for example, or at Parliament (Lewis 1945; McFarlane 1944). Relationships of this kind were not necessarily unstable (very often the indenture would be for life), though they were, unlike feudal tenures, not heritable. But there remained a large body of retainers gathered round a lord who were tied to him by nothing more than the acceptance of his fees and the wearing of his badge. It is this category of retainer which the statute of 1390 (a statute which deals in greater detail with this problem than any preceding it) aims to outlaw, and this form of service which contemporary records label as 'maintenance'.[6]

For different reasons, relations between lords and peasants were changing towards a cash-based economy in the world of the manor. The traditional manor was divided between the lord's demesne and the land which his tenants were allowed to work for themselves in return for their labour and certain traditional taxes they were obliged to pay the lord. Even before the plague of 1348 (which may have killed up to one-third of the population), this system was changing as it became unprofitable for the lord to work his desmesne directly, after the first quarter of the four-

6. Anno 13 Ric. II, Stat. 2. c. 3, 1389–90 (*Statutes of the Realm*, II. 74–5).

teenth century. In response to this, lords began to rent out their desmesne land to peasants, which involved the commutation of labour services for money rents. This process was quickened sharply by the effects of the plague, when the current of labour relations turned in favour of peasants: lords faced 'an acute shortage of labour; a collapse of demand for tenant land; [and] falling prices for arable produce as demand slackened' (Keen 1973, 192).[7] The net effect of these changes was to change the set of relationships between lord and peasant from relationships of traditional, permanent ties of loyalty and service, to contractual ties in which peasants worked for wages.

The reaction of the lords to this situation was to try to exploit their legal advantages, particularly over their unfree customary tenants, to restore their economic position: they insisted on their preferential right to the labour of their unfree tenants; they strictly enforced the payment of traditional manorial taxes; and, through legislation in the Statutes of Labourers of 1349, 1352, and 1388 they both limited the level of wages to pre-plague levels, and restricted the movement of peasants, thereby preventing peasants from seeking the most advantageous wages. It was the tensions created by this reaction which led, in part, to the Peasants' Revolt of 1381, where one of the main demands of the peasants was for their freedom, to release them from traditional, tenurial ties of service.[8]

England's economy remained an essentially agricultural economy throughout the medieval period; the thirteenth and the beginning of the fourteenth centuries were, nevertheless, periods of urban growth and expansion. The growth of towns implied, as it did all over Europe, a new set of formal liberties for citizens, in particular personal freedom, and freedom of movement. Citizens in towns held their land by 'burgage tenure', which involved free transferability of land, and rents paid almost exclusively in money (Platt 1979, Ch. 5).

If many groups in Langland's field (like many of the figures in Chaucer's company of pilgrims) do practise a non-manorial way of life, how does Holy Church respond to this in Passus I? Holy Church does certainly address herself to the question of material

7. For a more detailed analysis of changes to manorial life in the fourteenth century, see Postan (1971).
8. For accounts of peasant movements in the period, see Hilton (1969; 1975).

needs: the first part of her speech to Will concerns the basic
necessities of the body (food, drink, and clothing), and the use
of earthly money. In both cases, Holy Church acknowledges the
legitimacy of bodily and economic requirements: she says that
God ordained basic material remedies for bodily necessities, and
that earthly money should be used, according to the dictates of
reason, to provide for necessities – that Will should take it 'at
nede' (l. 56). But in both cases, she insists on the ways in which
these realms of need should be constrained by spiritual consid-
erations: she sets the needs of the body in contrast (if not exclusive
contrast) with those of the soul:

> Al is nought good to the goost that the gut asketh,
> Ne liflode to the likame that leef is to the soule,
>
> (I. 36–7)
>
> *goost*: spirit; *liflode*: sustenance; *likame*: body; *leef*: agreeable.

and she constrains earthly use of money by reminding Will of
Christ's words about one's debts to God: '"*Reddite Cesari* . . . that
Cesari bifalleth,/*Et que sunt Dei Deo*"'.

But the weight of Holy Church's reply falls, as we have already
seen, on the thematic word of her sermon, 'truthe', which has a
profound social force in addition to the moral and theological
senses we have already observed. As I mentioned, the first sense
of the word given by the OED is as follows: 'The character of
being, or disposition to be, true to a person, principle, cause, etc.;
faithfulness, fidelity, loyalty, constancy, steadfast allegiance. (See
also TROTH) . . .' This sense of the word is relevant to the
feudal notions of permanent loyalty between retainer and lord, as
well as to relations of horizontal loyalty between equals. In the
romance literature of the period we can see many examples of the
centrality of the word taken in both horizontal and vertical senses:
in the romance *Orfeo*, for example, the pattern of the narrative
is shaped by a series of acts of 'truthe' in the social sense: Orfeo
is true to his wife; Pluto is true to his word to Orfeo; and Orfeo's
steward is true to Orfeo on his return. In other romances we can
see just how important the concept is by observing how different
senses of the word compete, where the sense of 'fidelity' overbears the idea of strict moral uprightness: in the romance *Amis and
Amiloun*, for example, the fidelity of Amiloun to Amis takes
precedence over strict honesty, when Amiloun takes on the fight

for his friend in disguise, in what is an unjust fight; or in Chaucer's *Franklin's Tale*, Averagus insists that Dorigen's fidelity to her promise is more important than her moral obligation not to commit adultery, for 'Trouthe is the hyeste thyng that man may kepe' (l. 1479).

Within the aristocratic milieux of these romances, horizontal fidelity between equals is as important as vertical fidelity between retainers and lords; in Holy Church's sermon, the emphasis falls on the vertical fidelity between retainer and lord. She conceives of God as a feudal lord, who 'knyghted ten' to be feudal magnates over lesser angels:

> Cherubyn and Seraphyn, swiche sevene and another,
> And yaf hem myght in his majestee – the murier hem thoughte –
> And over his meene meynee made hem archangeles.
>
> (I. 106–8)

> *yaf*: gave; *meene meynee*: lesser retinue.

In this context, Lucifer's rebellion is given a specific social force in addition to its moral force – Lucifer is not only untruthful in a moral sense, he is also faithless to his feudal lord God in breaking 'buxomnesse' [obedience] (l. 113).

The direct relevance the theological senses of the word 'truthe' have for justice are also given a specific social force by Holy Church, in her reference to the earthly dubbing of knights by David, who made them 'sweren on hir swerd to serven truthe evere' (l. 99), where the service of 'truthe' clearly implies a fulfilment of knightly duties by enforcing the law, according to which knights should imprison transgressors, 'Til treuthe hadde ytermyned hire trespas to the ende' (l. 97).

Holy Church, then, takes up what might be described as a reactionary position with regard to the kind of society presented in the Prologue; she anchors her sense of theological truth and justice in specific social forms which can be described as feudal. Her commitment is to the kind of society implied by the space of the Prologue – an agricultural space bounded by the just lord's castle on the one hand, and his 'dongeon' on the other.

CONCLUSION

We have considered the way in which different senses of the word 'truthe' might help to illuminate the kinds of choice Langland makes in the Prologue and Passus I: his commitment to speaking without deceit determines his adoption of 'closed' discursive forms which are explicitly designed for moral reformation, and which reject the resources of fiction; his commitment to God as the source and model of justice determines the theological emphases Holy Church makes on the judgemental aspect of God; and his commitment to the social virtue of loyalty and fidelity determines Holy Church's emphasis on a feudal model of society.

Whereas other literary works whose theme is 'truthe' do, as I have mentioned, shape their narrative out of the *opposition* between different senses of the word (especially the *Franklin's Tale* and *Amis and Amiloun*), it seems clear that for Holy Church all the senses of 'truthe' form a coherent, self-supporting conceptual whole, in which theology and 'sociology' are not discrepant. If the rest of *Piers Plowman* did nothing but elaborate different aspects of this coherent cluster of ideas, then we would certainly describe the poem as conservative in a rather uninteresting way. But what I want to argue in the remaining chapters of this book is that each one of these choices – literary, theological, social – is put under searching scrutiny as Langland recognises, and confronts, the crises to which they lead. In particular, I want to argue that Langland's commitment to the idea of unremitting secular and divine justice leads him into positions of acute and fearful discomfort, and that in seeking a way out of this theological crisis he is provoked either to abandon or to seek to transform the social and ecclesiastical institutions to which he makes his initial commitment. I shall also argue that Langland, despite his initial commitment to 'closed' literary forms, ultimately creates a profoundly original and open-ended text. Whereas the discourse of Holy Church presents itself as unitary, it becomes clear in the poem that the concept 'Holy Church' contains many discourses, each with separate, often rival claims to authority.

Chapter 2

The First Vision:
Passus II–IV

PASSUS II: Will asks to be taught to know the false, in response to which Holy Church points out *Mede*, defining her as a principle inimical to law (ll. 1–51). Will observes preparations for the wedding of Mede and False, including the charter by which the territories of sin are to be distributed in this marriage (ll. 52–114). *Theology* objects to the marriage, insisting that Mede has a positive moral value; he argues that Mede should be taken to London where the propriety of her marriage with False should be judged in court (ll. 115–43). Mede and her retinue prepare to go to Westminster (ll. 144–88); the *King* hears that False is coming, and orders him and his companions to be arrested (ll. 189–205). False and his companions disperse on hearing this, leaving Mede alone to face the King (ll. 206–37).

PASSUS III: Mede is welcomed at Westminster and rewards those who receive her (ll. 1–100); the King offers *Conscience* as husband to Mede (ll. 101–13); Conscience refuses Mede, and declares why (ll. 114–69). Mede defends herself (ll. 170–229); Conscience replies by defining two senses of the word 'mede', one designating God's gift to men, the other the corrupting gifts of earthly society. Both of these are distinct from the payment of deserved wages (ll. 230–83). Conscience prophesies a world where justice and love, not mede, will rule (ll. 284–330). The passus ends with Mede and Conscience debating the propriety of receiving gifts (ll. 331–53).

PASSUS IV: Conscience still refuses to marry Mede unless *Reason* commands him to do so (ll. 1–5); Conscience fetches Reason, who comes to Westminster (ll. 6–46); *Peace* enters Parliament, and delivers a petition against *Wrong* (ll. 47–60); Wrong seeks the legal help of Wisdom and Wit, who seek to have Wrong released on bail; Mede also offers gifts to Peace to make amends for Wrong; Peace accepts the gifts, and prays for mercy towards Wrong (ll. 61–103); the King refuses any mercy (ll. 104–48); the judgement of the court is against Wrong, and the King sentences him, recognising the way in which Mede prevents the just exercise of law (ll. 149–95).

INTRODUCTION

In Passus I, then, Holy Church answers to the field represented in the Prologue essentially through different senses of the word 'truthe': the divine sense of the word implies standards of justice, while the word also means 'loyalty', and evokes a feudal ideal. Langland himself, or his narrator, also adopts discursive procedures which conform to a further sense of 'truthe' – that of 'stating the truth'. In this chapter, I will consider the action of Passus II–IV of the poem, involving the proposed marriages of Mede with False and with Conscience, and the trial of Wrong. Here, too, I will argue, Langland's thematic concern is with the social and legal senses of 'truthe'; and here, too, Langland's formal procedures as a poet are designed to elucidate 'truthe'. I will begin by considering the mode and genre of this section of the poem, before going on to discuss its social, and then its legal content.

PERSONIFICATION ALLEGORY

Before looking to the central action of the vision, I would like to define Langland's poetic mode in these passus by looking at a tiny example of personification allegory. In Passus IV the King orders Conscience to fetch Reason as a judge in the dispute about Mede's proposed marriage with False. Reason unhesitatingly joins Conscience, but as they travel to Westminister they are followed by two rather suspect characters:

Oon Waryn Wisdom and Witty his fere
Folwed hem faste, for thei hadde to doone
In th 'Escheker and in the Chauncerye, to ben descharged of thynges,
And riden faste for Reson sholde rede hem the beste
For to save hem for silver from shame and from harmes.

(IV. 27–31)

    fere: companion; *hadde to doone*: had business; *rede*: advise.

It might seem odd that the figure Wisdom, in particular, should
want to use money to be saved from harm. And if Wisdom *is* in
the business of bribery, it might seem more strange that Wisdom
and Wit should seek the advice of Reason, who is in the company
of Conscience. Either Langland is abusing words, or else he is
pointing up unexpected senses of words. In Middle English it is
clear that both 'wisdom' (along with its adjective 'wise') and 'wit'
can take shades of meaning which suggest practical, worldly
wisdom and cunning; we can observe these senses in Chaucer's
portrait of the Manciple in the General Prologue, for example,
where it is said that those who buy might take him as a model
'For to be wise in byyng of vitaille' (l. 569). Here 'wise' denotes
a capacity for shrewdness in practical, financial affairs, and it is
this sense, along with a practical sense of 'wit', which is placed
against another kind of wisdom in this way:

Now is nat that of God a ful fair grace
That swich a lewed mannes wit shal pace
The wisdom of an heep of lerned men?

(A. 573–5)

    lewed: ignorant; *heep*: great number.

In Chaucer's Prologue words of apparently stable and moral force
often begin to slide into ironic senses in this way (e.g. 'worthy',
'wise', 'good', 'noble'), but they do not shape the narrative. In
the example from Langland, on the other hand, we can see that
the meanings of words themselves, and the different senses of
words, actually form the narrative itself: the action of the narrative is shaped out of, as it were, listings under the dictionary
entries for the actants here, Wisdom, Wit, Reason, and
Conscience. We learn, through the action, that Wisdom and Wit
do have more suspect senses, and that they are dependent on

Reason for their suspect activity. This raises a question about the moral authority of Reason, but this question is answered in the action which follows, where Conscience warns Reason not to have anything to do with Wisdom and Wit, 'For Conscience knoweth hem noght' (l. 41): Reason, that is, is dependent on Conscience for moral guidance. Here, too, Langland differs from Chaucer, who allows different senses of words to develop and to attach themselves freely to unexpected concepts; Langland's Conscience, instead, acts from within the text as an unerring lexicographer, whose concern is to define and fix the senses of words according to moral criteria. It is clearly to the advantage of the suspect senses of 'wisdom' to take cover under larger, positive senses of the word; but when Conscience warns Reason about Wisdom and Wit by saying that 'there are wiles in hire wordes' (l. 34), the real force of that statement is that the words themselves are wily, containing traps for the unwary.

In this little sequence, then, we learn: (i) that Conscience is ultimately dependent on Reason, since the King will not accept Conscience's decision without Reason's approval; (ii) that 'wisdom' and 'wit' have pejorative senses; (iii) that even in those pejorative senses, they are dependent on Reason for advice; and (iv) that Reason depends on Conscience for moral counsel, to judge where he should exercise his intellectual skill. The passage, in short, neatly points to the conceptual overlapping of the senses of words, and warns the reader to be on guard against pejorative senses of one word which might masquerade under positive senses.

An example of this kind reveals at once the extremely explicit and analytical quality of personification allegory; any narrative action which uses personified concepts of its nature invites the reader to translate the action back into direct statements, to make statements out of the words from which the action originally sprang, in the way I have just done in the preceding paragraph. And this point leads to another, that personification allegory of its nature is necessarily reiterative, since the most a word can do as actant is to play out all its senses; beyond this, any action can only serve to reiterate those established meanings. Such a mode, in fact, offers very little scope for extended narrative action at all, since words can do little more than act out their range of pre-given meanings, such that dramatic action constantly threatens to collapse into direct statement (Griffiths 1985, 40). The action seems to be almost over before it has begun.[1]

Turning now to the main action of these passus, how is it possible that the action involving Mede should be sustained over three passus? The introduction Holy Church gives to Mede accentuates this problem, since it is in fact a conceptual definition she offers, a definition that would seem, in fact, firmly to delimit the scope of Mede's action. Will asks to know the false, in reply to which Holy Church points out Mede, and defines her in this way:

> 'That is Mede the mayde', quod she, 'hath noyed me ful ofte,
> And ylakked my lemman that Leautee is hoten,
> And bilowen h[ym] to lordes that lawes han to kepe.
> In the Popes paleis she is pryvee as myselve,
> But soothnesse wolde noght so – for she is a bastard,
> For Fals was hire fader that hath a fikel tonge . . .'
>
> (II. 20–5)

noyed: harmed; *ylakked*: disparaged; *lemman*: lover; *leautee*: justice/fidelity; *hoten*: called; *bilowen*: told lies about; *fikel*: treacherous.

The word 'mede' in Middle English means, in its broadest terms, 'reward'; MED lists the following senses under 1a:

(a) A gift; noble or royal endowment . . .
(b) a material reward; compensation (for work or services); wages, earnings, salary.
(c) a fee; ransom; reparation; the payment of a fee, a bribe; also bribery, graft.

It is clear that Holy Church wants to delimit the allowable senses of the word to within sense 1a (c), that of illicit rewards, since Mede is the 'daughter' of False, where the familial relationship implies inescapable semantic overlap; and the effect of these illicit rewards is to undermine justice – the word 'leautee' in Middle English is as close a Latin-based equivalent to the Germanic word 'truthe' as is possible, since it contains senses both of law-keeping and of keeping faith, or loyalty. Any action involving Mede, it would seem, must necessarily take place within these semantic limits (Stokes 1984).

The action of the poem seems to confirm the limited sense of

---

1. For Langland's personification allegory more generally, see Griffiths (1985), and Frank (1953).

the word 'mede' Holy Church wishes to impose, since it is proposed to marry Mede to False (ll. 52–114), where the narrative model of marriage also implies a fixed semantic relationship. But before the legal formalities of this marriage can be completed, a figure called Theology interrupts with a complaint that Mede should not be allied in this way. His objection amounts to a new definition of Mede:

> For Mede is muliere, of Amendes engendred;
> And God graunted to gyve Mede to truthe,
> And thow hast gyven hire to a gilour – now God gyve
>   thee sorwe!
> The text telleth thee noght so, Truthe woot the sothe,
> For *Dignus est operarius* his hire to have.
>
> (II. 119–23)
>
> *muliere*: legitimate; *gilour*: deceiver; *woot*: knows; *Dignus est operarius*: the labourer is worthy.

So Theology gives Mede a new lineage (saying that Mede is legitimate, born of Amendes), and proposes a new husband (Truthe). These familial affiliations serve, in effect, to delimit the senses of the word 'mede' in a way exclusive of Holy Church's definition: Theology insists that reward is legitimate, that it is produced by making amends, and that it is given to honest action, since, he says quoting Christ, 'the labourer is worthy of his wage' (Luke 10.7). This new sense conforms especially with the second main sense of 'mede' given by MED, under 2(a): 'Moral consequence or spiritual reward; requital, retribution, just deserts . . .; *theol*[*ogically*] grace, merit'.

At the heart of the action of these passus, then, is an ambiguity, a word which refuses to be tied down in any fixed way, and which can provoke exclusive and opposed definitions from two figures of apparently unimpeachable authority, Holy Church and Theology. There seems to be no authority from within the text who can fix the meanings of 'mede', and this is the very condition of Mede's freedom in the narrative: as long, that is, as she is semantically ambiguous, then the narrative can be sustained. We can see how Mede sustains narrative action, in a way the other unambiguous figures do not, in her journey to Westminster: when the King hears, from Conscience, that Mede is coming with her companions False and Favel, he unhesitatingly judges the unambiguous figures in this way:

'Now, by Cryst!' quod the Kyng, 'and I cacche myghte
Fals or Favel or any of hise feeris,
I wolde be wroken of tho wrecches that wercheth so ille,
And doon hem hange by the hals and alle that hem maynteneth'.

(II. 193–6)

favel: deceit; feeris: companions, wroken: avenged; hals: neck.

He does not condemn Mede; the unambiguous figures he does
condemn flee immediately and disguise themselves in the material world:

Falsnesse for fere thanne fleigh to the freres
And Gyle dooth hym to go, agast for to dye.
Ac marchaunts metten with hym and made hym abyde . . .

(II. 211–13)

As soon, that is, as the unambiguous words are recognised, the
narrative cannot sustain them in any interesting way; they can
only act out the meaning of the concept they denote, and they
disappear from view. Mede, on the other hand, is isolated in the
narrative, and remains the focus of action precisely because she
is ambiguous, and able to be attached freely in the text to different
concepts.

We noticed, in the little example of personification allegory
with which I began, that Conscience served as an 'unerring
lexicographer' from within the text. When Mede arrives at Westminster, it is Conscience to whom the King wishes to marry
Mede, where the King is clearly aligning himself with Theology's
definition of 'mede' as legitimate reward. Mede is therefore faced
with a difficult proposal, since Conscience, of all possible partners, is most likely to perceive the senses of 'mede' which are
morally unacceptable. Faced with this challenge, we can see that
it is in the interests of both Mede and her supporters to keep her
as ambiguous as possible, blurring any moral discriminations
Conscience might make. And when she arrives at Westminster,
the possibility of remaining ambiguous seems strong: the justices
who receive her promise Mede that she will be able to marry as
she pleases, 'For al Consciences cast [calculation] or craft [skill]'
(l. 19) – that she will be able to affiliate, that is, with whatever
concept she pleases.

When the match is proposed to Conscience, however, he
resolutely refuses to have anything to do with her, insisting on

her fickleness and the fact that the kind of reward she represents destroys justice (ll. 120–69). Mede's tactic in response is to confuse the semantic borders of both 'conscience' and 'mede': she points out that Conscience himself has used mede, particularly in the recent treaty with France, where Conscience advised the King to set aside his claims to French 'lordshipe for a litel silver' (l. 207). This is a reference to the treaty of Bretigny in 1360, in which Edward III had settled for a money payment and Aquitaine, in return for abandoning his claim to the French crown. It is possible to see how a policy of conscience might easily have preferred a money settlement instead of continued bloodshed in a war of aggrandisement, but Mede cunningly turns this against Conscience firstly by saying that he has relied on her (by accepting a money payment), and secondly by saying that she could have produced much *more* reward (by the spoils of war) (ll. 186–208).

Mede goes on to confuse the semantic borders between different senses of the word 'mede' itself, by focusing on apparently traditional practices of feudal largesse, and on the apparently innocuous reward of wages which pass between master and servant:

> It bicometh to a kyng that kepeth a reaume
> To yeve [men mede] that mekely hym serveth —
> To aliens and to alle men, to honouren hem with yiftes;
> Mede maketh hym biloved and for a man holden.
> Emperours and erles and alle manere lordes
> Thorugh yiftes han yonge men to yerne and to ryde.
> The Pope and alle prelates presents underfongen
> And medeth men hemselven to mayntene hir lawes,
> Servaunts for hire servyce, we seeth wel the sothe,
> Taken mede of hir maistres, as thei mowe acorde.
>
> (III. 209–18)
>
> *bicometh* to: is fitting for; *reaume*: realm; *yerne*: run; *underfongen*: receive.

This appeals both to the King's sense of his feudal obligations of largesse, and to his sense of justice in the mention of rewards given for services rendered – this last amounts, apparently, to nothing more than a description of fair wages. Mede foregrounds apparently positive senses of the word 'mede', those contained under senses 1a (a) and (b) above (Stokes 1984, 120–2). So there is nothing here which should necessarily offend Conscience, and it comes as no surprise, perhaps, that the King heartily endorses Mede's case (ll. 228–9).

The narrative is in need of resolution at this point, since not only is Mede's ambiguity increased, but it is clearly in her interests that this ambiguity be preserved. The only way the narrative can be resolved is by clarifying what senses of Mede are permissible, and this is exactly what Conscience now does. In the manner of an academic debate, he resolves the question at issue by defining, as he says, 'two manere of medes' (l. 231); 'mede' is an ambiguous term, meaning both the reward that

> . . . God of his grace graunteth in his blisse
> To tho that wel werchen while thei ben here,
>
> (III. 232–3)

and the kind of mede which represents bribes, which is used to 'mayntene mysdoers' (ll. 246–54) (where the word 'mayntene' is used formally, to designate the system of maintenance (MED sense 3(b); Alford GLD)). And he clarifies the definition of 'mede' by introducing new terms to denote payments which are not beyond desert, but strictly merited: he says that the wage taken by labourers 'is no manere mede but a mesurable hire' (l. 256), and that mede is not relevant to legitimate trading, which takes place on the basis of strict exchange: this 'is a permutacion apertly – a penyworth for another' (l. 258). In the equivalent C-Text speech (C. III. 285–405a), Conscience offers a formal term, 'mercede' (from the Latin merces) to denote this kind of strictly equitable payment (C. III. 209). The conceptual boundaries are carefully drawn now: 'mede' does indicate a reward distinct from the strictly equitable reward paid to a labourer, or paid in the strict exchange of trade, and this should prohibit Mede from using wages as an example of her own activity. At the same time, 'mede' of whatever kind (either from God or that used in acts of bribery) necessarily implies a reward beyond desert: men do not deserve salvation by strict justice, but only out of God's generosity or grace (even if there is some proportion between gift and works), just as those who receive bribes cannot be said to merit them.[2]

2. Important recent discussions of Conscience's distinctions between earthly and heavenly 'mede', and 'mesurable hire', all of which have greatly advanced our

If Conscience's lexical discriminations are to be convincing, then we should expect Mede to be restricted, in the narrative from here on, to representing bribery. This is in fact what happens: the narrative appears to be interrupted in Passus IV, since the question of Mede's marriage with Conscience is left aside, and instead the narrative focuses on the bill of Peace against Wrong. But in fact there is no conceptual break, since Mede enacts her pejorative senses in the trial of Wrong, thereby concluding the debate as to whether or not she can marry Conscience. In defence of the unambiguously guilty figure Wrong, goods are offered to the injured party Peace. Wisdom suggests that if any amends can be made (through paying Peace), then Wrong should be set free on bail, 'And so amenden that is mysdo, and everemoore the bettre' (l. 90). Theology had said that Mede was 'of Amendes engendred' in Passus II, and here Wisdom (of the practical, wordly kind I first described), cunningly plays on that idea to suggest the reasonableness of liberating Wrong (Stokes 1984, 143). The fact that Peace willingly accepts the gift reveals how the concept 'peace' wants nothing more than the quiet life, and is insufficient to guarantee real peace. The King, however, is concerned with the underlying conditions of his Peace. He now recognises the stable meaning of the word 'mede' as represented by Mede herself, resolutely refusing to allow Peace to be paid off in this way; instead, he insists that Wrong be judged, setting Mede in the same conceptual opposition with 'leaute' that Holy Church had first posed. Addressing Lawe, and, presumably, Wrong, he declares his sentence thus:

Mede shal noght maynprise yow, by the Marie of hevene!

---

understanding of Langland's theology, are Adams (1983; 1988a; 1988b), and Overstreet (1984). Adams and Overstreet disagree about 'mede' from God: is it 'mesureless' (Overstreet 1984, 286) or proportionate (Adams 1983, 400; 1988a; 97; 1988b, 230–1)? Overstreet states the question in this way: 'One might propose that in B Langland had in mind condign merit leading to eternal life (heavenly meed "mesurable") and wages (*mesurable hire*) as opposed to the *mede mesurelees* of bribery; but if so, what is the distinctive feature of meed that moves Langland to use the term for both heavenly reward and bribery?' (286, n. 92). Agreeing with Adams, I would reply that there is a difference between gifts which are undeserved absolutely (meesureless meed), and gifts which are in proportion, though (as gifts) not equal to deserving (heavenly meed). It is precisely this kind of gift which characterises the definition of *meritum de congruo* in the thirteenth and fourteenth centuries.

I wole have leaute in lawe, and lete be al youre jangling,
And as moost folk witnesseth wel, Wrong shal be demed.
(IV. 179–81)[3]
maynprise: serve as surety for (by offering bail money); *demed*: judged.

With the help of Reason and Conscience, then, the King has been
able to sentence the guilty figure Wrong; but this judicial sentence
relies on an intellectual act of defining the senses of the word
'mede': now the King uses the word unequivocally in sense 1a
(c), '. . . the payment of a fee, a bribe; also bribery, graft'. It is
this intellectual confinement of the word which allows for, and
presupposes, the legal confinement of Wrong in prison (Simpson
1986a, 13).

MEDE AND SOCIAL 'TRUTHE'

In considering personification allegory, we have seen how Langland's art is a 'clerkly' one, brilliantly playing as it does with the
meanings of words, and neatly manipulating the resources of this
kind of allegory, such that the narrative is sustained only so long
as there is any doubt about the meaning of the word 'mede'. So
far our consideration of these passus has been purely formal,
considering how Langland's personification allegory is designed
to elucidate verbal 'truthe'. Now I should like to turn to the
satirical content of Passus II–IV, and their representation of
society. Why should the definition of proper reward be so
important for Langland? What implications does the definition
have for Langland's commitment to the idea of 'truthe' in its
social sense, that of 'loyalty', or 'faith-keeping'?

Personification allegory, as Langland practises it, serves not
only to define the conceptual boundaries denoted by words
through their interaction with other words; it also defines the
social, institutional attachments of words. In Langland's hands,
that is, allegory of this kind is profoundly embedded in the
conceptual base of the institutions to which words like 'mede',
or 'conscience' attach themselves.

3. I here acknowledge what seems to me a misreading in my earlier article
(1986a), when I said (p. 13) that Mede is imprisoned; although the King seems
to be looking at Mede as he pronounces his sentence, it is strictly speaking
Wrong who is imprisoned, not Mede. This misreading does not affect the
substance of my argument there, about the intellectual confinement of 'Mede'.

The question of social 'truthe', then, can only be broached by considering the institutions which shape social relations. Mede's speech of self-defence (cited above), in which she says that kings, nobles, popes, prelates, teachers, priests and tradesmen all require or give mede (III. 209–27) points in fact to a series of social institutions (the monarchy; the aristocracy; the papacy; schools and universities; the parish church; and guilds), in each of which 'Mede' (actually nothing substantial herself) is what defines the relations between participants in those institutions.

So personification allegory, in Langland's hands, is necessarily raising questions about social institutions, since the concepts denoted by the personified words inevitably attach themselves to particular institutions. And we can also see why questions of economics, or of proper reward, should be of such importance to Langland, since it is precisely in the economic relations between people that 'truthe' in the social sense is either preserved or destroyed.

In particular, the fact that Langland chooses marriage nego-tiations as the model institution to present Mede serves his satirical purpose of attacking the way in which Mede subverts traditional ties of loyalty between people. I argued earlier that marriage serves Langland's personification allegory by offering a model through which the senses of words could be semantically linked (or not) with the senses of other words. But the specific details of Mede's proposed marriage to False also offer a critique of institutions – both of contemporary marriage practices, and, more generally, of the replacement of 'truthe' by financial reward in social relations of maintenance.

When, for example, Will first sees the wedding preparations for the marriage of Mede and False, he describes the retinue which is summoned to the wedding:

> As sisours and somonours, sherreves and hire clerkes,
> Bedelles and baillifs and brocours of chaffare,
> Forgoers and vitaillers and vokettes of the Arches;
> I kan noght rekene the route that ran aboute Mede.
> Ac Symonie and Cyvylle and sisours of courtes
> Were moost pryvee with Mede of any men, me
>   thoughte.
>
> (II. 59–64)

sisours: members of a sworn inquest, jurymen; bedelles: beadles, messengers of justice; brocours: commercial agents, middlemen; chaffare: trade; forgoers:

men who travelled ahead of a great lord, commandeering provisions; *vitaillers*: victuallers; *vokettes*: advocates or professional pleaders; *route*: crowd: *symonie*: the sale of a church office or benefice; *cyvylle*: civil law and its study (especially by church (canon) lawyers).

Mede has a whole 'retenaunce', or liveried retinue[4] of local, and particularly judicial officials at her service, who control both the secular and the ecclesiastical courts.[5] The scene evokes the late medieval phenomenon I described in Chapter 1, known in contemporary documents as 'maintenance', according to which a lord would strengthen his position by paying for the services of his retainers, rather than relying on the stock of vassals with which his feudal position supplied him. Whenever a lord appeared at great public occasions (being summoned to court, Council, or Parliament, for example), his retinue was required to ride with him. Mede herself is pictured as a great noble (she is a kinswoman to the King (II. 133), and her clothing designates her noble status (II. 7–16));[6] likewise the retinue summoned to her wedding, and with whom she rides to Westminster (II. 158–88), may be compared with the livery roll of late fourteenth-century baronial lords. The retinue of Edward Courtney, Earl of Devon, for the year 1384–85, for example, included seven knights, forty squires (among which number many estate officials), fifty-two yeomen, four minstrels, eight parsons, and fourteen men-of-law, including four sergeants retained to plead his causes in the king's courts (McFarlane 1973, 111).[7]

And if the retinue satirises the structures of 'bastard feudalism', or maintenance, the charter which formalises the marriage settlement attacks both contemporary marriage practices among noble families, and the lack of 'truthe' in social relations more generally.

4. The word 'retenaunce' can simply mean 'a retinue, a band of followers' (MED sense (a)). But among the instances given under this sense, there are examples of the contemporary practice of liveried retainers.

5. See the notes in Schmidt (1987a), though the reference to 'Civile' should now take into account Gilbert (1980) and Barratt (1982), who argue that 'Civile' represents civil jurisprudence as used by canon lawyers.

6. The Statutes of the Realm of Edward III place strict conditions on the wearing of dress and ornaments beyond one's income. Knights whose value is not above 200 marks, their wives, and their children shall 'wear not cloth of Gold, nor [Cloths], Mantle nor Gown furred with Miniver nor of Ermine, nor of no Apparel broidered of Stone, nor otherwise'. Mede wears all these categories of dress. (Anno 37 Edw. III, c. 10 (*Statutes of the Realm.* I. 380–1)).

7. For an account of maintenance and its relevance to *Piers Plowman*, see Baldwin, Anna (1981a, 24–31). I am much indebted to this study.

The *'maritagium'*, or marriage settlement drawn up by Mede's father follows the pattern of a permanent grant of lands, according to the model of a charter of enfeoffment; it begins with the standard opening of such a charter (*'Sciant presentes et futuri . . .'* (Alford *GLD*)), and is held at each point within the formulae of such a grant (II. 74a–114). The very precision of the legal model insists on the subversion of legality in the charter, since it seeks in every detail to legitimate illegality (Stokes 1984, 107). And the loyalty in social relations and in marriage specifically which the charter presupposes is necessarily absent, when the participants are Mede and False. McFarlane points out that 'bastard feudalism' developed its own characteristic documents, designed to create non-heritable contractual relations between the signatories, unlike the charter of enfeoffment, which is designed to create heritable property. But Mede belongs to the world of more temporary, non-tenurial relations: the only heritable rights in this charter are those created by the here unspoken divine sanctions against the capital sins, whereby (again parodying the standard forms of a charter) Mede and False are granted

> . . . to have and to holde, and hire heires after,
> A dwellynge with the devel, and dampned be for evere.
> (II. 102–3)

'Truthe' in marriage is here replaced by financial interest alone: the document states explicitly that False desires Mede simply because 'he woot hire riche' (l. 78). Like many of the noble marriages of the period, Mede's marriage is a financial transaction, whose motive is the increase of property, the kind of marriage satirised by the figure Wit in Passus IX, who counsels his listeners to be married 'for no londes, but for love' (IX. 177).[8]

So when Conscience rejects Mede in Passus III as a harlot, we can see that Langland is literally attacking falseness in marriage, and metaphorically attacking the instability of relations between people when they are based on profit; he says this about Mede:

> Wyves and widewes wantounnesse she techeth,
> And lereth hem lecherie that loveth hire yiftes
> . . .
> For she is tikel of hire tail, talewis of tonge,

---

8. For contemporary marriage practices in relation to noble households, see
   Starkey (1981).

As commune as the cartwey to [knaves and to alle] –
To monkes, to mynstrales, to meseles in hegges;
Sisours and somonours, swiche men hire preiseth,
Sherreves of shires were shent if she ne were.
(III. 125–35)
tikel: promiscuous; *talewis*: garrulous; *meseles*: lepers; *shent*: ruined.

The wives and widows in the first two lines here are those literal
wives, like the merchant's wife in Chaucer's *Shipman's Tale*,
whose sexual infidelity is at the same time presented as good business; but in saying that Mede herself is 'tikel of hire tail',
Conscience is using the sexual metaphor to suggest the way in
which relations of profit enter into all spheres of life, and destroy
relationships based on loyalty.

MEDE AND LEGAL 'TRUTHE'

We have seen how Langland's Mede is represented as undermining
the institutions of a 'leal' society – a society in which relationships
are constituted by faithfulness and loyalty. In particular, we have
seen how Langland pictures the corruption (as he sees it) of
specific institutions (e.g. the noble household; marriage), which
were in fact changing in the late fourteenth century. But if Langland portrays the corruption of social 'truthe' in this way, his
concern with the legal aspect of 'truthe' is dominant in these
passus, since the institutions in which Mede is most profoundly
and most threateningly embedded are legal institutions.

Holy Church's initial definition of Mede signals the specifically
legal aspect of Mede's activity; she says that Mede has disparaged
her lover 'Leautee', and told lies about him to 'lordes that lawes
han to kepe' (ll. 20–1). The word 'leaute' is listed in MED as
having a range of meaning overlapping with that of 'truthe':

(a) Uprightness, honourableness, honesty; truth; justice, fairness
    . . .
(b) loyalty, faithfulness;
(c) allegiance.

We have seen already how Mede threatens 'Leautee' in the senses
(b) and (c), but Langland places the word in a specifically legal
context, suggestive of sense (a), in saying that Mede has told lies
about 'Leautee' to those whose responsibility it is to maintain

justice. This is the sense in which the word 'leaute' is most frequently used in the poem – at the very end of Passus IV, for example, the King declares that he will have 'leaute in lawe' (l. 180)[9] Or in Passus XI, the just emperor Trajan uses the word, in apparent synonymity with 'truthe', when he encourages lords in this way:

> Lo! ye lordes, what *leautee* dide by an Emperour of Rome
> That was an uncristene creature, as clerkes fyndeth in bokes.
> Nought thorough preiere of a pope but for his *pure truthe*
> Was that Sarsen saved . . .
>
> (XI. 153–6) [my italics]
>
>   *sarsen*: pagan.

And one of Conscience's special complaints against Mede in his refusal to accept her as wife is that Mede obstructs the path of legal justice:

> Ther she is wel with the kyng, wo is the reaume —
> For she is favorable to Fals and defouleth truthe ofte.
> By Jesus! with hire jeweles youre justice she shendeth
> And lith ayein the lawe and letteth hym the gate,
> That feith may noght have his forth, hire floryns go so thikke.
>
> (III. 153–7)
>
>   *shendeth*: destroys; *lith*: lies; *letteth hym the gate*: blocks his way.

So Langland's satire on Mede picks up one of the central themes of Holy Church's sermon in Passus I, concerning the legal aspect of 'truthe', according to which it means 'justice'. In so doing, Langland is working within a well established literary tradition, known as 'venality satire'. This satire, which had developed in medieval Europe from the eleventh century, was directed chiefly against the use of money, and the way in which money corrupted the exercise of justice (Yunck 1963). Langland is certainly indebted to the conventions of this kind of satire, and would have been familiar with it through both Latin and French models (Yunck 1988). But however much he draws on literary traditions, his particular presentation of Mede's corruption of justice is firmly anchored in the specific legal institutions of fourteenth-century England.

We have already noticed that the retinue bidden to the wedding

---

9. On the larger significance of the concept 'leaute', see Kean (1964).

of Mede and False is peopled especially by local officals responsible for the enactment of both civil and ecclesiastical justice – the
'sisours and somonours, sherreves and hire clerkes' (II. 59). The
witty satire of Mede's journey to London makes the same point;
instead of riding *with* a retinue of local court officials, Mede and
the other abstract concepts of corruption ride *on* such officials.
Favel (Deceitful Speech) arranges for horses to be brought:

> And sette Mede upon a sherreve shoed al newe,
> And Fals sat on a sisour that softeli trotted.
>
> (II. 164–5)
>
> *sisour*: member of an inquest, juryman.

These are the officers of secular law (a sherrif was the King's chief
representative in a county (Morris and Strayer 1947, II. 53–73)
while a 'sisour' is a member of a jury, appointed by the sheriff).
Simony and 'Cyvylle', on the other hand, command a host of
church officials, responsible for ecclesiastical law, to be saddled
up – summoners (a minor official who cited alleged offenders to
ecclesiastical courts), deans, sub-deans and archdeacons (all officials of a bishop, archdeacons acting as judges in ecclesiastical
courts), among others.

As I have already shown, retinues of this kind were maintained
in the period; and they were used in practice to bring the institutions of local justice into line with the patron's interests. Juries,
for example, were not expected to decide a case on the basis of
evidence presented in court; instead, they were 'well-informed
neighbours who arrived knowing the answer' (McFarlane 1973,
116), and it is frequently found that the 'informing' of a jury costs
money, which indicates that they were bribed. Sherrifs, who
appointed the jury, could also be in the pay of the local patron
(Baldwin, J. F. 1913, 267; Morris and Strayer 1947, II. 67–8).

Retinues such as these represent the kind of corrupting influence
a lord could wield over dispensers of law in his own locality. In
Passus III and IV, however, the scene moves to Westminster,
where Mede must confront royal justice as dispensed in the
capital. When Mede first arrives, it would appear that here, too,
she will have no trouble in bribing the King's justices – the first
group of figures who 'receive' Mede at the court are, indeed,
justices, who are rewarded with treasures by Mede (III. 13–24).
Little scenes like this clearly exploit the resources of personifica-

tion allegory to bring a biblical text to life, as it were: later in Passus III Conscience cites Psalm 25 (l. 248a) to point to those who take mede: '*In quorum manibus iniquitates sunt; dextra eorum repleta est muneribus*' (Ps. 25.10) – 'In whose hands are iniquities: their right hand is filled with gifts'. Langland elaborates this biblical idea of receiving corrupting gifts by the model of courteously 'receiving' a guest. But in pursuing the idea of Mede at the King's court, Langland places such biblical ideas against the corruption of justice in a very specifically realised context of late fourteenth-century judicial institutions.

At the beginning of Passus IV the King sends for Reason, to be final arbiter in the proposed marriage of Conscience and Mede. But no sooner does Reason arrive than the whole question of the proposed marriage is apparently dropped, when the figure Peace places a petition before Parliament against Wrong, and the narrative follows the trial closely, until the sentencing of Wrong. This might seem like an awkward break in the action, but, as I argued earlier, it is in fact completely consistent with the intellectual content of the personification allegory: Conscience has defined Mede as bribery, and cannot therefore be married to her; the action of Wrong's trial confirms Conscience's definition, and confirms, as a result, the impossibility of any semantic overlap, or 'marriage', between 'conscience' and 'mede'. The court in which the King sentences Wrong, and recognises Mede for what she is, is the prerogative court of his Council, acting in its judicial function, and Langland's representation of the activities of this court is closely modelled on the judicial procedures of the King's Council in the fourteenth century.

The body known as the King's Council was constituted by officers of the King's household (such as the Chancellor and the Treasurer), legal officials (judges, and clerks of chancery), a select number of knights, and a select number of bishops and barons. Among its many other functions, the King's Council served a judicial role, to judge in those cases for which a solution could not be found at common law, or in those cases where the petitioner could not sue at common law because of the power of his enemies, and/or because the local courts were corrupt (Baldwin, J. F. 1913, Ch. 11).[10] The court was not bound by

10. For a discussion of how the procedures of the King's Council served as a model for the action of Passus IV, see Baldwin, Anna (1981a, Ch. 3).

common law, and made its decision on the strict equity, or justice of the case. It did not formally deal in any field of jurisdiction as distinct from other courts, but the cases it had most frequently to deal with were cases of violence, fraud, international law, and crimes which affected the rights of the crown, such as treason. The document by which plantiffs sought access to this special court was not the writ, but the petition, or 'bill', which was written in French or English (unlike the Latin writ of common law), and was composed (though not in any formal pattern) of the address, the complaint, and the prayer for a remedy.

In almost every respect, the trial scene of Passus IV conforms to the sketch of the King's Council in its judicial function which I have just given. The King is sitting in Council at the beginning of the passus (l. 8), and it is Reason (who becomes the King's household officer at the end of the passus), who tries the case. And the case itself is initiated by the petition, or 'bille' of Peace (l. 47). The offences of Wrong are clearly ones for which Peace has been unable to get redress at common law, for fear (l. 52, l. 60), and the offences themselves are characteristic of one stan-dard kind of offence which came before the Council – that of the violence committed by the maintained band of a powerful man (Baldwin, J. F. 1913, 265); what we are permitted to see here is the bully-boy world of maintenance as it might be practised in a locality, far from (but supporting), the polite, courtly world in which Mede is received at Westminster: Peace complains that Wrong

> . . . maynteneth hise men to murthere myne hewen,
> Forstalleth my feires and fighteth in my chepyng,
> And breketh up my berne dores and bereth awey my whete,
> And taketh me but a taille for ten quarters otes.
> And yet he beteth me therto and lyth by my mayde;
> I am noght hardy for hym unnethe to loke!

(IV. 55–60)

murthere: murder; hewen: servants; forstalleth: buys up goods and sells them at a higher price; chepyng: market; taille: a tally, or proof of debt (see Alford GLD); hardy: bold; for: on account of; unnethe: hardly.

What I have said about the trial of Wrong and contemporary legal practice so far might suggest that Langland's scene is a simple reflection of contemporary legal institutions. In fact, the scene presented by Langland is idealised, charged with a reforming spirit against the weaknesses and abuses of this court in the fourteenth century. The composition of the King's Council had been one of the most controversial issues of the period, with complaints against Edward II in particular, but also against Edward III in the so-called Good Parliament of 1376, centring on membership of the Council, a position which carried enormous power (Baldwin, J. F. 1913, Ch. 6). The names of the actants themselves in Passus IV suggest the normative impulse of the satire, designed as it is to reveal the basic concepts involved in the ideal practice of such a court: 'Pees' represents the phrase 'the King's Peace', and represents the law for which the King was directly responsible. And the figures on whom the King relies for judgement, Conscience and Reason, are themselves drawn from, and personify concepts at the base of contemporary English law: 'reson et conscience'; 'loy et reson'; 'ley et conscience' are all formulae to be found in cases coming before the King's Council. The Council-in-Chancery court was even referred to in the fifteenth century as the 'Court of Conscience' (Baldwin, Anna 1981a, 42).

But the most significant way in which the prerogative court of this scene diverges from contemporary practice is in the refusal of the King to offer Wrong any bail to release him from prison. These courts did exact heavy punishments on individual malefactors, but the court was consistently lenient against lords and knights committing offences with their large bands, normally releasing the felon on bail, rather than taking the risk of imprisoning him. And those who did pay a security as bail sought to have their obligations cancelled, which they were likely to obtain through channels of favour (Baldwin, J. F. 1913, 304–6). Wrong's associates Wit, Wisdom and Mede all attempt to persuade first the King directly, and then the King through Peace, to accept a financial surety:

> 'God woot', quod Wisdom, 'that were noght the beste!
> And he amendes mowe make, lat Maynprise hym have
> And be borgh for his bale, and buggen hym boote,
> And so amenden that is mysdo, and everemoore the bettre.'
>
> (IV. 87–90)

> *woot*: knows; *maynprise*: bail; *borgh*: one who stands as a surety, or pledge; *bale*: evil acts; *buggen*: buy; *boote*: remedy.

And Mede herself offers Peace a present in compensation, grate-
fully accepted by Peace, who then joins in the ostensibly
reasonable chorus of voices calling for a merciful sentence on
Wrong (ll. 94–103) (Stokes 1984, 143). But most of Wrong's
offences are criminal, not civil: his acts of rape, murder, fore-
stalling and maintenance (ll. 47–60) cannot be compensated for
by settling with Peace in the manner of a civil case; his offences
are against the King, and although the King is free to accept the
sureties offered to himself, he does not, as fourteenth-century
kings often did, accept them. With the help of Reason, he recognises that mercy to Wrong would be misplaced, and that the strict
enforcement of justice is the genuinely merciful act to those who
merit merciful protection against Wrong – if the King released
him, he says that Wrong would laugh it off, 'And eft the boldere
be to bete myne hewen' (I. 107). Reason declares the principle
of this strict justice in his summing up, saying that Wrong should
receive no mercy, unless 'mekenesse it made',

> For 'Nullum malum the man mette with inpunitum
> And bad Nullum bonum be irremuneratum'
>
> (IV. 143–4)
>
> nullum malum: no evil, inpunitum: unpunished; nullum bonum: no good; irre-
> muneratum: unrewarded.

This little personification allegory stresses the positive side of
justice: if someone commits no breach of the law, he will remain
unpunished, and every act of positive good will be rewarded. This
satisfying account of unfailing justice has its satisfying, if austere,
obverse, of course: anyone who does commit a breach of the law
will certainly be punished. The only exception to this is the clause
about mercy being given for genuine repentance ('mekenesse');
this is consonant with the King's earlier statement that Wrong will
be punished 'but lowenesse hym borwe' (l. 109), where the
surety, or 'borgh' of genuine repentance is preferred before the
financial surety offered by Mede. But this clause is not stressed
here, and in any case it is irrelevant to the incorrigibly illegal
figure Wrong. The justice which is stressed is the strict, unremitting justice administered by the King; anything short of this on
the side of mercy to Wrong is seen as an offence to justice, and
to genuine mercy.

The passus ends with a resounding representation of an idealised King's Council. Reason exhorts the Kingdom to reform by saying that he will have no pity until, in effect, pity will be unnecessary, since the reforms he envisages imply strict justice, one element of which concerns the King's Council: he will have no pity, 'Til the Kynges counseil be the commune profit' (l. 123). And the passus ends with Reason being appointed as a high officer to the King, and agreeing to stay forever with the King 'So Conscience be of oure counseil' (l. 193).

CONCLUSION

In conclusion, then, we can say that the action of these passus take up two of the senses of 'truthe' as used by Holy Church – the sense of 'loyalty', and the sense of 'justice'. The application of these senses here is to secular institutions, of baronial households, and, especially, to the institutions of both local and monarchical justice. We can also say that the textual procedure adopted by Langland here, that of personification allegory, is devoted wholly to the rational elucidation of 'truthe' in the simple sense of 'veracity'. In this action, then, Langland deploys venality satire in the interests of an idealised monarchy, and fills out the application of 'truthe', as Holy Church had used the word, in the secular sphere. However satisfying the resolution of these passus might be, it is only in the next vision, when 'truthe' is applied to the spiritual sphere, and to the discourse of penitence, that we realise the crisis to which unremitting stress on 'truthe' leads.

Chapter 3

The Second Vision:
Passus V–VII

PASSUS V: Will wakes from his vision, but soon falls asleep again (ll. 1–8); he now sees, and hears, Reason preaching to all the realm (ll. 9–59); after Reason's sermon *Repentance* provokes confessions from the seven deadly sins, which follow in the order Pride, Lechery, Envy, Wrath, Avarice, Gluttony, and Sloth; these confessions are followed by that of Roberd the Robber (ll. 60–477). The confession scene ends with Repentance's prayer to God for salvation (ll. 478–506). This produces Hope's clarion call (ll. 507–9b), at which the sinners leave on pilgrimage to seek Truthe. The first person they meet is a well seasoned pilgrim, who knows nothing of the shrine of St Truthe (ll. 510–36). At this point *Piers Plowman* offers his services to the pilgrims, declaring that he knows the way to St Truthe, since he is Truthe's worker (ll. 537–55). Piers refuses to be paid, and outlines the route to Truthe as a pilgrimage through the Ten Commandments to the charity and forgiveness of the New Law, where Truthe is found in the heart (ll. 556–629). The passus ends with some disreputable characters refusing to join Piers (ll. 630–42).

PASSUS VI: Piers announces that he must plough half an acre before he goes on pilgrimage; he gives instructions to different orders of society, including a representative of knighthood, as to how they might help the ploughing (ll. 1–56); Piers dresses for ploughing and promises a share of the harvest to all those who help (ll. 57–77); before he starts work, he draws up his will, in the manner of pilgrims about to leave on pilgrimage (ll. 78–104). The ploughing begins; many help Piers, but there are also many slackers, who resist the arguments and threats of both Piers and the knight (ll. 105–70). Piers now calls on *Hunger* to force the wasters to work; the threat of Hunger is instantly successful (ll. 171–98). Piers questions Hunger about the problem of beggary; Hunger replies that those unable to work should be given food, while everyone else should work for their sustenance, and eat with moderation (ll. 199–274). Before Hunger goes, he demands great quantities of food from Piers (ll. 275–301), such that workers are unwilling to work (ll. 302–19). The passus ends with a threatening prophecy about imminent famine (ll. 320–30).

PASSUS VII: *Truthe* sends a pardon to Piers, which also promises pardon to all those who fulfil their earthly functions faithfully: kings and knights, bishops, merchants, (rare) honest lawyers, honest labourers, and genuine beggars (ll. 1–104). A priest asks to see the actual wording of the pardon, that he might translate it into English, in response to which Piers unfolds the document. When he reads it, the priest denies that there is any pardon here at all (ll. 105–14). Piers tears the pardon and declares that he will no longer work so hard for physical food, but devote himself to penitential ploughing' instead (ll. 115–38a). The priest's and Piers's argument wakes Will, who reflects on the value of interpreting dreams, and on the meaning of this particular dream (ll. 139–201).

INTRODUCTION

The institutions Langland has been especially concerned to reform in Passus II–IV are those of secular law, and in particular the King's Council. The greatest single threat Langland sees to the just exercise of law is the undeserved profit represented by Mede, which blocks justice both through systems of maintenance, and through the bribery of courts. In Passus V–VII, however, the institutions Langland has in his sights are clearly ecclesiastical – he represents a cluster of practices controlled by the Church:

sermon, confession, pilgrimage, and pardon. The opening speech
of the vision proper signals the change from the secular to the
ecclesiastical, where Reason, who has been responsible for the
reformation of the King's Council in the previous passus, now
appears as a bishop, preaching a sermon. Will observes

> . . . how Reson gan arayen hym al the reaume to preche,
> And with a cros afore the Kyng comsede thus to techen.
>
> (V. 11–12)
>
> *arayen hym*: prepare himself; *comsede*: began.

This move to ecclesiastical institutions from those of secular
justice is not arbitrary, but instead reveals that for Langland
reformation of the secular realm is impossible without the more
profound reformation of the soul. This interdependence is implicit
in the fact that Reason, in his role of bishop, repeats (V. 24–59)
many of the injunctions he had made in his role as royal councillor
(IV. 113–33). But if reformation of the secular realm is dependent
on reformation of the soul, both kinds of reformation are also
parallel in their concern for the necessity to meet the standards of
a strict justice. Just as Mede and her followers seek to make
amends in order that Wrong might escape prison, so too do the
sinners of Passus V seek to make amends to their spiritual lord,
Truthe, in order that they, too, might be pardoned. It is only by
meeting the standards of the deified concept of justice, Truthe,
that the sinners can escape Truthe's 'dongeon'.

For both systems of justice, the earthly and the spiritual, Langland models the narrative on the institutions which embody
justice on earth and in the spiritual sphere – the King's Council
in Passus IV, and the penitential practices of confession and
pilgrimage by which the sinner seeks to meet the standards of
God's justice in Passus V and VI. In Passus IV the representation
of an ideal King's Council may stand as a satirical rebuke to the
questionable standards of the actual Council in the late fourteenth
century, but the institution itself is not attacked *qua* institution:
the very fact of presenting it in its ideal form itself implies Langland's faith in the structure of the institution as a *possible* ideal. In
Passus V–VII, however, I want to argue that Langland's
commitment to the standards of God's justice leads him to attack
the very institutional models on which the content of the narrative
is based. Despite his conservative ecclesiastical sympathies, his

commitment to 'truthe' impels him to question the practices upon which the narrative has been modelled. I will consider these passus firstly by discussing their satirical mode, and then by discussing the theological perceptions which inspire that satire.

ECCLESIASTICAL SATIRE

The narrative of Passus V–VII is modelled, as I have said, on a coherent cluster of ecclesiastical forms – sermon, confession, pilgrimage, and pardon.[1] The sermon provokes the confession of the seven deadly sins, which is heard by the confessor figure Repentance; and Repentance inspires the sinners to go on pilgrimage, in order to receive a full pardon for their sins, which is delivered by Truthe at the beginning of Passus VII. In following through this series of ecclesiastical forms, Langland is following standard definitions of the essential steps of penitence. According to standard penitential doctrine, sin involves two problems for the sinner: *culpa*, or culpability for the sin itself, and *pena*, or a debt which must be repaid before the sin can be pardoned. The steps of penitence are three: contrition of heart; confession of mouth (both of which allow a priest to absolve the *culpa* of sin); and satisfaction, which means the repayment of the debt, or *pena*, of sin through some act of restitution.[2] In this vision Reason provokes *contrition* through his sermon; Repentance hears the *confessions* of the contrite sinners; and in hope of absolute pardon, the sinners make *satisfaction* through their pilgrimage.

Langland's scheme is coherent, but the most immediate problems the reader faces in understanding the movement of these passus are the two interruptions to the conventional scheme on which the narrative is based: the pilgrimage is interrupted by Piers's ploughing of his half-acre, and when the pardon is finally opened, Piers tears it up. What is Langland's strategy in disrupting the standard penitential scheme upon which he has based his narrative?

Sermon and Confession

The discourses adopted by Langland in Passus V would seem to place the poem again, as it had been placed in Passus I, squarely

1. The argument of this section ('Ecclesiastical Satire') is heavily indebted to Burrow (1965).
2. These penitential steps are outlined in the poem at XIV. 16–21a.

back within the field of discourses employed by the Church:
Reason's *sermo ad status*, or sermon to different estates of society,
is delivered from a position of episcopal authority, and although
he cannot be said to have a formal theme in the way Holy Church
does in Passus I, his moral emphasis is similar to that of Holy
Church. He dislodges the words 'coveitise' and 'seke' from their
normal referents in exhorting his listeners to seek 'truthe':

> And ye that han lawes to kepe, lat Truthe be youre coveitise
> Moore than gold outher giftes if ye wol God plese
> . . .
> And ye that seke Seynt James and seyntes of Rome,
> Seketh Seynt Truthe, for he may save yow alle.
>
> (V. 52–7)

And if Reason's sermon seems to be projected from within the
discursive forms of the Church, so too are the confessions of the
deadly sins, who follow in the order Pride, Lechery, Envy,
Wrath, Avarice, Gluttony and Sloth. However intense in their
presentation, many of the details of these confessions are drawn
from the standard penitential manuals which provide frameworks
for self-analysis in the confession of sin. Chaucer's Parson, for
example, analyses the parts of envy in his penitential treatise by
saying that there are two 'speces', or types of envy: 'Ther is first,
sorwe of oother mannes goodnesse and of his prosperitee . . . The
seconde spece of Envye is joye of oother mannes harm . . . Of
these two speces comth bakbityng . . .' (X(I) 490–5), at which
point he goes on to define the different kinds of backbiting. The
opening of Envy's confession contains these two kinds of envy,
and their offspring backbiting, in dramatic form:

> I wolde be gladder, by God! that Gybbe hadde meschaunce
> Than though I hadde this wouke ywonne a weye of Essex chese.
> I have a neghebore neigh me, I have anoyed hym ofte,
> And lowen on hym to lordes to doon hym lese his silver,
> And maad his frendes be his foon thorugh my false tonge.
> His grace and his goode happes greven me ful soore.
>
> (V. 91–6)

wouke: week; *weye*: a standard of dry-goods weight; *lowen*: told lies against;
foon: foes; *happes*: chances.

Not only are the forms of the confessions, and many of their
details, based on the model of ecclesiastical penitential manuals,
but the sinfulness of the sins is often defined against their abuse

of standard ecclesiastical forms which could have saved them from sin. Envy, for example, puts his enviousness into intense relief in this way:

> And whan I come to the kirk and sholde knele to the Roode
> And preye for the peple as the preest techeth —
> For pilgrymes and for palmeres, for al the peple after —
> Thanne I crye on my knees that Crist yyve hem sorwe
> That baren awey my bolle and my broke shete.
> Awey fro the auter thanne turne I myne eighen
> And biholde how [H]eyne hath a newe cote.
>
> (V. 103–9)

   kirk: chirch; *roode*: cross; *bolle*: bowl; *broke*: torn; *auter*: altar.

In this powerful little example, we can see in the very posture of Envy how the humility and generosity of prayer is grotesquely transformed, and in the movement of Envy's eyes away from the altar how an obsessive concern with earthly standing has eclipsed the spiritual world entirely. Gluttony's sin, too, is defined against the ecclesiastical forms which could release him from it (Gray 1986); this is dramatically enacted by the fact that Gluttony is diverted to the pub on his way to church, 'his coupe to shewe' (ll. 297–300). But his (drinking) 'cup' takes precedence over his 'coupe' (*culpa*) of sin. And the pub scene itself is partly a parody of the ecclesiastical forms from which Gluttony has been diverted: the drinkers 'seten so til evensong, and songen umwhile' (l. 339); Glutton 'pissed a potel in a Paternoster-while' (l. 342), and 'blew his rounde ruwet at his ruggebones ende' (l. 343), which concludes the pub-scene proper, and as such seems to parody the blowing of the horn of Hope at the end of the confessions (ll. 507–8). And Sloth also defines his slothfulness in terms of his ignorance of the ecclesiastical forms which might protect him: he says that he knows the 'rymes of Robyn Hood and Randolf Erl of Chestre' (l. 396), while being ignorant of the Lord's Prayer; or that he never performs the penance enjoined upon him by the priest (l. 399); or that when he does go to church, he is satisfied to have heard the '*Ite missa est*', the end of the mass (l. 413).

These observations suggest that Langland is working unquestioningly within the conventional ecclesiastical discursive and liturgical forms of penance. The beautiful and resonant concluding prayer of Repentance (ll. 478–506), followed by the blowing of Hope's horn, suggests a confidence in these forms as represented in their ideal form by the confessor Repentance. The scene suggests that absolution for the *culpa*, or guilt of sin has been given, after the contrition and confession of the sinners, and that all that is now required is satisfaction, the paying of the *pena*, or penalty of sin. Strangely, however, this moment of hope is unmatched anywhere else in the action which follows – the pilgrims go on pilgrimage as the payment of their 'satisfaction', but the action is beset with doubts and spiritual anxiety, in which Langland's confidence in standard ecclesiastical penitential forms seems suddenly to have collapsed.

Pilgrimage

The sinners set off to seek St Truthe at line 510. Seeking St Truthe, as Reason had suggested (l. 57), as opposed to seeking the shrine of St James in Galicia, or the shrines of saints in Rome, itself suggests a transformation of the normal practice of going on pilgrimage: the essential idea of pilgrimage is retained, but its spiritual force is highlighted. The force of this idea is dramatically presented at the point when the pilgrims depart: without a guide, the first person they encounter is a pilgrim dressed in all the paraphernalia of contemporary pilgrimage – he has not only a staff, bag and bowl as the basic equipment of the pilgrim, but he is ostentatiously decked out with the signs of the shrines he has visited at Canterbury, Compostela, Sinai, Jerusalem and Rome. When, however, he is asked whether or not he knows the way to St Truthe, he reveals his ignorance of the spiritual meaning of his voyages in his complete ignorance of such a saint – no pilgrim, he says, has ever asked for *that* saint (ll. 535–6). At this moment, when the whole practice of pilgrimage seems to be under satirical threat, the figure Piers, a ploughman, suddenly presents himself to preserve at least the *idea* of pilgrimage: he says that he does know the way to Truthe, 'as kyndely as clerc doth hise bokes' (l. 538).

Piers first emerges in the poem, then, at precisely the moment when a standard ecclesiastical practice is under attack. His appearance serves to create a continuity for the idea of pilgrimage at the moment when it appears to have foundered in the pilgrim's spiritual ignorance; but this continuity is possible only at the expense of two of the normal qualities of pilgrimage. Firstly, Piers

proposes a *spiritual* pilgrimage, through the Ten Commandments
(ll. 561–608), whose final stage is in essence what an actual
pilgrimage should be – the 'pilgrim' comes to a castle, where

> Grace hatte the gateward, a good man for sothe;
> His man hatte 'Amende-yow' – many man hym knoweth.
> Telleth hym this tokene: 'Truthe w[oot] the sothe—
> I parfourned the penaunce that the preest me enjoyned.'
> (V. 595–8)

hatte: is called; *woot*: knows.

Piers outlines the way in which Truthe's standards of strict justice
can be met by paying the proper amends which erase the *pena* of
sin. It is precisely this *pena* which a normal pilgrimage is designed
to eliminate, but the only way that Piers proposes to achieve this
is by a spiritual, rather than a physical journey; the shrine at which
Piers wants his pilgrims to arrive is not some exotic sanctuary,
but rather the intimate sanctuary of the pilgrim's own heart,
where, Piers says,

> Thow shalt see in thiselve Truthe sitte in thyn herte
> In a cheyne of charite, as thow a child were.
> (V. 606–7)

The second way in which Piers's pilgrimage differs from the
normal pilgrimage is in the person of the guide himself.
Pilgrimage guides could certainly be secular figures (Chaucer's
Harry Bailly is the obvious example), but the pilgrimage Piers
offers to lead, as we have just seen, is of a spiritual kind, through
the Old to the New Law, by way of the Ten Commandments
and penitential doctrine. Piers would seem to be offering the
teaching normally offered by priests (it is Chaucer's Parson who,
naturally enough, offers a penitential treatise as a spiritual
pilgrimage), and Piers likens his knowledge to that of priests in
saying that he knows the way to St Truthe 'as kyndely as clerc
doth hise bokes' (l. 538). This comparison, which most immediately means that Piers knows the way as 'completely' as a cleric
knows his books (MED sense 3(d)), is not necessarily damaging
to the book-learning of priests, but it remains true that Piers's
knowledge of Truthe is not through books: 'Conscience and
Kynde Wit kenned me to his place', he says (l. 539), which
suggests another sense of 'kyndely', that of 'naturally' (MED
sense 1(a)). At the very point, then, when the ecclesiastical prac-

tice of pilgrimage requires a transformation to preserve it, a non-priestly figure emerges in the poem to lead that pilgrimage. And the first figure to abandon the pilgrimage proposed by Piers is a representative of an official ecclesiastical institution for the forgiveness of sin – a pardoner prefers not to go with Piers, and says that instead he will fetch his documents of pardon, his 'brevettes and a bulle with bisshopes lettres' (l. 640).

This might be the point at which we would expect the pilgrimage to become purely allegorical, and for Piers to lead the pilgrimage whose route he has sketched. In fact Piers does promise to lead the pilgrimage, but only *after* he has ploughed his 'half acre . . . by the heighe weye' (VI. 4). In the same way that the literal pilgrimage had been interrupted by the failure of the pilgrim to know the way to St Truthe, so too is the allegorical pilgrimage interrupted by what is explicitly registered as the 'long lettyng' of Piers's ploughing. But in the same way that the allegorical pilgrimage turned out to be the continuation of the idea of pilgrimage, so too does Piers's ploughing turn out to be the continuation of, and a definition of, the most real kind of pilgrimage, which in fact involves staying at home and fulfilling the demands of Truthe. The pilgrimage Piers leads turns out not to be through an allegorical country, but rather in the literal world of human relations around work and the production of food.

But this transformation of pilgrimage is not immediately evident: Piers, as I have said, promises to lead the pilgrims *after* he has ploughed his half acre (ll. 5–6). This temporal sequence, of ploughing, and *then* pilgrimage, is momentarily questioned at l. 56, where Piers says that he will dress himself as a pilgrim, and travel with the pilgrims until they find Truthe: the clothes he puts on in fact are those designed for ploughing – hanging, for example, his 'hoper at [his] hals in stede of a scryppe' (l. 61). But Piers goes on to insist that ploughing and pilgrimage are sequential by saying that, having sown the field,

> . . . sithenes wol I wende
> To pilgrymage as palmeres doon, pardon for to have.
>
> (VI. 63–4)

sithenes: afterwards.

But the reader cannot fail to register problems with this proposed sequence, since in making the distribution of labour for the sowing, Piers has done much more than to organise half a day's work (the time a half acre would take to plough); instead, he has taken this opportunity to redefine the essential relationships of a feudal society based on 'truthe': he orders the women to sew, either sacks for the wheat, or, in the case of noblewomen, church vestments (ll. 9–16). And a knight, as if in recognition of Piers's spiritual status, offers, astonishingly, to do the ploughing himself. But Piers resists this movement towards the blurring of earthly distinctions by courteously redefining the duties of knighthood:

> 'By Seint Poul!' quod Perkyn, 'Ye profre yow so faire
> That I shal swynke and swete and sowe for us bothe,
> And [ek] labour[e] for thi love al my lif tyme,
> In convenaunt that thow kepe Holy Kirke and myselve
> Fro wastours and fro wikked men that this world destruyeth'
> (VI. 24–8)
>   *faire*: graciously; *swynke*: work.

So instead of simply representing the labour required for the ploughing of half an acre, the poem is here redefining feudal society from the perspective of the peasant Piers, who willingly accepts his position in the society which he organises by virtue of his spiritual nobility (Simpson 1985). It is a society founded on that interlocking set of senses the word 'truthe' has, of 'loyalty', 'justice', and 'truth telling': the knight plights his 'trouthe' that he will keep his covenant with Piers (l. 34); Piers himself advises the knight to exercise justice only as long as 'Truthe wole assente' (l. 38); and Piers also advises the knight not to listen to the deceptive tales of minstrels, in order that he be 'trewe' of his 'tonge' (ll. 50–4). And the whole foundation of this true society is itself part of a penitential act, a pilgrimage to seek St Truthe.

What Langland has done, then, is to bring the narrative to the point that it had reached with the end of the confessions, with the sinners ready to perform the satisfaction, the *doing* of penance, again; but here that doing is defined not merely by reference to the ecclesiastical realm, but rather by reference to the essential relationships of an agricultural, feudal society, which Langland now reimagines as itself a penitential pilgrimage to Truthe, a way of meeting the standards of justice. For Langland the spiritual world is not separable from the material, and cannot be adequately catered for by reference to ecclesiastical forms of penitence, like pilgrimage, or simply by positing allegorical, spiritual pilgrimages of the kind Piers had sketched; instead, full spirituality of the kind Langland is committed to can be realised only through 'true' social relationships of interdependent labour. This is evident in the narrative of the second vision at precisely the moment we would expect Piers to leave on pilgrimage if the narrative had kept its promise to plough, and *then* to go on pilgrimage. In the manner of medieval pilgrims, Piers has a will made up before he departs on pilgrimage; ostensibly the prelude to departure, the will's conclusion confirms what we have already suspected, that the ploughing *is* the pilgrimage, and that honest work is the surest way of satisfying the penitential demands of 'truthe'. He says that with the goods that remain to him after distributing his goods fairly, he will work for God,

> And ben His pilgrym atte plow for povere mennes sake.
> My plowpote shal be my pikstaf, and picche atwo the rotes,
> And helpe my cultour to kerve and clense the furwes.
>
> (VI. 102–4)
>
> *plowpote*: plough-pusher; *pikstaf*: pikestaff (i.e. the staff of the pilgrim); *picche*: separate; *cultour*: ploughshare; *furwes*: furrows.

'Departing' for pilgrimage is constituted by staying at home, and continuing to work; Langland has subverted the model of his narrative by creating a new meaning for 'pilgrimage', directly opposed to the normal sense of the word, which involves leaving home.

Pardon

If Langland's satirical procedure with pilgrimage is to subvert the very model of his narrative, can the same be said for his treatment of the pardon, the final stage, and *raison d'être* of the pilgrimage? For the pardon, too, is unexpectedly 'interrupted', as it were, in Piers's tearing. Pardons certainly were abused in the late Middle Ages, with pardoners often promising pardons from both punishment and guilt, and illegally selling pardons (Kellog 1972), and it would be unsurprising to find Langland satirising their abuse.

The narrative of Passus VII begins with a confirmation of the basic pattern of ecclesiastical forms upon which the narrative of Passus V–VII has been based – after the sermon of Reason, the confession of the sins and the absolution of Repentance, and the pilgrimage, we are now offered the pardon:

Treuthe herde telle herof, and to Piers sente
To taken his teme and tilien the erthe,
And purchaced hym a pardoun *a pena et a culpa*
For hym and for hise heires for everemoore after;
And bad hym holde hym at home and erien hise leyes,
And alle that holpen hym to erye, to sette or to sowe,
Or any [man]er mestier that myghte Piers availe —
Pardon with Piers Plowman Truthe hath ygraunted.

(VII. 1–8)

teme: plough team; *a pena et a culpa*: from debt and from culpability; *erien*:
plough; *leyes*: fallow fields; *mestier*: occupation.

This pardon is one in which we can have confidence, despite the
formulae it uses. Satisfaction, the fulfilment of which is recognised by a pardon, or indulgence, strictly speaking only remits
the *pena* of sin; the pardon of Truthe follows the formula of papal
plenary indulgences (the 'pleyn pardon' of l. 102) in using the
phrase '*a pena et a culpa*', which could be misleading in suggesting
that the indulgence absolved the sinner from the guilt of sin as
well. But papal indulgences which did use the formula went on
immediately to say that is was applicable only to those who were
'truly confessed and penitent' (Sumption 1975, 142). Given that
this pardon is from Truthe, we must assume that the formula is
being used without deceit. Likewise, the promise that Piers's heirs
will benefit from this pardon makes an offer which no literal
pardon ever could make: we must interpret Piers's heirs as his
spiritual heirs, and consider Truthe's pardon to apply to all Christians who follow the model of Piers.

But if the Pardon from Truthe *is* regarded as having unquestionable authority, then why should Piers tear it up? I think there
are two, complementary answers to this question, one to be set
in the frame of Langland's satirical procedures, the other to be set
in the frame of his theology. In this section I am focusing on
Langland's satire and its procedures, and will restrict myself for
the moment to considering the tearing from this point of view.

We have already observed in Langland's treatment of the practice of pilgrimage that he structures his narrative on models he
is concerned to attack; the strategy of his satire, that is, is to lead
his audience to expect a familiar, standard pattern, before
suddenly pulling the carpet from beneath their feet by transforming standard practices into something quite new and

unexpected – pilgrimage is transformed into the spiritual act of staying at home and performing one's daily labour in a spirit of penitential humility and obedience. Can the same be said for his treatment of pardon? The priest who is present at the unfolding of the pardon certainly expects to play a standard mediating role between God and the laity in presenting the terms of the pardon:

> 'Piers', quod a preest thoo, 'thi pardon moste I rede;
> For I shal construe ech clause and kenne it thee on Englissh'.
>
> (VII. 105–6)
>
> *construe*: translate; *kenne*: teach.

As soon as the pardon itself is opened, however, expectations such as these are upset; it is true that the priest translates the pardon, but his position is certainly not that of the assured mediator between God and man, confidently enjoying his privileged position in an ecclesiastical practice; instead, he, like the audience of the poem, is unbalanced by the words of the pardon themselves, since they insist that there is no pardon, and that the confident expectation of such a document has been complacent and illusory:

> *Et qui bona egerunt ibunt in vitam eternam;*
> *Qui vero mala, in ignem eternum;*
>
> (VII. 110a–b)
>
> (Those who have done well shall go into eternal life; but those who [have done] evil [will go] into eternal fire.)

These are the words of the so-called 'pardon', and this is the priest's discomposed but technically accurate reponse to them:

> 'Peter!', quod the preest thoo, 'I kan no pardon fynde
> But "Do wel and have wel, and God shal have thi soule,"
> And "Do yvel and have yvel, and hope thow noon oother
> That after thi deeth day the devel shal have thi soule!"'
>
> (VII. 111–14)

Both the priest's paraphrase, and his dismissal of the 'pardon' as a pardon are accurate: the words of this document are of no use to the sinner looking for forgiveness; instead, as words with any practical force, they are of use only if they *precede* the act of sin. If they are read after the act of mortal sin, they do not absolve the sinner from that sin or pardon him from the penance pertaining to it – on the contrary, they simply insist on the inev-

itability of punishment. As a statement of strict justice they recall
the words of Holy Church in Passus I, in her account of Lucifer
and those who follow him:

> And alle that werchen with wrong wende thei shulle
> After hir deth day and dwelle with that sherewe.
>
> (I. 128–9)
>
> *wende*: go; *sherewe*: evil one.

The priest's words, then, are by no means untrue. But they are
complacent in not registering the terrible force of these words;
Langland seems to me to be recovering the relations of strict
justice which pertain between man and God *prior to* any
conditional reward of pardon; instead of recognising this
frightening truth which is staring him literally in the face, the
priest insists on looking for the comforting document which
would have him forget it. The construction he uses is satiric in
intent: 'there is no *pardon* here *but* "act well and be saved, and
sin and be damned"', where the 'but' ironically pretends that
what follows is a pardon, when in fact it serves to highlight the
fact that there is no pardon here whatsoever. Curiously, this is
exactly what Piers himself wants to say, though in a different,
unmocking sense: he, too, wants to say, in the context of
pardons being complacently handed out, that there *is* no
'pardon' but acting according to the demands of God's justice.
Since the priest has said exactly what Piers wants to say,
without understanding its real force, he leaves Piers with no
verbal retort possible. At this point Piers resorts to a physical
act of tearing the pardon in two, which simultaneously affirms
the nature of true 'pardon' from God, and attacks the
complacent practice of distributing ecclesiastical pardons. This is
an identical strategy to that which Langland had used in the
case of pilgrimage: the ploughing of Piers's half acre
simultaneously affirms the nature of true 'pilgrimage' and
attacks the normal practice of pilgrimage.

So our first answer to the question of Piers's tearing of the
pardon is that Piers is tearing not at the words of the pardon
itself so much as the paper document upon which they are
written – at 'pardon' as it is normally understood. In keeping
with his satiric strategy, which manifests itself in both large
narrative units and more local figures of thought, Langland sets

up 'pardon' as the model of his narrative precisely in order to attack it.[3]

This interpretation of the tearing of the pardon is confirmed, I think, when we look to the coda to the dream sequence at the end of Passus VII, where Will himself states explicitly that this is the meaning of his dream. Langland is wary about the satirical force of his poetry, and clearly wishes to distance himself from it; when Will is woken by the dispute of Piers and the priest, his position is one of studied ignorance about the meaning of his dream – he points to the difficulty of 'songewarie', or dream interpretation (l. 151), but takes heart from the example of biblical interpreters of dreams, Daniel and Jacob (ll. 151–67). This tentative approach is the prelude to what is in fact a fairly direct and explicit statement that

> . . . Dowel at the Day of Dome is digneliche underfongen,
> And passeth al the pardon of Seint Petres cherche.
>
> (VII. 172–3)
>
>   *digneliche*: worthily; *underfongen*: received; *passeth*: surpasses.

Will's statement of this position, despite some hedging and professions of complete faith in the authority of Rome, is unequi- vocally in favour of the superiority of good works over trust in paper pardons purchased from the Church with money.[4]

In conclusion, then, we can see that Langland's ecclesiastical satire in these passus works in a consistent, and brilliantly subver- sive way: his strategy is to use certain penitential practices, like pilgrimage, or the distributing of pardons, as the basis of his narrative, before he suddenly confronts the reader with the inad- equacy of such practices.

THEOLOGICAL THEMES: THE REWARD OF WORKS – A WAGE OR A GIFT?

But can the whole of the narrative of these passus (V–VII) be understood within the terms of the satire I have just described?

---

3. The strategy is central to the poem as a whole, and manifests itself in single figures of thought (Simpson 1986b) as much as in larger narrative units (esp. Burrow 1965).
4. This interpretation of the tearing of the pardon was first proposed by Frank (1951).

Certain important sections of it have been left entirely out of consideration, like the actual ploughing itself, which quickly disintegrates from the ideal society established by Piers. This disintegration would not be necessary for the ends of Langland's satire as I have described them. And certain important aspects of the narrative have been left unaccounted for: how, for example, do we account for Piers's evident anguish as he tears the pardon and renounces work in favour of prayers and penance (VII. 115–30)? His 'pure tene' might be accountable for as satiric 'tene', as it were, directed against the complacent priest, but if the whole point of this passage were simply to attack paper pardons by insisting on the value of good works ('Dowel'), then why should Piers *cease* to work, abandon his crucial position within the society of the field, and vow himself to a life of indigent penitence?

Consideration of these passages obliges us to look for further ways in which Piers's tearing might be understood. Beyond the insights provided by consideration of Langland's ecclesiastical satire, I think we should look to the theological issues behind this sequence of passus, and in particular to the standard of divine justice which rewards works in strict proportion to their merit. This theological question of strict reward, or wages, will also involve consideration of Langland's view of payment of peasants by their masters in late fourteenth-century England. I will be arguing that when the 'pardon' comes it shocks Piers by the strictness of its justice and by its complete lack of mercy. It proposes to reward men strictly according to their deserts, to wage them, with no conditional allowances made for repentance for sins committed. Piers tears the pardon, then, not only as a satiric act, but also as an act of profound anxiety before the strictness of the Old Law. He tears not only at the paper of the pardon, but also in anxious protest at the spirit of the words, despite their evident and unassailable truth.

When Langland discusses rewards from God, he does so in economic terms, of both wages and gifts: payments fully deserved, that is, and payments given out of the giver's generosity (Simpson 1987). In Passus II Theology had defined reward from God as 'mede', which, as we know from Conscience's definitions in Passus III, indicates a reward beyond desert, a gift:

For Mede is muliere, of Amendes engendred;
And God graunted to gyve Mede to truthe,
And thow hast gyven hire to a gilour – now God gyve thee sorwe!
The text telleth thee noght so, Truthe woot the sothe,
For *Digmus est operarius* his hire to have.

(II. 119–23)

muliere: legitimate; *gilour*: deceiver; *dignus est operarius*:
the labourer is worthy.

Theology indicates that God's reward is for honestly performed
works, with his image of the *operarius*, or workman. But the
reward given is not a wage strictly deserved: it is a 'mede' rather
than a 'mercede', to use the term used in the C-Text to denote
strictly deserved payment, which is given in exact proportion to
works performed. It may be helpful to cite that passage to recall
the exact distinctions Conscience makes. Having defined 'mede'
as the undeserved reward paid before payment is merited, Conscience goes on to define 'mercede' as a payment paid

When the dede is ydo and the day endit;
And that is no mede but a mercede, a manere dewe dette,
And but hit prestly be ypayed the payere is to blame
. . .
And ther is resoun as a reue rewardynge treuthe
That bothe the lord and the laborer be leely yserued.

(C. III. 303–9)

endit: ended; *prestly*: readily; *reue*: reeve; *leely*: justly.

If Theology uses the word 'mede' to denote reward from God,
this necessarily implies that reward from God to man is undeserved by man; and in the definition of 'mede' given by
Theology, we can see that such a reward from God does imply
that man has failed to deserve reward fully, as a 'mercede', or
'maner dewe dette for the doynge', since Theology's Mede is 'of
amendes engendred'. Theology's reward from God, that is, implies
a failure on man's behalf to merit full reward, which is compensated for by the making of amends, or penitence for sins
committed.

If Theology defines 'mede' as the model of man's reward from
God, Piers, on the other hand, merits a 'mercede', or wage. When
Piers first introduces himself he describes the payment he receives
from Truthe:

I have ben his folwere al this fourty wynter –
Bothe ysowen his seed and suwed hise beestes
. . .

For though I seye it myself, I serve hym to paye;
I have myn hire of hym wel and outherwhiles moore.
He is the prestete paiere that povere men knoweth:
He withhalt noon hewe his hire that he ne hath it at even.

(V. 542–52)

suwed: followed; to paye: to [his] satisfaction; presteste: readiest.

The terms of Piers's reward from God here evoke the definition
Conscience had given of a just reward, which is no 'mede' –
what 'laborers and lewede [leodes] taken of hire maistres, / It is
no manere mede but a mesurable hire' (III. 255–6). Piers, as the
apparently perfect Christian, does not require a gift from God
(even if God, out of his generosity, might give 'outherwhiles
moore'), but is able to meet the requirements of God's justice,
and to merit the 'mesurable hire', or 'mercede' proportionate to
his labour.

These two categories of reward, the wage and the gift, derive
from one of the most controversial doctrinal issues of the Christian tradition: how does man receive the reward of salvation, by
works or by grace? On the one hand, the Christian tradition as
it developed placed great emphasis on the existence of free will,
by which humans are responsible for their actions, and by which
they deserve or fail to deserve salvation by the worth of their
works. On the other hand, the Judeo-Christian tradition conceives
of man as radically debilitated by the wound of orginal sin, so that
it is only through the free gift (or grace, from Latin *gratia*) of
redemption that God has rendered humanity capable of good
deeds and salvation (Adams 1983, 369–70).

To stress the importance of works and independent human
virtue in achieving salvation is to undermine the omnipotence of
God, since it renders God *obliged* to reward virtue; it also undermines the omniscience of God in making His knowledge
dependent on the decisions of humans. The doctrine which
stressed the independent possibility and worth of human works
was labelled as Pelagianism, after the late fourth-century British
monk Pelagius, who was considered to maintain this position. On
the other hand, to stress the omnipotence and omniscience of God
in awarding salvation through His grace as a gift, is radically to
diminish the worth of human action, and can lead to a position

which attributed salvation only to God's predestination of souls. This was the position of St Augustine's (AD 354–430) later writings.

The images of 'gift' and 'wage', then, arise out of this larger doctrinal debate concerning the nature of reward from God: if the reward God gives is a wage, then man deserves it and God is obliged to give it (the potentially 'Pelagian' position); if the reward God gives is a gift, then man has not deserved it, and God is not obliged to give it (the more Augustinian position). Langland's use of these images is not original, and he is indebted to central currents of fourteeth-century theology in his use of them. For fourteenth-century theologians the questions of how man could be said to merit from God was of central importance. Theologians drew on a thirteenth-century distinction between two kinds of merit, *condign* merit and *congruent* merit. Condign merit is an absolute, strict merit, whereby man can be said to merit the reward of salvation absolutely and justly. Congruent merit, on the other hand, is relative and conditional, whereby man receives reward from God out of God's generosity (Obermann 1957, 149–51, 155–59; 1963, 169–74). When we look to the image used by theologians to describe these two kinds of reward, we see that they described condign reward as wages, and congruent reward as a gift (Overstreet 1984, 281–7). The early fourteenth century theologian Durandus of St Pourçain, for example, defines two kinds of merit, correlating them with two kinds of debt:

> Just as there are two kinds of debt, so too are there two kinds of merit. One is condign debt, which is debt in a simple sense. [This debt pertains] when, for example, it is just that a labourer, through the nature of his work, be given a reward on account of the equality between the work and the payment. The other kind of debt is congruent debt, where such a reward is not deserved through the nature of the work, but rather through the generosity of the giver. For it is allowed to offer some generous gift which someone did not merit condignly. Condign merit pertains to the first kind of debt, while congruent merit pertains to the second kind.[5]

The categories of reward offered by this passage correspond exactly to the categories of reward from God defined in *Piers*

---

5. Durandus of St Pourçain (1556). I cite the Latin text (Simpson 1987, 94), with slight emendation of the edition.

Plowman: 'mercede', or 'mesurable hire' (a wage) corresponds with condign reward, and 'mede' (a gift) with congruent reward. Besides being indebted to this theological tradition for his categories of rewards, it should not be forgotten that Langland is also indebted to the Bible for images of salvation as a wage for works performed, found in the Parable of the Vineyard, for example (Matthew 20. 1–16), and at John 4.36: 'And he that reapeth receiveth wages, and gathereth fruit unto life eternal'.

But if Langland is indebted to these theological and biblical traditions for his images of rewards from God, his application of them in the narrative of his poem does not stop at the level of abstract theological argument. Instead, Langland connects issues of theological reward with contemporary issues of payment between lords and peasants in later fourteenth-century England. When we turn back to the ploughing of the half acre with the question of rewards for works in mind, we notice that Piers first vows to work for the knight for love (B. VI. 25), in return for the protection of the knight. When the ploughing itself begins, however, this feudal image of labour relations gives way to a representation more characteristic of labour relations in the later fourteenth-century. The knight plays almost no part in the ploughing, and Piers is represented as a peasant landholder organising peasant labourers, and paying them wages on a contractual basis. It is Piers who decides who will be hired:

> At heigh prime Piers leet the plough stonde,
> To oversen hem hymself; whoso best wroghte,
> He sholde he hired therafter, whan hervest tyme come.
>
> (VI. 112–14)
>
> *heigh prime*: = 9 a.m

And after the attack of Hunger, each poor man is

> . . . wel apaied to have pesen for his hyre.
> And what Piers preide hem to do as prest as a sperhauk.
> And [Piers was proud therof], and putte hem to werke
> And yaf hem mete as he myghte aforthe and mesurable hyre.
>
> (VI. 195–8)
>
> *apaied*: pleased; *pesen*: pees; *prest*: ready; *aforthe*: afford.

The form of labour here is contractual wage-labour where the payment is 'mesurable hire' and the person hiring is Piers, not the knight. One recent scholar remarks that 'far from being traditional, this social model represents one of the most recent developments in rural life' (Baldwin 1981a, 61), and many historians comment on the phenomenon of the wealthy peasant in the period, who either owns or leases land, and who engages wage labourers (Hilton 1969, 44–6; Postan 1942, 11–12; Bolton 1980, 237–9)

Initially, Langland's presentation of the ploughing of the half acre would seem to be satirical in intent: it is modelled closely on contemporary practices, and its attack on the failure of the peasants to work can be paralleled to attacks made in parliamentary documents contemporary with *Piers Plowman*. When, for example, Piers threatens the slackers with hunger, they pretend to be maimed and unable to work:

> Tho were faitours afered, and feyned hem blynde;
> Somme leide hir legges aliry, as swiche losels konneth,
> And made hir [pleynt] to Piers and preide hym of grace:
> 'For we have no lymes to laboure with, lord, ygraced be ye!'
>
> (VI. 121–4)

faitours: dissemblers; *feyned*: pretended to be; *aliry*: as if they were paralysed; *losels*: wretches; *konneth*: know how.

This scene dramatises the complaints of parliamentary bills comtemporary with the poem; in the Parliament of 1376, for example, a bill of Labourers complains that when labourers are requested to work according to the regulations of the Ordinance of Labourers, they suddenly leave their service 'and become mendicant beggars, to lead an idle life', when they are 'strong of body, and could easily contribute to the common profit by living by their labour and service, if they wished to serve'. It goes on to request that it be forbidden under penalty to sustain such 'fautores mendinantz & beggeres' by almsgiving, and that all such beggars be chained and taken to the nearest prison until they are returned to their own territory and made to work according to the statutes (*Rotuli Parliamentorum* (Strachey (1767–77), II. 340)).

The representation of peasant recalcitrance to the constraints of law more generally echoes the complaints of contemporary documents. The acute labour shortage caused by the Black Death of 1348 gave much greater power to peasants in their demands for higher wages, and gave them greater scope for movement in search of the best labour terms. The main preoccupations of the Statutes of Labourers of 1349, 1352 and 1388 are to restrict the level of wages to pre-Plague levels on the one hand, and to restrict freedom of movement on the other; the Statute of 1349, for example, legislates that 'every man and woman . . . of what condition he be, free or bond, able in body . . . not living in merchandize, nor exercising any craft, nor having of his own whereof he may live . . . shall be bounden to serve him which so shall him require; and take only the wages, livery, meed, or salary, which were accustomed to be given in places where he oweth to serve . . .'.[6] The fact that these statutes had to be repeated and stengthened implies their powerlessness to control the labour market; this powerlessness of the law is represented in Langland's text by the unsuccessful intervention of the knight, whose help Piers enlists against wasters:

> Curteisly the knyght thanne, as his kynde wolde,
> Warnede Wastour and wissed hym bettre:
> 'Or thow shalt abigge by the lawe, by the ordre that I bere!'
> 'I was noght wont to werche,' quod Wastour, 'and now wol I
>   noght bigynne!' –
> And leet light of the lawe, and lasse of the knyghte . . .
>
> (VI. 164–8)
>
> *kynde*: nature; *wissed*: instructed; *abigge*: pay the penalty.

And even after the successful intervention of Hunger, who does provoke a flurry of work, the labourers revert to demanding high wages (l. 312), and to dismissing the King and his Council, 'Swiche lawes to loke, laborers to greve' (l. 317).[7]

Scenes such as these are clearly satirical up to a point. In the context of the pardon, however, their ultimate force is theological. If Piers's payment by God is a wage, such payment embodies, as we have seen, a just and deserved payment, distinct from a gift. Through his works alone, Piers seems able to merit reward condignly from God. But when we see the image of a wage-labour market in practice on earth, Langland represents the labourers as incapable of meriting the just and deserved payment of wages. What is expected of the labourers is that they fulfil the demands of strict justice through their works. The same is true of all other estates mentioned in the pardon of Passus VII.

---

6. Anno 23 Edw. III, 1349 (*Statutes of the Realm*, I. 307).
7. The connection between these scenes and the contemporary labour situation is revealingly discussed by Aers (1980 Ch. 1).

1–104, which could be summarised in the lines concerning labourers:

> Alle libbynge laborers that lyven with hir hondes,
> That treweliche taken and treweliche wynnen,
> And lyven in love and in lawe, for hir lowe herte
> Haveth the same absolucion that sent was to Piers.
>
> (VII. 60–3)

libbynge: living; *wynnen*: gain wealth.

But it is precisely this demand which the labourers as they are represented are incapable of meeting (Simpson 1987). And it is, in my view, this radical incapacity which the 'pardon' reveals in its austere statement of strict justice: those who do well (i.e. those who merit a wage) will be rewarded with salvation; those who sin will be damned.

Just as the King in Passus IV insisted on the strictness of justice in the earthly realm by refusing pardon, so too does Truthe (as we would expect from the deification of Justice) insist that no pardon will be given to sinners. But whereas the King's insistence on strict justice in the earthly realm is satisfying in its unremiting judgement of crime, Truthe's unremitting judgement of sin (to which, according to the Christian tradition, all humans are susceptible) is frightening in its implications. It is for this reason that Piers tears in protest at the words of the 'pardon'. Piers acts in anxiety before the demands of 'truthe', much in the way that other figures in literature contemporary with *Piers Plowman* do: Gawain, when told that he failed in 'lewte', shudders and blushes in anxious confusion (*Sir Gawain and the Green Knight*, ll. 2366–72); Averagus, faced with the strict demands of 'truthe', 'brast anon to wepe' (Chaucer's *Franklin's Tale*, V. 1480). And Will himself, faced with Scripture's austere text 'Many are called but few chosen', becomes anxious 'al for tene of hir text' (XI. 115), just as Piers, much later in the poem, attempts to beat off the devil 'for pure tene' as the devil collects souls according to strict justice (XVI. 86.)

If man is incapable of satisfying the demands of God's justice through works and, as such, incapable of deserving *wages* from God, then must he rely solely on God's gift, or grace? In facing Piers with the impossibility of deserving works, some scholars have argued that Langland is adopting an Augustinian position, in firm rejection of Pelagianism (e.g. Baker 1980). The promise of pardon, these scholars argue, leads the reader to trust in the possibility of independent, meritorious good works, until it actually arrives, when the reader is suddenly faced with the clear neccessity of committing himself to God's grace.

This is not the only possibility, however: it may be the case that man is unable *condignly* to merit reward from God through works without grace, but that he remains able to merit reward from God conditionally, or *congruently*, by acting within the terms of a pact made between God and man out of God's generosity. This certainly involves a gift from God, since He is not *obliged* to make a pact of this kind, but such a pact would not necessarily invalidate good works. In fact, the poem presents such a pact being made with man in Passus XIX, where Christ offers true pardon to Piers out of His generosity. In the account of Christ's life given in Passus XIX, it is said that Christ gave

> To alle maner men, mercy and foryifnesse;
> [To] hym, myghte men to assoille of alle manere synnes,
> In covenaunt that thei come and kneweliche to paye
> To Piers pardon the Plowman – *Redde quod debes*
> (XIX. 185–8)

> *hym*: i.e. Piers; *kneweliche to paye*: acknowledge satisfactorily (by meeting the terms of); *Piers pardon the Plowman*: Piers Ploughman's pardon: *redde quod debes*: repay what you owe.

The word 'covenant' here indicates that this is a pact with man; according to this pact, the possibility of forgiveness is acknowledged, and the possibility, even the necessity, of repentance being achieved by the effort of the sinner is registered. The sinner, that is, must 'pay what [he] owes'. This pact is represented as being operative as long as the world continues; only at the end of time will Christ come to make definitive judgement within the terms of this pact. And only here does the act of Christ's judgement resemble that of the unremitting 'pardon' of Passus VII:

> Anoon after an heigh up into hevene
> He wente, and wonyeth there, and wol come at the laste,
> And rewarde hym right wel that *reddit quod debet* –
> Paieth parfitly, as pure truthe wolde.
> And what persone paieth it nought, punysshen he thenketh,
> And demen hem at domesday, boths quyke and dede –

The goode to the Godhede and to greet joye,
And wikkede to wonye in wo withouten ende.

(XIX. 192–9)

wonyeth: dwells; *reddit quod debet*: repays what he owes; *parfitly*: perfectly;
demen: judge; *quyke*: living; *wonye*: dwell.

This reference forward in the poem is to the dispensation of
Christ, which does institute a pact according to which man can
meet the standards of a mitigated truth, or justice, by the works
of penitence. But in the context of Passus VII Piers does not seem
to be in full possession of this knowledge. He does recognise that
he must transform his ploughing into the 'work' of penitence:
'Of preieres and of penaunce my plough shal ben herafter'
(l. 120), he declares after the tearing of the pardon. But he seems to
be in an Old Testament world; the text of the Psalm he cites
suggests his trust in God's goodness, despite the austerity of the
'pardon': *Si ambulavero in medio mortis / Non timebo mala, quoniam
tu mecum es*' (Ps. 22. 4–5) ('Though I walk through the valley of
the shadow of death, I will fear no evil: for thou art with me'),
but it does suggest at the same time that Piers cannot see confidently beyond the 'eye for an eye, tooth for a tooth' world of
Truthe's 'pardon'. If Piers, and the audience of the poem, *could*
see clearly beyond this statement of strict, Old Testament justice,
then much of the rest of the poem would be rendered otiose. I
am not of course suggesting that Langland's original audience
would have been unaware of the Christian promise of mercy, but
rather that Langland is concerned: (i) to restate the fundamental
relationship of justice between God and man, in which man simply cannot merit condign reward from God of his own efforts; and
(ii) to leave undecided the question of exactly *how* man can read-
just the imbalance between himself and God: by grace alone; or
by the establishment of a pact wherby God, out of His mercy,
does allow merit to good works, and particularly to the good
works of penitence? Certainly the most pressing question which
this sequence of passus throws up concerns the value of works,
and it is precisely this question, 'What is Dowel'?, which
dominates the sequence of passus which follow.[8]

---

8. I therefore agree with Adams (1983; 1988a) that the tearing of the Pardon does
   not represent an Augustinian affirmation of 'grace alone'; I disagree with him

CONCLUSION – THE CRISIS OF JUSTICE

In Chapter 1 I observed that Langland began his poem by adopting the genres of estates satire in the Prologue, and sermon in Passus I, and I argued that he exploited these genres for their most authoritarian and dogmatic potential. It will be obvious that the sequence of Passus V–VII cannot be described as 'closed' in the way that the Prologue and Passus I could be: the meaning of the second vision is, I think, deliberately 'open', in so far as it poses questions in a dramatic way rather than making declarations in a dogmatic way. If Langland exploits literary forms to more open-ended, exploratory ends in this way, it is also true that he seems to have questioned the institutions which produce and are sustained by the genres used in the Prologue and Passus I. Estates satire is traditionally exercised in support of a feudal ideology, just as the discourses of Holy Church are produced from an authoritarian ecclesiastical ideology. At the end of Passus VII both these ideological attachments which seemed so firm at the beginning of the poem, come under serious pressure.

On the one hand, Piers represents a much more personal unmediated religious culture at the end of Passus VII. It is the ploughman who takes upon himself the responsibility of praying for his soul, without reference to the institution of the Church. Piers's holiness, indeed, is defined against the complacency of the learned priest, who mocks at what he sees as Piers's ignorance by asking him who taught him to read. Piers answers by pointing to the superior knowledge of Conscience, which comes through hardship, and which does not, clearly, need to be mediated by the institution of the Church:

'Abstynence the Abbesse,' quod Piers, 'myn a.b.c. me taughte,
And Conscience cam afterward and kenned me muche moore.'
(VII. 133–4)

kenned: taught.

Whether or not Piers can read, he certainly knows the Bible (he

---

in his argument that the semi-Pelagian position is evident in the scene as it is presented (1983, 403–4; 1988a, 96–7); in the dramatic structure of the poem, it seems essential to me that this solution should be unavailable at this point; the scene poses a critical problem, which is worked out in the following vision. The *solution* is the one to which Adams points, but it is not (in Passus VII) yet visible in the text.

cites a passage of the Scriptures to the priest); and even if Piers is uncertain of how to escape from the stricture of the 'pardon', Langland's spiritual sympathies are clearly with the lay ploughman rather than with the official representative of the Church.

And if Piers seems to distance himself from the authoritarian ecclesiastical culture represented by figures like Holy Church, he also detaches himself from his position within feudal society. In the estates satire of the Prologue, ploughmen had been placed in the structure of feudal society where we might expect them to be placed – at the bottom:

Thanne kam ther a Kyng: Knygthod hym ladde
. . .
The Kyng and Knyghthod and Clergie bothe
Casten that the Commune sholde hem [communes] fynde.
The Commune contreved of Kynde Wit craftes,
And for profit of al the peple plowmen ordeyned
To tilie and to travaille as trewe lif asketh.
(Prol. 112–120)

casten: decided; communes: food; contreved: devised; craftes: skills.

When Piers organises the ploughing of the half-acre, this feudal structure is preserved, since Piers agrees to work for the knight all his life if the knight protects both Piers and the Church. But in that case the feudal structure is preserved only by acknowledging Piers's moral and spiritual superiority: it is the knight who offers to plough himself, in response to which Piers courteously agrees to maintain his traditional role of labouring – the hierarchy is preserved, but from the 'bottom up'. At the end of Passus VII, however, Piers seems to abandon his place in the world of earthly food-production altogether, with the biblical authority of Matthew 6.25:

We sholde noght be to bisy aboute the worldes blisse:
Ne soliciti sitis, he seith in the Gospel
And sheweth us by ensamples us selve to wisse.
The foweles in the feld, who fynt hem mete at wynter?
Have thei no gerner to go to, but God fynt hem alle.
(VII. 126–30)

blisse: happiness; ne soliciti sitis: do not be over concerned; ensamples: examples; wisse: instruct; gerner: granary; fynt: provides for.

The figure Hunger had, like Piers, attacked the wasters on the field, and urged the necessity of labour, by appealing to scriptural authorities and to 'Kynde Wit', or experience (VI. 231–52). But the labour Hunger activates has a purely physical, material impulse, and it is not surprising that labour relations collapse again, once those physical needs have been satisfied (VI. 302–30); Hunger, that is, necessarily contains a rationale for labour, but just as surely involves the cessation of labour once it has been satisfied. Piers himself does not abandon labour or food-production, but he does spiritualise them – prayer and penance will be his 'plough', and his food will be the 'payn' of penance, where the pun on French *pain* ('bread') and English 'pain' neatly encapsulates the transformation of earthly into spiritual food. After the ploughing itself, which had been reduced to a purely physical, despiritualised act under the compulsion of Hunger, Piers sees no possibility of living in the world and preserving his soul. Langland's poem, whatever its audience, seems to me to be profoundly concerned with the issue of living a spiritual life while remaining in the world, and keeps returning to it. Holy Church's speech had first outlined the relation of the spiritual and the material in Passus I, suggesting no particular problems in accommodating them both; Piers, however, confronted with the austere text of the 'pardon', sees no possibility of such accommodation, and abandons the earthly field. The issues raised by penance have created strains which Langland's conception of active life in the world seems unable to bear. It is also true that the issues raised by penance seem unable to be contained within a narrative modelled on ecclesiastical penitential practices; a new discourse is called forth, which is what we see in the following vision.

Chapter 4

The Third Vision:
Passus VIII–XII

PASSUS VIII: Will, awake, asks many men, including two
friars, what Dowel is; he is unsatisfied with their answer,
and falls asleep (ll. 1–70). The first figure he meets is
Thought, who declares what Dowel, Dobet, and Dobest
are (ll. 71–108); Will is unsatisfied with his answer, and
continues to argue with Thought until they meet *Wit*. Wit
is asked by Thought on Will's behalf how the elements
of doing well, better and best should be distinguished
(ll. 109–29).

PASSUS IX: Wit replies that Dowel dwells in the body; his
allegory of the body involves him in discussion of God
as Creator and of Inwit, the highest part of man's soul
(ll. 1–74); after a short exhortation to almsgiving, Wit
defines the Dowel triad (ll. 75–104); he then redefines
Dowel as the wedded state, and expands on marriage
(ll. 105–99); he concludes with another two definitions of
the Dowel triad (ll. 200–7).

PASSUS X: *Dame Study*, Wit's wife, berates Wit for
teaching Will, and attacks the misuse of reason by
teachers and clerics (ll. 1–136); Wit withdraws, and Will
humbly promises life-long obedience to Study (ll. 137–
48). Study teaches Will the way to her cousin *Clergy*,
outlining the disciplines over which she has command,
and acknowledging her incapacity to understand theology
(ll. 149–217). Will moves on to Clergy, by whom he is
well received (ll. 218–27); Will asks about the Dowel
triad, and Clergy offers his answer (ll. 228–63). Clergy

goes on to satirise incompetent and otherwise inadequate priests, and prophesies that a king shall come to reform the Church (ll. 264–327). After Clergy's mention of a reforming king, Will asks if Dowel is secular lordship, to which *Scripture* replies in the negative (ll. 328–68). At this point Will makes a broad objection to the teaching he has received: he argues, on the basis of Scripture, that man is predestined, regardless of his learning, and sometimes regardless of his moral worth – many wise men have been damned, just as many wicked men and women have been saved (ll. 369–472a).

PASSUS XI (containing an inner-dream): Scripture chastises Will for self-ignorance, and Will falls asleep, into a dream within a dream, or inner-dream (ll. 1–5). Will is taken by Fortune into the 'land of desire', from where he observes the world; he is led by Fortune and her companions into a state of careless abandon, or recklessness, until he grows old, when Fortune becomes his enemy (ll. 6–62). Will appeals unsuccessfully to the friars for help (ll. 63–83); after the friars' betrayal of him in his need, Will asks *Lewtee* if he (Will) is justified in publicly denouncing the friars, to which Lewtee responds in the affirmative (ll. 84–106a); Scripture agrees with Lewtee about denouncing sin, and cites the parable of the marriage feast, to which many are called but few are chosen (ll. 107–14); Will trembles in fear at this text, arguing with himself about the likelihood of his own salvation; he declares, by analogy with statuted law, that sinful Christians will certainly be punished by God unless God shows mercy. Scripture agrees with this argument (ll. 115–39a). At this point *Trajan*, a saved pagan, affirms the value of just action in attracting God's grace, and goes on to stress the importance of love beyond observance of the law (ll. 140–229a); Trajan argues that the model of loving patience is found among the poor (ll. 230–80a); he ends by criticising priests who take money unjustly, or who are ignorant (ll. 281–318). Will now has a new experience within the inner-dream: he is taken by *Kynde*, or Nature, to witness the natural world, in which all creatures except humans act according to Reason, which in this context designates the principles of divine law manifest in nature (ll. 319–67); Will accosts *Reason*, to ask why he allows humans to err in this way; Reason rebukes Will for his question, and argues that suffrance is a prime virtue: God 'suffers' (i.e. both allows and suffers), and so too should men not blame others, since no one is without sin (ll. 368–402). Will awakes from this inner-dream, and encounters a figure who says that had Will been patient in the dream, he would have witnessed much more (ll. 403–39).

PASSUS XII: The new figure announces himself as *Imaginatif* (ll. 1–9a); he warns Will to amend himself, and argues that Will should concern himself more with his soul than with the writing of his poetry (ll. 10–19). Will defends his poetry, first as play, then as work essential to his search for Dowel (ll. 20–8). Imaginatif defines the Dowel triad, stressing the relative unimportance of either intellectual or material endowment. Grace is more important, and is to be found among the humble (ll. 29–63a). Book-learning and learning from observation (clergy and kynde wit) have their value, but are unable to comprehend grace. In developing this point, Imaginatif passes in review Will's arguments against Clergy and Reason (ll. 64–274). Will asks if pagans can be saved, to which Imaginatif answers with a vigorous affirmative (ll. 275–95).

INTRODUCTION

As I argued in the introduction to the last chapter, the penitential discourses of the second vision are proposed as a way of completing the political discourses of Passus II–IV: the reformation of the political order is impossible without the deeper reformation of the soul through penitence. But, as we saw in the last chapter, the penitential discourses of the second vision offer no sense of closure: they highlight radical inadequacies in the Church's dispensing of pardons, and they also highlight an essential theological question as to whether man is saved by grace alone, or whether works ('dowel') have any role in salvation. So the discourses of penitence themselves provoke recourse to other ways of writing and thinking. This is what we find in the third vision, where Langland invokes the discourses of education – those discourses which train the soul to analyse and resolve the theological question of 'dowel', or works. Before we look to the vision as a whole, let us refocus the question of works and salvation.

In Passus I Holy Church, as I argued in Chapter 1, sees the nexus of different meanings of 'truthe' as unproblematic: meeting the standards of God's 'truthe', or justice, seemed necessarily to involve meeting the standards of 'truthe', or loyalty, required through one's works in a feudal society. At the end of Passus VII, however, it is apparent that man cannot meet the standards of God's justice independently, and that the status of the works by which men try to meet it is therefore uncertain. In an attempt to meet the demands of the pardon sent by 'Truthe', Piers abandons his 'trewe', loyal labour for a life of eremitic penitence. Different facets of the word 'truthe', that is, tend to pull apart at this point in the poem.

If the value of works *is* uncertain, then we can see why Will should ask the question he so insistently does in the third vision: 'What is Dowel?'. The "pardon" from Truth had affirmed, in its austere way, ' "Do wel and have wel, and God shal have thi soule" ' (VII. 112); but in the ploughing we have observed the stark evidence that man cannot 'do well' independently. In the next vision, then, the question Will asks in his first encounter is whether or not the friars know 'where that Dowel dwelleth' (VIII. 13), and he repeats this question, in different forms, to Thought, Wit, Study, Clergy, Scripture, and Imaginatif in the same vision.

By the end of this third vision, at the end of Passus XII, it seems that some solution to Will's question has been arrived at. The conclusion of Passus XII recalls the end of the second vision: the verse from Psalm 22 (Vulgate) that Piers cites as he abandons the field in Passus VII ('though I walk through the valley of the shadow of death, I will fear no evil, for thou art with me'), is repeated at the very end of the third vision. But whereas this passage is cited by Piers in faithful but unillumined 'tene', here it is associated with a confident affirmation of the value of human action before God. It is said that even the just pagan might be saved by his just action:

Ne wolde nevere trewe God but trewe truthe were allowed.
And wheither it worth or noght worth, the bileve is gret of truthe,
And an hope hangynge therinne to have a mede for his truthe
. . .

Si ambulavero in medio umbre mortis &c.
The glose graunteth upon that vers a greet mede to truthe.

(XII. 288–92)

allowed: accepted; *worth*: is; *glose*: interpretation

At the end of this vision, then, the question of the value of works would seem to have been answered; it might be noticed, however, that this passage affirms that God grants 'mede', rather than 'mercede' to truth: man, that is, does not merit a wage from God through his independent action, but rather receives a reward for his just works out of God's gift. The position Langland seems to have arrived at here could be described as a 'semi-Pelagianism', a position which acknowledges some kind of gift given by God to man, but which at the same time affirms the value of good works in receiving that gift (Adams 1983; 1988a).

This is the general solution to which the poem provisionally arrives; to put this solution into proper focus, however, and to understand the difficult but passionate process of intellectual struggle by which Will arrives at it, we must consider the structural principles of the vision, and in particular the coherence of the cluster of personifications Will meets. From there I will go on to define the style of this section of the poem, before looking to its central theme. In discussing the theme of this section, it is necessary to understand something of the theological context in which Langland is writing, and I will introduce the relevant background material here. After discussing the inner-dream, I will conclude by discussing the ways in which certain authoritative discourses are subverted in this vision, and by considering the role of Imaginatif in Passus XII.

STRUCTURE AS DETERMINED BY PSYCHOLOGY

Passus I–VII of *Piers Plowman* are largely within traditions of satire, either estates satire, venality satire, or ecclesiastical satire. But however much they are pointed towards society as a whole, these passus tend, ultimately, to theological questions about the ways in which man can merit salvation from God. In Passus VIII–XII Langland takes up this theological question and poses it explicitly. Will changes from being the largely passive observer he has been in the first two visions, to being much more active in the third vision. Here he interrogates himself, and in particular his reason, for answers to the question which preoccupies him.

Before the vision proper, Will meets a pair of academically trained friars, 'maistres of the Menours', in a waking episode. They offer a self-congratulatory answer to Will's question by saying that Dowel dwells with themselves. They offer Will an argument that Dowel, or Charity (as they define Dowel), saves a man from deadly sin (VIII. 27–57). Their answer is complacent, but more importantly it does not resolve Will's problem, since it confuses 'Dowel', or action in accordance with strict justice, with charity and forgiveness. There is nothing unorthodox about their reply that charity saves man from mortal sin. But Will's question is one which undermines the complacency of orthodox doctrine, since he is questioning the fundamental relations of justice between man and God, which stand *prior* to the Christian dispensation of forgiveness and charity. What Will wants to know is what value dowel has if Truthe, or justice, demands 'dowel', and if man is unable to perform it. Will expresses dissatisfaction at their reply, and, with this brief resort to standard sources of theological clarity briefly exhausted, he sleeps and turns instead to his own reason for answers.

The figures he encounters are, in order: Thought, Wit, Study, Clergy, Scripture, and Imaginatif. (I have omitted consideration of the inner-dream of Passus XI for the moment.) What coherence do these figures have among themselves? And what semantic force does the word 'Will' have in the context of these figures?

The essential idea behind this interrogation of the self is the Neo-Platonic dictum 'know thyself'.[1] Pursuing this idea, Christian writers developed literary forms structured around self-analyses, where the actants are the constituent parts of the soul. This can be seen in, for example, St Augustine's *Soliloquies*, where the Augustine persona questions his own reason. The text begins in this way (translating Alfred's Old English version):

1. This is a very large tradition, with many medieval branches; the best discussion of its twelfth-century, monastic expressions, and their relevance to Langland's poem, is Wittig (1972).

Then he [Augustine] related, repeatedly questioning his mind and pondering various and remarkable things, and especially concerning himself: what he was, whether or not his mind and his soul were mortal and transitory, or immortal and eternal; and concerning his own good: what it was . . . and what good was best to do and what evil best be left aside (ed. Carnicelli 1969, 48–9) [my translation].

Augustine is answered at this point by what he assumes is his own reason, and the work proceeds from this point as a dialogue between 'himself' and his reason, where the reason draws knowledge from Augustine.

When we turn back to *Piers Plowman*, we notice that the actants Thought, Wit and Imaginatif are parts of the reason, while Will clearly represents the poet persona, Will Langland. In the context of these rational powers, we might, however, be able to assign a different semantic force to 'Will'. Christian philosophers inherited from classical philosophers a division of the soul into a cognitive power and an affective power: into a part of the soul which thinks, and perceives the truth on the one hand, and a part which feels, and desires the good, on the other. Common Latin terms for these two basic parts of the soul are *ratio* for the thinking part of the soul, and *voluntas* for the desiring part. When these terms are translated into the vernacular, there are different words used for both of them, but 'will' is the term most often used in Middle English for *voluntas*. In a late fourteenth-century text, *The Cloud of Unknowing*, for example, the author states that the soul has 'two principal worching myghtes, reson and wille'.[2] He defines 'reson' as a 'myght thorou the whiche we departe the iuel fro the good, the iuel fro the worse, the good fro the betir, the worse fro the worste, the betir fro the best' (p. 116); and 'wille' he defines as a 'myght thorou the whiche we chese good, after that it be determinid with reson; & thorow the whiche we loue God, we desire God, & resten us with ful likyng & consent eendli in God' (p. 116).

Langland's 'Will', then, when set in the context of the rational part of the soul, takes on a meaning of Latin *voluntas*. This is the force behind the remark that Thought 'cam and called me by my kynde name' (VIII. 72), where 'kynde name' could mean 'own name' (MED sense 2(a)), but can also mean 'natural name' (MED

---

2. Ed. Hodgson (1944, 115). Letter forms have been modernised.

sense 1(a)). Given that the will is a natural power of the soul, then Will's 'kynde' name is 'will'. The *Cloud* author's remark that the will chooses the good 'after that it be determined with the reson' further illuminates the ideas behind the series of encounters between Will and Thought, Wit, and Imaginatif: we can see that this series of encounters represents a process of knowledge, whereby the will desires to know something, and consults the reason to 'determine' it. The reason replies with information not only about Dowel, but also (gratuitously) about Dobet and Dobest, 'the good fro the betir . . . the betir fro the best'.

This opposition between the will and the reason is in fact fairly common in basic instructional literature in the vernacular. Simple instructional lyrics work within it, and insist that the will must be subject to the reason, lest it desires irrationally. A small thirteenth-century lyric puts it this way:[3]

> Hwenne-so wil wit oferstieth
> Thenne is wil and wit for-lore,
> Hwenne-so wil his hete hieth
> Ther nis nowiht wit icore . . .

oferstieth: surmounts; *forlore*: ruined; *hete*: passion; *hieth*: quickens; *nowhit*: not at all; *icore*: chosen.

And many, more sophisticated poems of the period work within this basic distinction. *Pearl*, for example, begins with the dreamer being emotionally controlled by his will, when his reason instructs him otherwise:

> A deuely dele in my hert denned,
> Thagh resoun sette myseluen saght.
> I playned my perle that ther watz spenned
> With fyrce skyllez that faste faght;
> Thagh kynde of Kryst me comfort kenned,
> My wreched wylle in wo ay wraghte.
> (ll. 51–6)

deuely dele: desolating grief; *denned*: lay deep; *saght*: at peace; *playned*: lamented for; *watz*: was; *spenned*: imprisoned; *skyllez*: arguments; *faght*: contended; *wraghte*: was pained.

3. Ed. Brown (1932), no. 39. Letter forms have been modernised. Reference should also be made to *The Conflict of Wit and Will*, edited Dickins (1937), where a series of Middle English examples are listed. See Davenport (1988), for a discussion of this and other internal dialogues in Middle English.

Or Gower in the *Confessio Amantis* often refers to the opposition between the will's desire to love, and the reason's counsel against passionate love. The lover, in whom reason and will contend, personifies the two powers in this way:

Reson seith that I scholde leve
To love, wher ther is no leve
To spede, and will seith therayein
That such an herte is to vilein,
Which dar noght love, and til he spede,
Let hope serve at such a nede:
He seith ek, where an herte sit
Al hol governed upon wit,
He hath this lyves lust forlore.
        (III. 1179–87) (ed. Macaulay 1900)

therayein: against this; *vilein*: cowardly, base; *spede*: is successful; *lust*: pleasure;
forlore: lost.

So Langland is working within a commonplace scheme in his presentation of the meeting between Will and Thought, Wit and Imaginatif. The series of meetings could, in fact, be described as an extended play on the traditional will/wit topos. The fact, however, that the rational part of the soul is divided into more than one part indicates that Langland, unlike many of his contemporaries, is using a more elaborate psychological scheme. Most vernacular writers used the will/wit topos for moral ends, setting the will as an obstreperous and misleading force against the moral director wit. More sophisticated psychological schemes were available, however, for writers interested in the actual process of thinking and abstraction, and in the sources of true knowledge. In particular, writers could draw on a model provided by Aristotle's *De Anima*, whose influence in the Middle Ages was felt through Latin translations (between *c.* 1150 and 1268) of the Greek text, and of the Arabic commentary of Avicenna (980–1037) (Dod 1982). Although it became a university textbook for students in the Faculty of Arts in Paris later in the thirteenth century (Lohr 1982, 85), the *De Anima* met resistance by university authorities in Paris earlier in the century, being banned in 1231 (Kaulbach 1985); this produced attempts to harmonise Aristotelian with Augustinian psychology, and it is from works of this kind (as well as from earlier works engaged in the same syncretising enterprise) that Langland may have drawn his concept of the soul, which combines Aristotelian and Augustinian elements.[4]

In the Aristotelian scheme the soul of man is seen within the context of all nature. Man's soul is a hierarchy of powers, some of which he has in common with the rest of nature, some of which are unique to himself, and some of which he shares with the angels. Leaving aside the vegetative power man has in common with plants, man's soul has sensible powers, which it shares with animals, and rational powers, which animals do not possess. The process of apprehension in this scheme is essentially a series of abstractions, whereby one perceives bodily forms through the outward senses (sight, hearing, taste, touch, smell). These impressions are received and stored by the inward wits. These are: (i) common wit (*sensus communis*), which receives and distinguishes between the impressions of the senses; (ii) imagination, which stores the images produced by the senses; (iii) *imaginativa*, which divides and combines images; (iv) estimation, which understands the intention of a particular impression, in the way a lamb understands the intention of a wolf; and (v) memory, which makes a store of these intentions (Harvey 1975, 39–48). The purely abstractive, and uniquely human role of reason then comes into play, which can perceive the abstract essence of an object without continued reference to particular bodily images stored in the imagination; and finally, through the intellect, man can join the angels in contemplation of the divine forms, or Ideas. In addition to these cognitive powers, man has appetites, or desires, which fall into a twofold division: man has sensitive appetites, which he shares with animals (irascible, which makes him instinctively shun what he fears, and concupiscent, which attracts him to what his senses desire); and a rational appetite, or will, which makes him desire the truth perceived by the reason as good. This he does not share with animals.[5]

This is a coherent and sophisticated psychology of mind,

4. The other important source for faculty psychology is Boethius, who provides two *loci* in which the powers of the soul are described: *Consolatio Philosophiae*, V, prose iv, and, less explicitly, *De Trinitate* ii. The absorption of Greco-Arabic psychology in the West is lucidly presented by Michaud-Quantin (1949).

5. An influential tract, which presents this, along with other, psychological schemes, is the *Tractatus de divisione multiplici potentiarum animae*, by Jean de la Rochelle, ed. Michaud-Quantin (1964).

linking man with the corporality he perceives on the one hand and with universal essences on the other. It is more sophisticated, in fact, than was necessary for many vernacular writers of the late Middle Ages, whose interests were moral rather than philosophical. In such a situation, writers in late fourteenth-century England who wished to develop terminology to cope with the range of concepts here were obliged to find their own English equivalents. Of the few writers who do present the scheme, or variations of it, we find a range of terminology,[6] and some garbled versions of the scheme itself.[7] Chaucer draws on elements of this psychology with confidence (Minnis 1981, 77–8), but Langland is the only writer who draws on a psychological scheme to shape the extended structure of his narrative. Aspects of the psychology of the third vision correspond to elements of the more philosophical psychology derived from Aristotle; in following visions, Langland draws on the more religious conception of the soul characteristic of Augustine.

I am unable to link each psychological element of Langland's narrative with corresponding elements of Aristotelian derived psychology, but I think the poem is broadly indebted to this tradition.[8] In further chapters I will show how the narrative right up to its end is shaped around psychological structures; within the bounds of Passus VIII–XII we can say that Langland is indebted to a scheme which is broadly speaking Aristotelian, for these reasons: (i) the fact that understanding is presented as progressive, whereby Will's question is treated at different, and progressively deeper psychological levels; (ii) the name and the role of Imaginatif, which can be securely placed within the Aristotelian model.

6. Chaucer translates the Boethian list of *sensus, imaginatio, ratio, intelligentia* as 'wit', 'ymaginacioun', 'resoun', 'intelligence' (*Boece*, V. iv, 150–60). The fifteenth-century text *Pecock's Donet*, ed. Hitchcock (1921), lists the outward wits (i.e. the senses), the inward wits (as 'comoun witt, ymaginacioun, fantasye, estimacioun and mynde'), and adds Reason and Free Will as the specifically human components of the soul.

7. *The Lay Folks' Catechism*, ed. Simmons and Noloth (1901), lists the five inward wits, for example, as 'wyl, resoun, mynd, ymaginacioun and thogth' (p. 19).

8. One source of his knowledge may have been the eclectic pseudo-Augustinian text, the *De Spiritu et Anima* (PL 40. 779–831), which presents this scheme, along with other, Augustinian psychological schemes (which also influence Langland), albeit in a confusing way. For Langland's possible knowledge of this text, see Schmidt (1968, 363–4; 1969, 144) and Wittig (1972, 212).

I shall give a brief exposition of each actant in turn, beginning
with the psychological concepts, before looking to the pedagogic
actants.[9]

Thought, Wit and Imaginatif

Thought

Will falls to sleep in a 'doute' (VIII. 70); the first figure he meets
is tall and like Will himself; he knows Will's 'kynde name', and
says that he has followed Will for seven years, and asks Will why
he (Will) has not seen Thought sooner, at which point Will recognises Thought, and puts his question to him. What are we as
readers to make of this information?

The word 'thought' is used in Middle English to designate one
of the inward wits, but in a way which does not clarify *which* of
the inward wits is being referred to.[10] Another possibility might
be to look at poetic texts. In Spenser's *Faerie Queene* Guyon visits
the castle of Alma, or soul. Alma takes Guyon to visit the three
chambers of the castle's turret. The first of these is that of Phan-
tastes, a melancholy figure, whose chamber is full of false
imaginings, 'idle thoughts and fantasies'. This image is drawn
from the Aristotelian model, where the *sensus communis* is sometimes called *fantasia* when it is not subject to reason.[11] The image
of being melancholy and full of 'idle thoughts' is clearly relevant
to Chaucer's *Book of the Duchess*, which begins with a melancholic
dreamer who has 'so many an ydel thoght', and whose head is
full of 'fantasies' (ll. 1–29). This sense is not exactly right for
Langland's 'Thoght', though, who is not irrational.

Looking further at the use of 'thought' in Middle English,
however, we can see how the obsessive quality of the dreamer's
thought in the *Book of the Duchess* might be relevant. OED lists
under sense 4(b) for 'thought' 'meditation, mental contemplation;

9. In the discussion of the psychological and pedagogic actants which follows,
   I am indebted at points to work kindly shown to me by Nicky Zeeman; her
   material will be presented as part of a Cambridge Ph. D.
10. For example *The Lay Folks' Catechism*, where, as I have said, the scheme is
   in any case garbled, and the elaboration of 'thought' not suggestive of any link
   with a specific inward wit: 'loke thy thowght be groundyd in the ioy of heuyn
   . . .' (p. 19).
11. See, for example, Jean de la Rochelle (1964, 72–3).

perplexity, puzzled condition of mind', and under 5 'anxiety, or distress of mind'; both these senses could be present in *Book of the Duchess*, 504, describing the Black Knight, who 'argued with his owne thoght'; the dreamer apologises for disturbing the Black Knight's 'thought' (l. 524), and wishes to know more of his 'thought' at l. 538. Turning back to Langland's 'Thoght', we could say that he represents a superficial state of rational reflection (rather than a psychological faculty as such). The fact that he has followed Will for 'seven years' (a conventional period), without Will recognising him might suggest that it is only now that Will recognises the problem that has been perplexing him for a long time in its explicit form. It is also relevant to mention that poems (or sections of poems) often begin in a state of 'thought': this is true of Langland's fourth vision, for example, where Will has 'muche thought' about the previous vision (XIII. 4), before he lies down 'longe in this thoght' (XIII. 21) and sleeps; it is also true of Lydgate's *Temple of Glas* (another dream poem), and of Hoccleve's *Regement of Princes*.

Just as the Black Knight 'argues' with his own thought, so too do Will and Thought 'dispute' (l. 116) until they come to Wit. Thought serves as a mean between Will and Wit, which might suggest the idea of a perplexing problem being presented to the reason for deeper consideration. This idea, of thought being a state preliminary to understanding, is behind Trevisa's usage: 'To brynge here hertes out of thought that hereth speke of laborinthus, here I telle what laborinthus is to menynge' (Babington 1865, I. 311).

Wit

Wit is grave of aspect, gentle in speech, and commands more respect than Thought (VIII. 124). When Thought intercedes on Will's behalf, he puts his request in this way: 'Here is Wil wolde wite if Wit koude teche' (l. 127). This is a neat formulation, with the two verbs 'wolde' and 'wite' expressing the basic action of these passus, of the *will* desiring to *know* ('witen') (Dillon 1981). The will/wit opposition in this line recalls the very frequent use of this opposition in Middle English generally, as in the examples we have already seen. This suggests that Langland's Wit represents the reason.

Wit introduces a complexity here by offering a picture allegory of the body in his definition of Dowel. He says that the body is like a castle (the castle of *Caro*), made by Kynde from the four elements, and containing the soul. Dowel, he says, guards the soul, but the constable of the castle itself is 'Sire Inwit', who had five sons 'by his firste wyve' (IX. 1–24). Later he says that Inwit is in the head, serves the soul, and is 'gretteste' after the grace of God. What does 'Inwit' mean?

In Passus XIII Langland uses 'inwit' to mean 'the collection of inward wits', as opposed to the outer wits, or senses (XIII. 288). Here, however, Inwit seems to be granted much higher status in the hierarchy of the soul (just below God Himself) than the inward wits. Even medieval writers who used the Aristotelian psychological scheme drew on a different, Augustinian scheme in their description of the upper reaches of the soul (e.g. the influential twelfth-century pseudo-Augustinian tract, *De Spiritu et Anima*). According to Augustine, the reason has an upper and a lower part, with the upper part looking towards contemplative wisdom, and the lower part towards worldly prudence. This is the way the *De Spiritu et Anima*, for example, describes the upper and lower reason: '. . . the reason divides itself in two, that is into an upper and a lower reason: the upper reason is wisdom, the lower prudence . . .'.[12] It is this higher reason that Wit (the lower reason) denotes by 'Inwit'. Inwit's 'first wife' (l. 19) must be the body, whose 'fyve faire sones' (l. 19) are the senses.

Imaginatif

The only other natural faculty of the soul Will meets in this vision is Imaginatif (Reason, whom Will meets in Passus XI, is not a faculty of Will's soul; he is a principle of justice and order in the universe (Alford 1988)). Will meets Imaginatif when he wakes from the inner-dream of Passus XI, and Imaginatif reflects on the dream that has gone before until the end of Passus XI, and in Passus XII reflects back on, and resolves, the important issues of the vision as a whole. Study had said to Will in Passus X that 'Ymaginatif herafterward shal answere to youre purpos' (l. 117),

---

12. '. . . Et dividit se ratio in duo, scilicet in seorsum et deorsum: sursum in sapientiam; deorsum in prudentiam . . .' (*PL* 40. 787) [my translation].

suggesting that the whole vision will be reflected on, and resolved by Imaginatif; when he announces himself at the beginning of Passus XII, it is clear again that his role is one of moral reflection across time, both towards the past and the future:

> I have folwed thee, in feith, thise fyve and fourty wynter,
> And manye tymes have meved thee to [m]yn[n]e on thyn ende,
> And how fele fernyeres are faren, and so fewe to come;
> And of thi wilde wantownesse [whan] thow yong were,
> To amende it in thi myddel age, lest myght the faille
> In thyn olde elde . . .
>
> (XII. 3–8)
>
> *mynne*: meditate; *fele*: many; *fernyeres*: past years; *faren*: passed.

In Aristotelian psychology, the *imaginatio* is a relatively low faculty – that which stands immediately behind the common wit (*sensus communis*) to receive and retain images produced by that faculty. The *Cloud* author describes the imagination as the 'myght thorow the whiche we portray alle ymages of absent and present thinges' (p. 117). Langland uses the form 'imaginatif', however, rather than 'imaginacio(u)n'. In accounts of the Aristotelian scheme, writers distinguish between *imaginatio* and *imaginativa*; whereas imagination is purely passive, *imaginativa* has the power to divide and compose images. When this power is subject to reason, then it has the power to think through images.[13] This deliberative power is denoted, for example (above mere 'imagination'), by Chaucer's reference to the '*heigh* ymaginacioun' of the fox as he plans to capture the cock in *The Nun's Priest's Tale* (l. 3217). When we turn back to Langland's Imaginatif, we notice that he is certainly subject to reason in his power to resolve many arguments which have preoccupied Will, and that he certainly uses images, in, for example, his argument about the salvation of the learned man being like the more probable salvation of the man who can swim (XII. 155–86).

13. This is the argument of Jean de la Rochelle (1964, 76), where '*cogitativa*' is given as a synonym for *imaginativa*, when the *imaginativa* is subject to reason. Kaulbach (1985) and Minnis (1981) both seek to provide accounts of the imagination which offer a deliberative function to the faculty. Kaulbach locates Langland's sources closely here with the Aristotelian tradition, as commented by Avicenna. See also White (1986) for the connections between Imaginatif and Kynde.

Study, Clergy and Scripture

So far I have considered only the natural faculties of Will's soul (or, more accurately, of the soul of which Will/the will is a part). Will also meets, however, three other figures who are clearly not part of the human soul, and who mediate between the meetings with Thoght and Wit on the one hand, and with Imaginatif on the other: Study, Clergy, and Scripture. What place do they have in the psychological scheme I have outlined?

It is a commonplace of medieval studies that medieval writers respected written authority, rather than trusting purely to their own experience. This perception is relevant to the structure of the third vision, where Will can learn only so much through the uninformed exercise of his reason, before requiring information from sources of written authority, and particularly from Scripture, the ultimate written authority. In order to read Scripture, however, Will needs first to be taught to read, and then to handle theological questions, through meeting first Study, and then Clergy. In the *De Spiritu et Anima*, we read the commonplace idea that 'the soul is distinguished by the reason, by which it is taught in the best arts and instructed in exceptional disciplines, in order that it should treat of human things, and taste of divine things'.[14] It is precisely this instruction of the reason that we see at the beginning of Passus X, when Study rebukes Wit for teaching Will:

> 'Wel artow wis,' quod she to Wit, 'any wisdomes to telle
> To flatereres or to fooles that frenetike ben of wittes!' –
> And blamed hym and banned hym and bad hym be stille.
>
> (X. 5–7)

> *frenetike*: crazed; *banned*: reproached.

These figures, then, represent an educational hierarchy and progression, from the basic instruction of Study to the higher institutions of learning in Clergy, whose textbook is Scripture.

Study

Study is married to Wit, and Langland indulges himself (especially

---

14. 'Ratione insignita est anima, qua artibus docetur egregiis et disciplinis instruitur eximiis, ut divina sapiat et humana tactet' (*PL* 40. 793) [my translation].

after Wit's speech about marital harmony) to present their
marriage as one in which Study is the domineering, 'schoolma'mish'
wife, before whom Wit becomes 'so confus he kouthe noght loke,
/ And as doumb as a dore nail drough hym aside' (ll. 138–9).
When Will submits to her authority and discipline, he offers to
obey her all his life, as long, he says, as she teaches him what
Dowel is (ll. 144–8); instead of accepting his service, however,
Study says that she will send Will on to her 'cosyn' Clergy.[15] In
not telling Will what Dowel is, and in sending him on to Clergy,
Study is representing an educational tradition according to which
one passed from study of the secular, liberal arts, which cannot
teach morality (or 'dowel'), to study of theology. The idea that
the arts themselves could not teach moral virtue was a commonplace. A mid-thirteenth-century preacher quotes Seneca as saying
that 'we instruct our children in the arts not in order that they
may learn virtue, but rather that they should prepare the soul for
the reception of virtue' (cited Simpson 1986c, 53). Study sends
Will on to Clergy with the password of the Trivium (grammar,
rhetoric, and dialectic) and some other arts (ll. 170–81), and with
the map of an allegorical landscape, passing through suffrance,
poverty, sobriety, and simplicity of speech (ll. 159–69). These are
clearly the characteristics of the ideal student, since they are
characteristic also of Chaucer's Clerk (General Prologue,
ll. 285–308) (about whom it is said, it might be noticed, 'of studie
took he moost cure' (l. 303)). And in not accepting Will's offer of
life-long service, too, Study is within a standard educational
tradition that students should not 'grow old in the arts', and that
they should move on to the Faculty of Theology (which is why
there is, perhaps, a quiet satire of the Clerk in Chaucer's prologue,
since the Clerk remains in the arts, in 'study', rather than moving
on to theology).

Clergy

Study is incapable of understanding Theology. After giving Will
his password of liberal disciplines to pass to Clergy, she goes on
to say that Theology confuses her completely, since love, which
is unintelligible, is at the centre of theological consideration:

Ac Theologie hath tened me ten score tymes:

The moore I muse therinne, the myst[lok]er it semeth,
And the depper I devyne, the derker me it thynketh.

(X. 182–4)

tened: troubled; *mystloker*: mistier; *devyne*: ponder.

The author that Study *can* understand is Cato, whose *Distichs* formed a basic textbook for schoolchildren in the Middle Ages. She says that Cato teaches to repay enemies in kind, whereas the Theology teaches the contrary, that we should love our enemies (ll. 191–9).

In acknowledging this incapacity, Study conforms to a standard educational structure, whereby students move from preliminary learning to theological study. In universities a student passed from the Faculty of Arts to that of Theology if he wished to proceed as a theologian. In Langland's poem Study does not represent university study in the arts (which involved study of the three philosophies – natural and moral philosophy and metaphysics) (Courtenay 1987, 15–36); rather, she represents the grammar school, the preliminary educational institution, among whose textbooks is Cato, and whose domain of instruction is the verbal arts especially. But Clergy, as 'cosyn' to Study, does represent, in my view, the institution of university theological learning. The word 'clergie' in Middle English can mean simply 'the clergy (as distinguished from the laity)' (MED, sense 1(a)), and, by association, 'the learned men of a country' (sense 1(c)). This second sense gives rise to a further sense of 'knowledge, learning, doctrine', and 'pure clergy', which denotes 'higher learning, theology' (sense 3(a)). We find a will, for example, which makes a donation 'so that . . . may be founded . . . Quenes collage to . . . augmentacion of pure clergie, namely of the Imparesse of alle sciences and faculltees, theologie' (cited MED sense 3(a)). It is this sense, I think, which is personified by Langland's 'Clergie'. It is certainly true that the kinds of questions raised by Will with Clergy are of a specifically theological nature.[16]

16. The word 'clergie' in *Mum and the Sothsegger*, ed. Day and Steele (1936), while not denoting specifically theological learning, denotes university learning: in seeking 'clergie' the narrator goes to Cambridge, Oxford and Orléans (ll. 319–23).

Scripture

If Cato is the textbook for the knowledge of Study, then Scripture, or the Bible, is Clergy's text, and, in Langland's allegory, Clergy and Scripture are married. It could be noticed, however, that Scripture is being used in a specific way, adduced in academic debate. In Passus I Holy Church had used scriptural texts, but in a purely dogmatic way; and in the passus to follow (XV–XVIII) Will enters profoundly into the allegorical interpretation of Scripture. In Passus X, instead, Scripture occupies a middle ground between these two extremes of the purely dogmatic instruction and intimate, allegorical understanding; Scripture is being used actively by Will, but the scriptural texts are being used as counters in theological, academic arguments (e.g. B.X. 374a). There is one tiny point about Scripture, which seems to me characteristic of a distinctively academic approach to Scripture: she is attentive to the authenticity of the text in her arguments. In replying to one of Will's arguments, she opens her statement of position by saying 'but if scryveynes lye' ('unless copyists lie') (X. 329), which shows a remarkable awareness of the fragility of the text of Scripture. Scripture is herself aware, that is, that the truth of what she has to say is dependent on the accuracy of the copyists who have copied the Bible from other copies.

Concluding our discussion of the structure of Langland's psychological and educational allegory, then, we can say that these figures do form a coherent group; they have a set of relations between themselves which suggests this coherence. (Thoght is a 'mean' between Will and Wit; Wit is married to Study; Study is the cousin of Clergy; and Clergy is married to Scripture. Only Imaginatif, who reflects on the whole process, fittingly stands unrelated to any one of the other figures.) Langland's narrative in these (and following) passus could be described as a *Bildungsroman*, the story of the soul's education, both through natural, psychological faculties, and through formal educational institutions. The structure of the narrative is itself formed around the structure of the soul's education.

STYLE

As I have said, the first figures Will encounters on this educative journey are two friars, 'maistres of the Menours, men of grete witte' (VIII. 9), where the title 'maistre' is being used in a formal way, to denote the academic degree of *magister*, or 'master'. And the style of Will's speech to these friars confirms the academic level of the encounter, and in effect sets the dominant stylistic register of the third vision. In reply to the friars' complacent assertion that Dowel lives with them, Will replies in a formal, academic manner:

> '*Contra!*' quod I as a clerc, and comsed to disputen,
> And seide, 'Soothly, *Sepcies in die cadit iustus*.
> Sevene sithes, seith the Book, synneth the rightfulle,
> And whoso synneth,' I seide, '[certes] dooth yvele, as
>   me thynketh,
> And Dowel and Do-yvele mowe noght dwelle
>   togideres.
> *Ergo* he nys noght alwey at hoom amonges yow
>   freres'.
>
> (VIII. 20–5)
>
> *contra*: against [this]; *sepcies in die cadit iustus*: the just man
> falls seven times a day; *ergo*: therefore.

The process of argument here is syllogistic, using a two-part major premise: Will draws his first major premise from Scripture, which is necessarily true; he adds another which is logically necessary (that sinning is 'doing evil'); his minor premise is that 'dowel' and 'do-evil' cannot be together. The conclusion which follows (introduced by the '*Ergo*'), is that Dowel cannot therefore be amongst the friars.

Will's argumentative procedures are drawn directly from the dialectical models of university debate, as we might expect in a vision which is about the education of the soul. (Dialectic is the name given to the art of constructing arguments in Roman and medieval education, and formed a basic part of preliminary education in the Trivium.) Will argues as one who

> . . . should konne and knowe alle kynnes clergie,
> And answere to arguments and also to a *quodlibet*,
>
> (XV. 379–80)

where a '*quodlibet*' is a testing kind of university debate, in which any question can be put to a master. If the institutions which produced the characteristic discourses of the first two visions were the Church and the monarchy, in the third vision it is educational institutions which provide the discursive forms for much of the poetry. It is also true that, within these educational encounters, satire is often used; many speakers attack the traditional objects of satire: Wit attacks contemporary marriage practices; Study attacks uninformed theological speculation; and Clergy attacks avaricious religious. The status of satire itself comes under scrutiny in this vision, and I shall return to it, but it remains true that the framing discourse is that of academia.

Langland's narrative here is marked lexically by the use of many scholastic, university terms which are not often found in vernacular writing contemporary with *Piers Plowman*. This is true of the following terms, for example: '*Contra*' and '*Ergo*' of Will's argument at VIII. 20–5 (also X. 341); 'motif' (X. 115), meaning 'a proposition, an assertion; argument, proof, justification' (MED sense (a)); 'repreven' (X. 341), meaning in its academic sense, 'to refute, disprove' (MED sense 2(b)); 'balled reason' (X. 54), meaning 'a glib or crafty argument' (MED sense 8(b)).

And at certain points the shape of the verse is determined by the argumentative joints, or articles, of a scholastic *quaestio*, or question, the basic unit of academic debate in medieval universities. Within each article, one rehearses the 'resons of bothe two sides, / The pro and the contra as clergie askith' (*Mum and the Sothsegger* (ed. Day and Steele 1936), ll. 299–300). At X. 328, for example, Will engages in formal dispute with Scripture (Boitani 1982, 93). After a prophecy that the secular power shall amend the Church, Will returns to his central preoccupation by asking a *question*: 'Thanne is Dowel and Dobet,' quod I, '*dominus* and knyghthode?' (X. 328). Scripture replies by *objecting*, with authoritative passages from the Old and New Testaments, and from Cato, to the effect that kingship, knighthood and wealth generally are of no value, and are even hindrances to salvation (X. 329–40). To this Will offers a *contra*, by arguing that New Testament authority proves that anyone baptised will be saved, rich or poor (X. 341–3). At this point Scripture makes a *response*, which first takes care of Will's point about all baptised being saved by stating that this is said with regard to pagans, who might be baptised at the last moment and be saved. But he goes on to return to the main issue (whether or not riches help or hinder the rich Christian to salvation) by elaborating the argument he has already made that riches and earthly power are more likely to hinder the possibility of salvation.

This pattern of argument follows that of the scholastic *articulus*, or article, a form of treating a problem developed in medieval universities in the late twelfth and thirteenth centuries. It is designed to incorporate necessarily within its structure all the authorities and arguments most powerfully opposing the argument that the writer himself wishes to make, in order to force him to test the truth of his own position by rebuttal. Its features are: (i) statement of the question; (ii) objections, putting arguments for one or other side of the question; (iii) a *sed contra* ('but, against . . .'), which appeals to an authority against the objections; and (iv) a determination of, or response to the question, which resolves it by answering opposing arguments raised either in the objections or the *sed contra*.[17] A glance at any scholastic treatise confirms the pattern of this argument (e.g. Aquinas, ed. Gilby 1964), and it is clear that Langland is working within this formal dialectical tradition in many of the encounters between Will and his interlocutors. When Will says at the beginning of this vision that he 'as a clerc . . . comsed to disputen', it is this formal mode of debate to which he is referring. Just as he interrogates the rational faculties of his soul, so too are the rhetorical modes of the text accordingly analytical, or what medieval theoreticians called 'definitive, divisive, and argumentative'.[18]

THEME

Having considered the structure and style of this vision, we must now turn to its central theme, concerning the status of good works before God. This is, as I have argued, the question which the 'pardon' from Truthe places so forcefully before Will: the document sent by Truthe had promised pardon for the·sins which men inevitably commit. When it comes, the 'pardon' puts even the possibility of pardon into radical doubt, since it insists that the only 'pardon' is to 'dowel', or not to require pardon. If this is the case, then man must either trust wholly to God's grace, or gift, to be saved, or there must be some other sense in which 'dowel' can merit a genuine pardon from God.

At the beginning of the third vision, however, Will is unable

17. For the historical development of this procedure, see Chenu (1969).
18. For the late medieval exposition of these textual procedures (*formae tractandi*) and their close relation to rational, psychological faculties, see Simpson (1986a).

to perceive how works might be of any value, since all he can think of is how man is simply unable to perform meritorious good works which satisfy the demands of God's justice. In the encounter with the friars at the beginning of the vision, Will's argument that Dowel cannot be among the friars themselves takes its impetus from his scriptural point that even 'the just man sins seven times a day' (VIII. 21). Will begins the vision, then, with an inescapable sense of man's incapacity to meet the standards of God's justice.

What answers do the powers of the soul Will meets give? Do they clarify for Will the status of good works in their answers to Will's often repeated question 'Where (or what) is Dowel?' It seems to me that they do not, since they each repeat, in different ways, the point that Dowel is to obey the law; if this is their reply, then it does not advance Will beyond the statement of the 'pardon' itself, since this is exactly what that document, and its preliminary glosses in the body of Passus VII, had said.

Thought, for example, gives this answer to Will's question:

Whoso is trewe of his tunge and of his two handes,
And thorugh his labour or thorugh his land his liflode wynneth,
And is trusty of his tailende, taketh but his owene,
And is noght dronkelewe ne dedeynous – Dowel hym folweth.

(VIII. 81–4)

liflode: sustenance; tailende: reckoning; dronkelewe:
given to drink; dedeynous: arrogant.

The word at the centre of this definition of 'dowel' is 'trewe': as the spiritual guide to Truthe, Piers Plowman tried to fulfil each of these demands. But how useful is this to Will? As a definition of Dowel, it recalls the admonition to labourers in the glosses to the 'pardon' itself, which declared that all labourers who 'treweliche taken and treweliche wynnen' will receive the same pardon as Piers (VII. 60–3). And it also recalls the nexus of 'truthe' we observed in Holy Church's speech of Passus I, where being 'true' in speech and honest in one's dealings with men was felt to meet the standards of God's 'truthe', or justice. It is precisely this definition of Dowel which had provoked Will's search in the first place, and it is unsurprising that Will should feel that this solution to the problem does not get him very far, in so far as it is no solution at all, but rather a restatement (which is what we would expect from 'Thoght', representing a state of perplexity over a given problem).

If Thought does not advance Will, we might expect more from Wit. In fact, however, Wit's answer to Will's problem is of no more help, since he, too, stresses obedience to law at a basic level. He gives two answers to the question of what 'dowel' is: (i) to dread God (IX. 95 and 204); and (ii) to 'doon as lawe techeth' (IX. 200). The life he sees as representative of this basic level of fulfilment of the law is that of wedlock, which was often conceived in the Middle Ages as a basic, imperfect, but satisfactory state of life (morally below that of widows and virgins) (Bloomfield 1958):

> [In this world is Dowel trewe wedded libbynge folk],
> For thei mote werche and wynne and the world sustene.
>
> (IX. 108–9)
>
> *libbynge*: living.

In his role as the lower, more prudential aspect of the reason Wit stresses practical common and moral sense in the making of marriages, that couples should not be matched for financial interest, but rather for love (ll. 161–78). And in keeping with the role of wit in the Will/Wit opposition, he stresses rational control in sexual activity: men should marry to avoid fornication, and, once married, they should make love only within season (i.e. not in periods of fasting or menstruation) (ll. 179–99).

But Wit's definitions, while clearly having a conventional moral authority behind them, are of no use to Will. Piers, after all, is a married man (VI. 96), whose role it was to 'werche and wynne and the world sustene'. After the crisis provoked by the 'pardon', however, Piers abandons this role, and it is precisely the inadequacy, before God, of working in the world which also provokes Will's own search.

Wit's definitions of Dowel, then, like Thought's, stress obedience to the law, or 'truthe'. As powers of the cognitive, or rational part of the soul, this might not surprise us. After all, the rational part of the soul is designed for the perception of the truth, and it is the rational part of the soul which must be brought into play in deciding matters of justice. In Passus IV, we might remember that it is the personification of Reason who is responsible for the ultimate judicial sentence of Wrong in accordance with Truthe (who determines 'hire trespas to the ende' (I. 97)), and it is Reason who refuses any mercy to Mede or Wrong. Reason is, of course, the personification of a legal concept of justice rather than of the ratiocinative power of the individual soul; but the very fact that the same word is used of both indicates their close relation: the perception of justice requires the exercise of reason. The reason is precious because of this power it has for recognising justice, but this is also its profound limitation; for in the third vision, we see that the rational faculties are incapable of recognising anything *but* justice – Thought and Wit reiterate that Dowel is 'to doon as lawe techeth' (IX. 200).

And like Reason, or 'Truthe', Wit seems embedded in an Old Testament world. It is Reason who articulates the concept of strict, Old Testament reward in the secular court of Passus IV, in his statement that Wrong should not go unpunished:

> For '*Nullum malum* the man mette with *inpunitum*
> And bad *Nullum bonum* be *irremuneratum*'.
>
> (IV. 143–4)
>
> *nullum malum*: no evil, *inpunitum*: unpunished; *nullum bonum*:
> no good; *irremuneratum*: unrewarded.

And it is Truthe who sends the 'pardon' to Piers, which insists on the same Old Testament principle of strict justice in the spiritual sphere. Moreover, the exempla cited by Wit are, on the whole, drawn from the Old Testament (he cites *Genesis* for the creation (ll. 32–50), for the misconception of Cayn (ll. 119–26) and for the vengeful, punishing Flood (ll. 127–42)). And his response to these exempla itself insists on the propriety of punishment – he says that in the Flood children paid for their ancestors' sins (l. 143), which, he says, is against the spirit of the 'Gospel' (here meaning the New Testament), which claims that sons shall not carry the iniquity of the father. In fact the 'gospel' text he cites is from the Old Testament book of Ezechiel (18.20), but he defends this kind of punishment, by arguing that in fact children do bear the moral characteristics of their parents. He even completely mistakes the spirit of a citation which is from the New Testament in support of his case 'Do men gather grapes of thorns, or figs of thistles?', which, in its context (Matt. 7.16), has nothing to do with the qualities inherited by children from their parents. Wit talks wholly from within an Old Testament world: he stresses a life of law and justice, especially as exemplified in wedlock, as the life of Dowel. (It is interesting to note that wedlock is closely associated with the Old Testament period for Langland, as a scene in Passus XVI (ll. 77–85) indicates.)

Study, as I have said, does not offer a definition of Dowel. This is in keeping with educational traditions which stress the preparatory role of the liberal arts, as a preparation for the study of virtue. It is true, however, that she, too, seems to inhabit an Old Testament world of strict repayment. She confesses her incapacity to understand Theology because it has love at its centre. Cato teaches us to repay enemies in the same manner in which they treat us. Study can understand this doctrine (and she, as the instructor in basic school textbooks, is responsible for teaching Cato), but Theology, she recognises, bids us to love our enemies (ll. 191–206). Study respects this doctrine of love, but is clearly unable to understand or explain it.

Neither can Clergy help Will with his question. For like Thought and Wit, Clergy's definition of Dowel points to the satisfaction of a minimum basic level of the Christian life:

> 'It is a commune lyf,' quod Clergie, 'on Holy Chirche to bileve,
> With alle the articles of the feith that falleth to be knowe:
> And that is to bileve lelly . . .'
>
> (X. 230–2)
>
> *falleth*: it is proper; *lelly*: faithfully.

So all these definitions have in common an insistence on obedience to a basic, 'trewe' or 'leal' level of secular or spiritual life: the words at the centre of the definitions of Dowel are 'trewe', 'trusty', 'lelly' – words, that is, which stress conformity to the standards of 'Truthe'. There is nothing unorthodox about these definitions – they are absolutely standard moral doctrine. One of the remarkable things about this vision of *Piers Plowman* is, however, that it is precisely these absolutely standard restatements of moral doctrine which lead Will to despair. Having been instructed by Clergy and Scripture, Will turns against the sources of his instruction and attacks them. Having progressed to the higher stages of theological learning, Will marshalls the knowledge gained from his teachers to attack their enterprise (in the way intelligent students often do!). He confronts Scripture with the doctrine of predestination from Passus X. 369, which he could have only learnt through higher theological learning. But this doctrine of salvation wholly by divine grace and election is one which leads Will to despair. For if men are saved by God's prior decision, then what, it could be asked, is the value of moral effort, and what is the value of learning itself?

This is the way Will begins his reproachful attack on Scripture and Clergy:

'This is a long lesson,' quod I, 'and litel am I the wiser!
Where Dowel is or Dobet derkliche ye shewen.
Manye tales ye tellen that Theologie lerneth,
And that I man maad was, and my name yentred
In the legende of lif longe er I were,
Or ellis unwriten for som wikkednesse, as Holy Writ witnesseth:
Nemo ascendit ad celum nisi qui de celo descendit

(X. 369–74a)

lerneth: teaches; yentred: entered; legende of lif: Book of Life;
nemo ascendit . . . descendit: no one ascended into heaven, but that he descended from heaven.

For the first time in the poem, Will the dreamer argues at length here (right up to 472a, without a pause), and his argument is full of verve. His first target is learning and its uselessness: he cites Solomon and Aristotle as examples of wise men who have been damned, and he cunningly manipulates a standard allegory of the Church as the ark of the faithful: if it is the ark, then what about the learned clergy, who are the carpenters of the ark of the Church? The carpenters of Noah's Ark were drowned (X. 396–410). This argument is learned, drawing on the learning Will has acquired from his instructors, but it is hostile to the very idea of learning which it sees as useless.

But why should Will attack learning as useless here? As I see it, this is the sequence of thought which leads inevitably towards scepticism about the value of learning: Will's instructors each insist, in their different ways, on the importance of obeying the law; this provokes Will to adopt the predestination position, since the one thing Will is sure of is man's incapacity to meet the standards of God's law: if man cannot therefore be saved by 'dowel', then the only alternative seems to be salvation by God's predestination of souls by grace. But if this is the case, then what is the value of learning? Learning will not help us perceive the mind of

God Himself, as is implicit in the fact that the learned are often damned (X. 375–410).

And not only is the value of learning radically questioned here, but beyond that the value of all moral action and effort is threatened. Will cites the examples of the thief saved on the cross, of Mary Magdalene, David and Paul: 'wh[o myghte do] werse?' Will asks, and yet they are in heaven (X. 411–38). The exempla of the penitent sinners, so often used as a *counter* to despair, are here, then, used in a way which might provoke despair: if they are saved, and if everything is in God's unknowable decision anyway, then why struggle to meet the standards of God's justice by 'doing well'? (Collins 1985). Will does not explicitly say that good works are of no value, but stresses the unknowability of what constitutes such works, and the fundamental incapacity of humans to match the standards of God's justice. 'For sothest word that ever God seide was tho he seide *Nemo Bonus*' ('No-one is good') (X. 438).

It is at this point that the authentic text of the A-Text ends. We should not confuse Langland the poet with Will – we simply do not know why Langland the poet stopped writing the A-Text at the point he did. It is nevertheless true that the text has reached a point of crisis: from the austerity of the 'pardon', Will has interrogated the faculties of his reason to discover the status of works before God. They have been unable to advance him beyond the austere injunction of the 'pardon', which Will realises cannot be met. In response to this, Will takes up the more Augustinian position of predestination, whereby man's salvation is entirely in the hands of God's gift and decision, regardless of man's merits. In this scheme, there seems to be no place for the moral efforts of individual Christians, and no place for the effort of learned enquiry into the value of works.

Will's position here is in fact one which can be correlated with central issues of fourteenth-century theology. At the end of the thirteenth century, there had been a powerful reaction against the increasingly philosophical tendency of thirteenth-century theology, under the influence of Aristotle and his Arab commentators. In 1277 the Bishop of Paris, Etienne Tempier, condemned 219 theses which could be traced to the Aristotelian identification of reality, intelligibility, and necessity. Against the movement to 'philosophise' God into a predictable, intelligible principle, the

Condemnations of 1277 asserted the centrality of God's absolute power (*potentia absoluta*) and incomprehensibility. They insisted on the all-powerful, unknowable, Old Testament God, as it were, against the God of the philosophers (Gilson 1955, 406–8; Grant 1982). This had immediate and profound consequences for the question of how man achieves salvation, since man cannot predict God's decision in any way; and it is remarkable how the central questions of fourteenth-century theology are massively reduced to relatively few preoccupying questions, including the' relation between man's free will and God's will. Grace and predestination, 'for the first time since the Pelagian controversy of the fourth century, . . . became central problems' (Leff 1957, 10; Courtenay 1987, 253–8).

One of the most forceful proponents of the neo-Augustinian, predestination position was Thomas Bradwardine (*c.* 1300–49). That late fourteenth-century vernacular writers regarded his *Summa de Causa Dei* (1344) as the near contemporary *locus classicus* for the question of predestination is suggested by the narrator's comment in Chaucer's *Nun's Priest's Tale*. 'Was it predestined that Chaunticleer flew into the yard?'; the narrator playfully suggests the question, but pretends ignorance:

> But I ne kan nat bulte it to the bren
> As kan the hooly doctour Augustyn,
> Or Boece, or the Bisshop Bradwardyn.
> (VII. 3240–2)
> *bulte it to the bren*: sift it to the husks (resolve the argument).

Bradwardine asserts 'God's grace to the exclusion of all merit. His intention was to win back for God all power which he [Bradwardine] considered to have been usurped by men'. This allowed 'no independent freedom' to men at all, and is the 'essence of his system' (Leff 1957, 15). The Nun's Priest says that there has been 'greet altercacioun' and 'disputisoun' 'in scole' concerning this matter (ll. 3237–8), and it was clearly regarded as a central theological issue of the middle and late fourteenth century (it is, incidentally, the question debated at length by Troilus in Book IV of *Troilus and Criseyde*).

Langland not only presents the doctrine of predestination; he also reveals the emotional effects of such a doctrine. Like Troilus, who is in 'despeir' (both amatory and philosophical) as he confronts the doctrine of predestination (IV. 954), so too is Will represented as being on the brink of despairing abdication of moral effort: For '*quant OPORTET vient en place il ny ad que PATI*' ('When *must* comes on the scene, there's nothing for it but *endure*' (X. 436)). From within the purely rational psychological resources of his current vision there is no escape from this position. He must resort to more profound sources of knowledge, or approach what he knows in a different way, before he can resolve his problem. He does this in the inner-dream of Passus XI, a vision set into the third vision. I have avoided discussion of this dream until this point, since it has its own coherence, but now we must consider the ways in which this inner-dream answers to Will's questions.

THE INNER-DREAM (XI. 5–402): FORTUNE, LEWTEE, SCRIPTURE, TRAJAN

This is a complex vision, and I cannot discuss its every part. I will argue that this vision is the turning point of the poem, since Will first makes crucial recognitions about the possibility of God mercifully recognising the merits of human action. For the first time since the 'pardon', Will advances beyond the intellectual and emotional blockage at which he had arrived.

The inner-dream has two parts, each inspired by a separate visionary experience: (i) Will is shown a 'mirour that highte Middelerthe' at XI. 9. In this visionary experience the figure of Fortune and her followers charm Will into a state of reckless, youthful abandon, until he suddenly grows old and recognises the gravity of his situation. This vision provokes a series of linked reflections from three figures, Lewtee, Scripture and Trajan; (ii) at XI. 320 Will is shown another vision of 'Myddelerthe', this time by Kynde, or Nature, which provokes a discussion between Reason and Will. At XI. 404 Will wakes out of the inner-dream and reflects on the whole experience with Imaginatif, until the end of Passus XI. I will discuss the vision of Nature later, but for the resolution of the question of works and salvation, we should concentrate on the first of these visionary experiences, the vision of Fortune.

Fortune, Lewtee, Scripture

Langland is the only English writer (to my knowledge, the only medieval writer), to have used the device of the dream within a dream. He does so, I think, as a way of engaging deeper, more emotional aspects of the self in the resolution of intellectual problems. The inner-dream cannot be regarded as a straight continuation of the intellectual argument in the previous passus; it is more of a replay of certain central issues, which provoke Will to see them in a different, more intense and personal light. It begins with Scripture dismissing Will's intellectual ingenuity; before his argument about predestination, Scripture had not 'scorned', or derided Will (X. 329), but at the beginning at Passus XI she does precisely that (XI. 1). She cites the first line of a widely influential twelfth-century monastic text, which stresses the importance of self-knowledge above knowledge of things external to the self (Wittig 1972, 212), as a way of dismissing Will's cunning, witty deployment of arguments in favour of predestination and against the value of learning. Will begins the dream, then, in a state of emotional tension, weeping 'for wo and wrathe of hir speche' (XI. 4).

He does not witness the vision of Fortune, so much as participate in it; the figures Will first meets in the vision (Fortune and her followers), are inspired from scriptural sources (I John 2.15–16), but Will is not treating sources as mere counters in an argument here, so much as being personally involved in the narrative with them. The blandishments of Fortune pick up and underline the point of intellectual despair at which Will had arrived in Passus X, since Fortune and her followers lead Will to a state of moral laxity. Will's arguments about the salvation of the famous sinners in Passus X held the seeds of a *laissez faire* morality within it, given his point that sinners are saved and the learned damned: what, it could be asked, is the value of moral and intellectual effort? It is this state which is represented as a biographical experience, rather than an intellectual argument, in Passus XI. One of Fortune's followers is Rechelesnesse, who encourages Will to put everything into God's hands, and enjoy the interim:

'Folwe forth that Fortune wole – thow has wel fer til Elde.

A man may stoupe tyme ynogh whan he shal tyne the
  crowne.
"*Homo proponit,*" quod a poete, and Plato he highte,
"And *Deus disponit,*" quod he, "lat God doon his wille".'

                                    (XI. 35–8)

that: what; *tyne*: lose; *homo proponit*: man proposes;
deus disponit: God disposes.

The 'lat God doon his wille' might sound like 'Thy will be done',
but Rechelesnesse uses it in a context where its implications are
for complete abandon to the sensual will for the time that one is
not confronting the will of God.

In keeping, however, with the quality of this inner-dream, in
which the moral implications of concepts are felt in intensely
personal terms, Will suddenly grows old. He follows the advice
of 'Coveitise of Eighes' to seek a pardon from the friars whenever
he sins, since their absolution is given so easily in return for
monetary payment, 'Til', he says, 'I foryat youthe and yarn into
elde' (XI. 60). In his penniless old age, however, the friars refuse
to have anything to do with him. He complains against them, and
approaches a figure called Lewtee to ask whether or not he has
the right publicly to attack the friars. 'Lewtee', as we saw in
Chapter 1, is as semantically close a Latin based word to the key
word of Langland's first two visions, 'truthe', and clearly personifies a concept of justice which legitimates 'truthe' telling: he
encourages Will to attack the friars (XI. 84–106a).

So satire is defended here on the grounds of strict justice. This
is satisfying as long as it applies to the practice of the satirical poet;
but the defence of blaming on the grounds of strict justice also
has theological implications, for God, too, can blame on the
grounds of strict justice. And, in fact, the movement of the poem
suddenly opens out into these wider theological implications. For
the figure Scripture agrees with Lewtee, but extends the principle
of strict justice (by which satire would be legitimated) to God's
own action. Scripture suddenly reintroduces the really central
issues of the third vision as a whole – that of God's justice and
the frightening incapacity of man to meet its standards:

'He seith sooth,' quod Scripture tho, and skipte an heigh and
  preched;
Ac the matere that she meved, if lewed men it knewe,

The lasse, as I leve, lovyen thei wolde
The bileve o[f Oure] Lord that lettred men techeth.
This was hir teme and hir text – I took ful good hede:
'*Multi* to a mangerie and to the mete were sompned;
And whan the peple was plener comen, the porter unpynned the
    yate
And plukked in *Pauci* pryveliche and leet the remenaunt go rome.'

(XI. 107–14)

> *sooth*: the truth; *meved*: raised; *lewed*: ignorant; *teme*: theme; *multi*: many;
> *mangerie*: feast; *sompned*: summoned; *plener*: fully; *pauci*: few.

The parable Scripture chooses as her text (Matt. 22. 1–14) is one
which stresses both the openness of God's invitation, and the
austerity of His judgement (the lord in the parable invites his
associates to the wedding feast of his son; they refuse to come and
are punished; the lord then commands his servants to go into the
streets and invite everyone to the feast; many come, but one who
is found not to be properly dressed for a wedding is violently
punished). *Cleaness* (roughly contemporary with *Piers Plowman*),
highlights more than any other contemporary poem the vengeful
inscrutability of the Old Testament God; the exempla used in the
body of this poem are all drawn from the Old Testament, but the
Prologue introduces the idea of God's austere demand for spiritual
purity with this New Testament parable. The poet interprets the
filthy clothes of the guest who is cast out in this way (addressing
each member of his audience):

Hit arn thy werkez wyterly, that thou wroght hauez,
And lyued wyth the lykyng that lyghe in thyn hert

(ll. 171–2)[19]

> *hit arn*: they are; *wyterly*: certainly; *hauez*: have; *lykyng*: desire.

This interpretation seems inevitable, but in the context of Will's
certainty that the truest word that God ever said is 'No one is
good' – '*Nemo bonus*' (X. 438, discussed above under 'Theme'),
then this interpretation is particularly frightening, and one which
would indeed cause men to love less 'the bileve . . . that lettred
men techeth' (XI. 110). Certainly Will (who as the will, after all,
knows the 'lykyng' that lies in the heart) responds to this text in
fear and anxiety; he trembles 'al for tene' (XI. 115), which recalls

19. Ed. Andrew and Waldron (1978). Letter forms have been modernised.

the exact emotion Piers felt before the same recognition of God's justice before he tears the pardon (VII. 115). And instead of disputing with others, Will turns the problem to himself, as one of immediate and intense personal, rather than merely theoretical concern:

> And in a weer gan I wexe, and with myself to dispute
> Wheither I were chose or noght chose . . .
>
> (XI. 116–17)
>
> *weer gan I wexe*: became perplexed.

We seem to be back, then, at the point of Will's departure in the third vision, facing the austerity of God's judgement. Here, however, as he sees his problem in a more experiential way, he makes crucial recognitions which, in my view, are the intellectual and emotional pivot of the whole poem. It seems to me that from this moment, as Will encounters the text of Scripture directly and personally, his conversion, or '*vita nuova*' ('new life') begins.

After the state of despair that his academic theological training had induced, Will now makes crucial recognitions for himself concerning the possibility of acceptance by God, without dismissing the claims of God's justice. He begins by saying that Christ called 'us alle', 'Sarsens and scismatikes, and so he dide the Jewes', which develops the openness of invitation by the lord in the parable. Unlike non-Christians, however, Will recognises that Christians have a claim to entry by Christ's redemption, and by their baptism (XI. 123–4a). This legal claim, however, brings its own obligations, and does not serve as an automatic entree into heaven. The obligation is that the Christian, as under a legal contract, is unable to renounce his Christianity (XI. 125–6). Should he try to renounce his status through sinning, he will be prohibited entry into the lord's feast, as it were. Will makes this last point by analogy with contemporary relations between lords and serfs:

> For may no cherl chartre make, ne his c[h]atel selle
> Withouten leve of his lord – no lawe wol it graunte.
> Ac he may renne in arerage and rome fro home,
> And as a reneyed caytif recchelesly aboute.
> Ac Reson shal rekene with hym and rebuken hym at the laste,
> And Conscience acounte with hym and casten hym in arerage,

And putten hym after in prison in purgatorie to brenne,
For his arerages rewarden hym there right to the day of dome . . .

(XI. 127–34)

chartre: charter; chatel: property; leve: permission; arerage: a state of debt; reneyed: forsworn; caitif: wretch; rekene: settle accounts; acounte: make accounts; brenne: burn.

This might sound like a repetition of the point that has been made so often in the third vision, that God's justice, through those ministers of justice Reason and Conscience, will punish those who, like Will, roam 'rechelessly' about. The image of putting the sinner/serf in prison recalls both contemporary legislative documents,[20] and, theologically, the Parable of the Wedding Feast, where the ill-dressed guest is cast into 'outer darkness'. But there is a crucial difference between the image of justice enforced here, and the bare stipulation of the 'pardon' that those who do not 'Dowel' will be damned. For here the relations between lord and serf are not those of absolute divine law, but rather those of positive, or man-made law: the serf who has fallen into 'arerages', or debt, is like the Christian who has become the 'serf' of sin; but this comparison suggests that the Christian might be able to meet the standards of God's justice, if, like the indebted serf, he can repay his debt according to the standards of an agreed contract, or pact between lord and serf. That Will does think this is possible is certain from the last two, unbearably postponed lines of the citation which follows, which I omitted from the end of the previous quotation:

Ac Reson shal rekene with hym and rebuken hym at the laste,
And Conscience acounte with hym and casten hym in arerage,
And putten hym after in prison in purgatorie to brenne,
For his arerages rewarden hym there right to the day of dome,
But if Contricion wol come and crye by his lyve
Mercy for hise mysdedes with mouthe or with herte.

(XI. 131–6)

20. The Statutes of Labourers of 1349 and 1351, for example, legislate that serfs unwilling to work for their customary lord shall be imprisoned until they can find a surety, or bail (Anno 23 Edw. III, 1349 (Statutes of the Realm, I. 307)). The Statute of 1360 restates the previous clauses of the Statute of 1351, but revokes the possibility of bail (Anno 34 Edw. III, c. 9, 1360 (Statutes of the Realm, I. 366)).

Here, for the first time since the prayer of Repentance at Passus V. 479, the poem makes a firm and hopeful affirmation of God's merciful acceptance of repentant sinners.[21] And, for the first time in the third vision, a figure agrees with Will. Scripture rejoins in this way:

> 'That is sooth', seide Scripture; 'may no synne lette
> Mercy al to amende, and mekenesse hir folwe;
> For thei beth, as oure bokes telleth, above Goddes werkes:
> *Misericordia eius super omnia opera eius.*'
>
> (XI. 137–9a)
>
> *lette*: prevent; *misericordia . . . eius*: His mercy [is] above all His works.

Just as Will's arguments about predestination at the end of Passus X can be paralleled with central positions in fourteenth-century theology, so too can this new, more hopeful position, which does recognise the possibility of man bringing himself out of debt with God through a statuted pact established between man and God.[22] Bradwardine, the theologian whom I

21. My view of this scene is seriously at odds with Adams (1988a), who describes the dreamer's position here as one of 'smug, stagnant orthodoxy' (p. 100) (cf. Adams (1983, 387–8)). The positive reasons for my reading are stated above (especially the affirmation of mercy, and the comparison with positive law, both essential concepts in the development of the theological argument (the second allowing the first). In his article of 1983, p. 387, Adams argues that Will ' . . . attempts to convince himself, through an elaborate feudal analogy, of the indefectibility of baptismal grace . . . ' The 'elaborate feudal analogy' is in fact statuted law (see note immediately above) of considerable contemporary importance, given the high incidence of runaway serfs following the Black Death; the fact that Will draws his model of theological judicial proceedings from statuted human law is important too, since Will is making the recognition that God will act not according to absolute justice, but rather according to a statuted pact between man and God. Neither does Will try to convince himself 'of the indefectibility of baptismal grace'; on the contrary, Will's argument is that being baptised involves legal constraints, which cannot be abjured by the Christian; should he try to do so, he will be cast into prison. At the same time, Christians have an advantage over non-Christians in being released from prison, by virtue of their baptism. But this advantage is capitalised on not through the mere fact of baptism, but rather by contrition.

22. My argument presupposes that Langland had some contact with university learning. See Courtenay (1987), pp. 91–106 and p. 378 for evidence of London as an academic centre in the period, and for the argument that it is unnecessary to hypothesise an Oxford or Cambridge connection for a poet who shows awareness of university learning. Courtenay also points out that the issues and scholars occasionally mentioned in works of literature are 'principally those of the first half of the century' (p. 378). That Pelagianism was still an issue in the later fourteenth century is suggested by ecclesiastical legislation of 1368, which bans some Pelagian conclusions (Wilkins, III. 76).

mentioned as representative of the Augustinian, 'grace alone' argument, wrote against theologians whom he regarded as 'Pelagian' – his tract on this subject is called *Summa De Causa Dei Contra Pelagium* (*The Sum in Defence of God Against Pelagius*). It is the ideas of these theologians to which we must now briefly turn. A representative figure to choose might be the Dominician Robert Holcot (d. 1349), who, like Bradwardine, was part of the household of Richard De Bury, Bishop of Durham, and who, like Bradwardine, was influential for vernacular, literary figures in the later fourteenth century.[23] Like Bradwardine (and consistent with the currents of fourteenth-century theology), Holcot accepts the post-1277 view of an all-powerful, omniscient God, whose standards man can meet through grace alone. Unlike Bradwardine, however, Holcot sees this absolute power (or *potentia absoluta*, as the theologians called it), as mitigated by God's ordained power, or *potentia ordinata*. According to this ordained power, God freely commits Himself to stand by the rules and pacts that He has established with man. At this point, it could be objected that man can only meet the standards of those established pacts through God's grace anyway, in which case one might as well simply accept the 'grace alone' position, and abandon any hope in man's independent efforts. To this objection Holcot replies that part of the pact is that God is (freely) committed to give His grace to all those who do what is in their natural powers. God is in no way obliged to institute this pact, but having done so, He can be counted on to stick by it: 'constrained necessity does not in any way apply to God; [but] the necessity of reliability pertains to God by His promise and pact, or statuted law, and this is not absolute necessity, but conditional necessity' (Holcot 1494, *Lectio* 145 B).

To recall the distinctions made in Chapter 3 between condign and congruent reward from God, Holcot is saying that although man does not merit salvation condignly, or absolutely, nevertheless he can merit salvation congruently by 'doing what is in him' ('*facere quod in se est*'): '. . . our works do not merit eternal life condignly through their natural goodness, but

---

23. For Holcot, see Smalley (1960). In vernacular poetry Holcot is named, for example, by Thomas Hoccleve, *La Male Regle*, l. 249.

congruently only, since it is congruent, or fitting that God, through His infinite power, should reward a man acting within his finite power' (Holcot 1494, *Lectio* 35 B). These concepts clarify why Will should be able to express his sudden confidence in God's mercy: like the runaway serf, the Christian sinner can meet the conditional standards freely established by God if he 'does his what is in him' through penitence for sins committed. At last Will is able to see how works, even though they clearly cannot match the standards of God's absolute justice condignly, can nevertheless meet the standards of His conditional justice congruently. Man is dependent on God to have freely made this pact, but he does, nevertheless, have the dignity of choosing freely himself to do his best. He need not denigrate all human powers in the way the Bradwardinian, 'Augustinian' position would have him do.

Trajan

This more hopeful and dignified position to which Will comes is the position described as 'semi-Pelagianism' by modern commentators, and 'Pelagianism' by contemporary figures like Bradwardine. That there are potentially Pelagian elements in Will's (and Scripture's) position here is certain from the next character who speaks, Trajan. The medieval legend of Trajan had it that Saint Gregory, the sixth-century pope, once heard a story which testified to the pagan emperor Trajan's sense of justice. He interceded with God on Trajan's behalf, and Trajan was saved.

As the legend is presented in Passus XI, it certainly looks like an example of pure Pelagianism. Here, after all, is an example of a pagan who is saved, and saved through his 'pure truthe', or justice (XI. 155) (Gradon 1983). Will seems to be swinging from the extreme of despair he felt at the end of Passus X to the other extreme of spiritual presumption here, since Trajan seems to be a man, not even Christian, who is saved by independently meeting the standards of God's justice. It is even said that he was saved 'nought thorugh preiere of a pope but for his pure truthe' (XI. 155).

I think that to regard the speech as presumptuous would be wrong, and that we should rather see it as broadly, if liberally consistent with the *semi*-Pelagian position I have just outlined. Will has said that Christ invited all humans, 'Sarsens and scismatikes, and so he dide the Jewes' (XI. 120). Will himself has covered the case of Christians who might be saved by the merciful pact freely made by God with man. Trajan takes up the more problematic case of the pagan (he calls himself a 'Sarsen' (XI. 156)) who was saved without the benefit of baptism. He begins his speech with 'baw for bokes!' not because he disagrees with Scripture – everything he says insists on his complete agreement with Scripture about God's mercy – but rather because, he is saying, one does not necessarily require the benefit of Scripture to understand the imperative of acting according to 'truthe'. But Trajan is not saying that he was saved simply because he was just (which would seem to grant no special status to baptism), but rather because Pope Gregory prayed for a just man; Gregory, he says, 'wepte and wilned me were graunted grace' (XI. 148). He is a special case, who would not have been saved without Gregory's intercession, but the grace granted through this intercession is granted not because 'a great pope discovered him, but because a just man was discovered' (Wittig 1972, 255).

And more importantly, the speech which follows to l. 317, which I attribute to Trajan,[24] is not that of a speaker presumptuous in his own justice. The initial emphasis of the speech is the superiority of love to law (XI. 170–83); it then moves to praise of almsgiving and poverty, for in patiently borne poverty the soul is readier for contrition. As a walnut, bitter on the outside and sweet in its kernel, so too with poverty:

> So is after poverte or penaunce paciently ytake,
> Maketh a man to have mynde in God and a gret wille
> To wepe and to wel bidde, wherof wexeth mercy,
> Of which Crist is a kernell to conforte the soule.
>
> (XI. 261–4)

is: (it) is; *maketh*: (which) makes; *mynde in*: thought to; *wexeth*: grows.

The speech is certainly delivered wholly from within a Christian perspective – Langland is not interested in classical morality

---

24. See Wittig (1972), p. 255, n. 143 for an account of possible speakers of this speech. Kane and Donaldson (1975) make an unnecessarily severe decision, to offer a single line to Trajan at XI. 171, but to cut him off in mid-sentence, with another speaker (whose identity is unclear) taking over.

for its own sake in the way Dante is. But the fact that Trajan is saved is proof that Langland acknowledged the coherence of classical morality, and this passage (along with XII. 285–92) is the closest he gets to what might be called 'humanism'. Christians should be all the more inspired by a speech from a just pagan, since they are not in his special category, and they may, instead, 'cleyme . . . entree' (XI. 123).

DECONSTRUCTION

I have spent so much space analysing the structural elements and the argument of the third vision because it is the most difficult section of the poem, requiring most elucidation. As I hope my exposition will have demonstrated, the argument of this vision is essential to the progress of the poem after the crisis of the 'pardon'. It will be clear, nevertheless, that this section of the poem is essentially argumentative in nature, designed in elucidate theological doctrines.

If it were *only* argumentative, however, we might want to object that it could have been set forth in a much simpler and straightforward way. The first answer to that objection might be to say that Langland is not simply presenting theological doctrines, but that he is also presenting the way in which such doctrines are perceived through the intellectual, moral and emotional biography of an individual. This is true, but what I want to focus on in the penultimate section of this chapter is the way in which Will's biography also entails the exhaustion of authoritative discourses. What seems to me extraordinary about these passus is the way in which Langland adopts the genres of authoritative institutions and reveals their limitations. It is in exhausting the potential of these discourses, and in revealing their limitations, that Langland's real originality lies. Much of the argument does not advance Will, but it does advance Langland's larger purpose of examining the bases of authoritative institutional discourses. Having discussed the *structure* of the third vision at such length, then, I would like to discuss its 'deconstructive' current – the way in which it subverts the literary and academic forms it apparently adopts. I shall concentrate briefly on two genres, each of which claims authority for itself: satire; and academic debate.

Satire

Many figures in the vision practise kinds of satire: Wit attacks the marriage market in Passus IX (ll. 161–99); Study attacks amateur lay speculation in theological matters in Passus X (ll. 51–136); and Clergy attacks corrupt religious in the same passus, before he prophesies their downfall (X. 289–327). We can see an appropriateness in the kind of satire practised by each of these figures, but embedded in Clergy's exposition of the Dowel 'triad' is an idea which runs *counter* to this satirical current of the poetry. Dobest, says Clergy, is 'to be bold and to blame the gilty' (X. 256). But as Dobest, the superlative of the adverbial triad 'well, better, best', this has immediate implications for anyone who is not perfect, and it is these implications which Clergy goes on to explicate:

> Ac blame thow nevere body and thow be blameworthy
>
> . . .
>
> God in the Gospel grymly repreveth
> Alle that lakketh any lif and lakkes han hemselve
>
> . . .
>
> Why mevestow thi mood for a mote in thi brotheres eighe,
> Sithen a beem in thyn owene ablyndeth thiselve?
>
> (X. 258–62)

lakketh: blame; *lakkes*: faults; *mevestow thi mood*: do you get angry; *mote*: speck; *beem*: plank.

The problem of telling the truth openly was clearly of great interest in Langland's England; it had been a traditional theme of medieval satire (Ferguson 1965), and became a pressing issue of the late fourteenth century: we have already seen how cautious Langland is at certain points of satirical attack (e.g. Prol. 110, 209–10, VII. 149–95), and the early-fifteenth-century work in the *Piers* tradition, *Mum and the Sothsegger*, registers dangers in free speech which are verifiable from other sources.[25] Langland is clearly preoccupied with the problem of satire himself: in the inner-dream of Passus XI he encounters the figure Lewtee, or justice, and asks whether he is justified in attacking the friars. Lewtee has no hesitation in confirming Will's right. He cites

25. See Barnie (1974), appendix B, pp. 142–5 for the dangers of political comment in late-fourteenth-century England.

traditional checks on satire (e.g. never to publish individual faults (Miller 1983, 81–2), but cites both canon and civil law in defence of plain speaking (XI. 91–106a).[26]

These defences of declaring the truth in 'retorik', or poetry, sound very like the defences made in *Mum and the Sothsegger*. And the idea of telling the truth in poetry is evidently one to which Langland is committed, as I argued in Chapter 1. But Langland's set of problems is wider than that of the *Mum* author. Will meets Lewtee in an intensely personal inner-dream, in which his intellectual and moral biography is being played through in a concentrated way. Lewtee defends judging others, but only in the context of God's austere judgement – immediately after his speech Scripture confirms it with 'he seith sooth' (XI. 106), and presents the idea of strict judgement from a divine point of view. It is precisely the austerity of divine judgement which has been preoccupying Will throughout the third vision, and it is, as I have argued, immediately after this encounter that Will recognises the possibility of God's *mercy* beyond His judgement. Langland's problematic for satire is not simply, then, whether or not it is legal to judge, or *'licitum'*, as Lewtee says; instead, he implicates his practice of satire in his moral and intellectual biography. The need for forgiveness, that is, is one of the central recognitions Will makes with regard to his moral life more generally, but this recognition must also embrace Langland's practice as a satirist. If God is prepared to be merciful despite the fact that no one is worthy (*'Nemo bonus'*), then the satirist concerned with the theological implications of his satire must consider his own readiness to judge. Interestingly, this is exactly what Trajan says immediately *after* Will's crucial encounter with Scripture. Trajan represents the best that man is capable of independently, who has nevertheless required God's mercy to win salvation. It is this figure, the just man who nevertheless requires mercy, who encourages forebearance in the self-knowledge of human fallibility:

> Forthi lakke no lif oother, though he moore Latyn knowe,
> Ne undernyme noght foule, for is noon withoute defaute.
>
> (XI. 213–14)
>
> *forthi*: therefore; *lakke*: blame; *undernyme*: rebuke; *foule*: bitterly.

26. Compare *Mum and the Sothsegger* (ed. Day and Steele 1936), ll. 737–57, and notes.

And in the same passus Reason rebukes Will in particular for blaming others. In the second of the 'mirror' visions of Passus XI, the vision of Kynde, Will sees all creation except man following a natural and moral order. He rebukes the personification of this rational order, Reason, by asking him why he does not follow man and be sure that man, too, like the rest of creation, does not sin. In the context of this inner-dream, when Will has discovered that man's own efforts, his 'doing well', *can* earn him salvation before God, it is clear that a necessary concomitant of that is the freedom to choose whether or not one makes that effort. A necessary concomitant of merit through works before God, that is, is the free will to choose or not to choose to make the effort to 'do well'. God must therefore suffer man to act as he likes, according to his will. This is exactly what Reason says (ll. 375–81): 'Who suffreth moore than God?', he asks, where 'suffreth' embraces senses of both 'allows' and 'suffers' (Schmidt 1986, 36–7). But Reason goes on to relate this divine suffrance to the suffrance of man:

> 'Forthi I rede,' quod Reson, 'thow rule thi tonge bettre,
> And er thow lakke my lif, loke if thow be to preise.
> . . .
> For man was maad of swich a matere he may noght wel asterte
> That som tyme hym bitit to folwen his kynde.
> Caton acordeth therwith – *Nemo sine crimine vivit!*'
>
> (XI. 385–402)
>
> *asterte*: escape; *bitit*: befalls; *kynde*: nature;
> *nemo sine crimine vivit*: no one lives without fault.

Whereas earlier in the third vision the idea that 'noon is withoute defaute' had produced spiritual despair in Will, here it is the occasion to recognise God's mercy and suffrance, and the concomitant suffrance required of man. It may be relevant here to remark that the very text chosen by Imaginatif in Passus XII to defend the value of learning is the text written by Christ, '*Nolite iudicare et non iudicabimini*' – 'Do not judge, that you may not be judged' (Matt. 7.1) (XI. 89a).

Despite the fact, then, that Langland adopts the genre of satire and exploits it for its most authoritarian potential in the first vision, without questioning his own role as satirist, here in the third vision it is clear that he is deeply reflexive about his own poetic practice, and that he has implicated himself as poet into the theological resolutions which he reaches. 'Truthe' in Passus I demanded satire; here the crisis to which pure 'truthe' leads provokes a searching reflexivity about the premises of satire. In Passus I Holy Church had warned lords from her position of unquestioned authority, to be meek in their legal judgements,

> For the same mesure that ye mete, amys outher ellis,
> Ye shulle ben weyen therwith whan ye wenden
>   hennes.
>
> (I. 177–8)
>
> *amys*: wrongly; *wenden*: go.

Here, in Passus XI, Langland recognises the bearing such advice has on his own practice as a satirical poet. It is true that the poem does not by any means abandon satire after this point, but that satire must be intimately conscious of the almost divine prerogatives it assumes.

Academic Debate

As I argued earlier in this chapter, the two dominant genres of Passus VIII–X are those of satire and academic debate. We have seen how satire might be 'deconstructed' in this vision. Can the same be said for academic debate? The procedures of academia are clearly a privileged discourse within the vision. Authoritative figures representing the educational establishment attack those who adopt such procedures without properly understanding them. Study, for example, mocks the inexpert theological speculation of non-clerics:

> I have yherd heighe men etyng at the table
> Carpen as thei clerkes were of Crist and of hise myghtes,
> And leyden fautes upon the fader that formede us alle,
> And carpen ayein clerkes crabbede wordes . . .
>
> (X. 103–6)
>
> *carpen*: speak; *myghtes*: powers; *leyden fautes*: laid blame.

Study herself seems to treat Will as if he were one of these speculative laymen; her complaint against Wit at the beginning of the passus is for putting 'margery perles/Among hogges' (X. 9–10), which is a standard text (Matt 7.6) in the Middle Ages for writers wishing to preserve the knowledge of an elite for that elite. In the same way that the Church defended its sole claims to theological hegemony in the period by various measures (including forbidding schoolmasters to teach theology (Wilkins, III. 317), and suppressing the use of the vernacular in sophisticated theological discussion (Hudson 1982)), Study first insists that Will remain unlearned, humbly accepting basic church doctrine without further investigation:

> Wilneth nevere to wite why that God wolde
> Suffre Sathan his seed to bigile;
> Ac bileveth lelly in the loore of Holy Chirche.
>
>   (X. 119–21)
>
> *wite*: know; *suffre*: allow; *bigile*: deceive; *loore*: teachings

In what follows, however, we can see that Langland is not prepared to leave the matter there – in humble, lay acceptance of dogma; instead, Will is given access to the knowledge of Study, and, beyond this, Will becomes aware of Study's limitations and of the necessity to pass beyond her, to her cousin Clergy. But neither is Langland prepared to leave Will's education here, humbly accepting the theological teaching of university learning. As I have argued, Will turns against the source of his theological instruction once he has been instructed: he turns on Clergy and Scripture and argues that, given the doctrine of predestination, all learning is useless. He points out that 'plowmen and pastours' 'percen with a Paternoster the paleys of hevene', whereas many learned men have cursed the time when they knew any more than 'Credo in Deum patrem' ('I believe in God the Father') (X. 450–72a).

These arguments are not without force in the poem as a whole, given the fact that it is the apparently unlearned figure Piers, taught by Conscience, who is more spiritually gifted and knowledgeable than the priest of Passus VII. Does this mean that Langland has completely 'deconstructed' academic procedure, by using it to get himself into a position from which he can subvert it? I do not think so; it is Will, rather than Langland speaking here, and Will is speaking from a position of scepticism and despair.

It remains true, nevertheless, that the vision as a whole does recognise the clear limitations of academic discourse as it proceeds through the institutions which promote such discourse. Will expresses dissatisfaction with the instruction he is given by his rational and academic mentors by saying that he requires to have 'kynde knowynge' of Dowel, as distinct from the instruction he has been given. This is true of his encounters with the friars (VIII. 58) and Thought (VIII. 111). Or when he acknowledges the authority of Study, he promises to serve as long as she can teach him 'kyndely' to understand Dowel (X. 148); Study does not accept this service, but sends him on to Clergy, who, she says, will teach Will 'kyndely to knowe what is Dowel' (X. 217).

As an adjective, the word 'kynde' in Middle English means, in its primary sense, 'natural' (MED sense 1(a)).[27] The idea of 'kynde knowynge' had been introduced into the poem by Holy Church in Passus I; Will asks her how he might know 'truthe' in himself, at which point Holy Church castigates Will for not having learnt enough Latin in his youth; if he had, Holy Church seems to be saying, he would know that it is a 'kynde knowynge that kenneth in thyn herte' what 'truthe' is (I. 140–5). This is an interesting speech coming from the authoritarian teacher Holy Church, since what Holy Church is saying is that Will knows *naturally* what the truth is, in which case, he needs no other teacher than his own heart. Holy Church, that is, seems to be opening the way for the obsolescence of her own position as teacher.

But if Will desires *natural* knowledge in the third vision, then why is he interrogating figures which represent educational institutions, since the knowledge they can offer is necessarily acquired, and not natural? It seems to me that Langland recognises the usefulness of acquired arts of learning in pointing beyond themselves, to a kind of knowledge which is more profound, more experiential, and more 'natural'. What Will is doing is to interrogate the 'Latyn' that he should have learned in his youth (I. 141), as a way of moving beyond the teaching of 'Latyn', or formal education. Study, for example, neatly turns her grammatical acumen to undermine the purely intellectual quality of Will's search. With regard to Wit's elaborate definition of Dowel, she berates those who build clever intellectual constructs:

27. For the concept of 'kynde knowynge', see Davlin (1971, 1981), and White (1988, Ch. 2).

And tho that useth thise havylons to [a]blende mennes wittes
What is Dowel fro Dobet, now deef mote he worthe,
Siththe he wilneth to wite whiche thei ben alle.
But if he lyve the lif that longeth to Dowel,
I dar ben his bolde borgh that Dobet wole he nevere.

(X. 131–5)

havylons: tricks; *ablende*: blind; *worthe*: be;
siththe: since; *but if*: unless; *longeth*: pertains; *borgh*: surety.

Whereas Will has been looking for a *concept*, 'Dowel' (which he pictures as a person), Study neatly points out that the word 'dowel' is, quite simply, a verb and not a noun at all: she asserts that Will must 'lyve the lif' that pertains to Dowel, and she insists on this verbal aspect in the next line when she short-circuits the syntax of Dobet's usage as a noun, and uses it instead as an infinitive verb ('Dobet wol he nevere . . .'). Study's grammatical skill, which we would expect of her as the instructor of grammar, is used here, then, to undercut the analytical casuistry that Wit had used. If Will does not *do* better, then a mere concept of Dobest will be of no use to him at all. So even if Study cannot give a 'kynde' knowing of Dowel, she can at least exercise her own grammatical skill to point to her own limitations, and this, in turn, points in the direction of more profound modes of knowing.

And in Passus XI we can see how Will might deploy the clerical education he has received in a more 'kynde', or experiential way. Will's training in theological questions brings him to the crisis at the end of Passus X, when it is clear that analytical discussion is not going to get him any further; the inner-dream of Passus XI comes as a response to this impasse, and, as Joseph Wittig (1972) has argued, works within more monastic, twelfth-century traditions of self-knowledge. But it is in Will's encounter with Scripture that the turning point comes; what we might expect to be the most dogmatic encounter of the poem, where Will confronts the one unassailable text of the Christian tradition, turns out instead to be a moment of profound and inspired reading. Will's meetings with Study have taught him to read, as his meeting with Clergy has taught him to argue about theological matters in an academic way; but when Will actually arrives at the ultimate textual authority of his tradition, Scripture, the encounter is not one of passive, subservient reading and receiving of school-

knowledge; instead it is an inspired act of reading, which underlines the necessity of understanding truth in the self. Will has been
brought to this point through external educational authorities and
institutions, but precisely at the point to which they bring him,
he recognises their limitations, and the necessity to seek truth
within the self.

IMAGINATIF

In Passus XII, the points I have just made about the value of
learning are made from within the poem by Imaginatif. Imaginatif
recognises that the manner of Will's search is as much the subject
of his search as its ostensible subject. Its ostensible subject is the
definition of Dowel, but its manner, through different sources of
knowledge, becomes equally important. Imaginatif defines two
sources of knowledge, 'Clergy' and 'Kynde Wit', which is basically a version of the 'auctoritee' and 'experience' pair so common
in Middle English literature.[28] Clergy represents theological
knowledge gained from books, whereas Kind Wit represents the
knowledge gained from observation:

> . . . kynde wit cometh of alle kynnes sightes –
> Of briddes and of beestes, [of blisse and of sorwe],
> Of tastes of truthe and [oft] of deceites.
>
> (XII. 128–30)
>
> *kynde wit*: knowledge through experience; *kynnes*: kinds; *briddes*: birds; *tastes*:
> experiences.

These two sources of knowledge seem to me to embody the two
'mirrors' through which Will was instructed in the inner-dream:
the dream of Fortune is animated by scriptural citations, and leads
to Scripture after it, while the dream of Kynde was a vision of
the natural world. Imaginatif even calls clergy and kynde wit
'bothe . . . *mirours* to amenden oure defautes' (XII. 95). But even
if Imaginatif recognises the value of both these sources of knowledge, he also points to their limitations:

> Clergie and kynde wit cometh of sighte and techyng,
> As the Book bereth witnesse to burnes that kan rede:
> *Quod scimus loquimur, quod vidimus testamur.*

28. The author of the *Book of Privy Counselling*, ed. Hodgson (1944), uses the same
    words for the pair as Langland (e.g. pp. 162–3).

Of *quod scimus* cometh clergie, a konnynge of hevene,
And of *quod vidimus* cometh kynde wit, of sighte of diverse peple.
Ac grace is a gifte of God, and of greet love spryngeth;
Knew nevere clerk how it cometh forth, ne kynde wit
    the weyes.

(XII. 64–9)

clergie: knowledge through book-learning; *burnes*: men; *Quod vidimus . . .*
testamur: we speak what we know and we testify what we have seen; *quod*
scimus: what we know; *konnynge*: knowledge; *quod vidimus*: what we have
seen.

Imaginatif can recognise the limitations of the wisdom gained
from books and from nature, but the bulk of his speech in Passus
XII is taken up with an 'imaginative' (in the medieval sense of the
word) commendation of both these sources of knowledge: he uses
many images to counter Will's arguments about the uselessness
of learning (e.g. XII. 99–100, 103, 105, 161–9, 198–201).

What is strange to a modern reader, however, is the fact that
Imaginatif should be so unsympathetic to imaginative writing (in
the modern sense of the word 'imaginative'). He clearly wants to
defend the institutions of divine and secular learning, but the
opening of Passus XII suggests that he has no sympathy for the
act of writing poetry. He begins by warning Will of the dangers
to his soul, and of the importance of spiritual foresight; instead
of heeding these warnings, Will writes poetry:

And thow medlest thee with makynges – and myghtest go seye thi
    Sauter,
And bidde for hem that yyveth thee breed; for ther are bokes ynowe
To telle men what Dowel is, Dobet and Dobest bothe,
And prechours to preve what it is, of many a peire freres.

(XII. 16–19)

medlest thee with makynges: you dabble in verse making; *sauter*: psalter.

Imaginatif's criticism of Will takes its impetus from a powerful
current of medieval literary theory, that the truth derives from
auctoritas, and that it has been stated in the past: there are 'bokes
ynowe' to tell Will what he wants to know; not only this, but
the truth has its own, perfectly adequate means of institutional
dissemination: 'prechours', and 'many a peire freres'.

That Langland would dispute with the first of these points (that
truth derives from authority), I doubt: his poem is profoundly
aware of the authority of Scripture, for which 'God was the

maister,/And Seint Spirit the samplarie' (XII. 101–2). But that he
would dispute with the second point (about the adequacy of the
institutional means of disseminating the truth), is equally clear.
We need only remember the 'peire of freres' Will meets at the
very beginning of the third vision, whose answer about Dowel
was perfectly orthodox but equally inadequate to the urgency of
Will's question. But beyond this single point, it will be clear that
my own sense of the passage of the third vision is that it adopts
but exhausts the discourse of at least one authoritative institution,
that of academia. The movement of the poetry is generated out
of the need to move beyond each interlocutor, as they are found
wanting, and some kind of resolution in the poetry only becomes
possible once Will has registered the force of the biblical passage
for himself in Passus XI. The movement of these passus, that is,
stands as a counter to any complacent notion about the adequacy
of institutions to disseminate truth to individuals.

Will's actual reply to Imaginatif's criticism relies at first on a
conventional, but in this context fairly spineless defence of poetry:
poetry is amusing, refreshing play; whereas this is normally a
defence of reading poetry (e.g. in the Prologue of Henryson's
Fables), Will uses it to defend the writing of poetry – he plays
'whan', he says, 'I make' (XII. 22). After this fairly lame excuse,
however, Will proposes another account of his 'makynges' which
at the same time asserts that his (playful) poetry constitutes his
work, and that Imaginatif is wrong to suggest that the Church's
dissemination of truth is adequate:

> Ac if ther were any wight that wolde me telle
> What were Dowel and Dobet and Dobest at the laste,
> Wolde I nevere do werk, but wende to holi chirche
> And there bidde my bedes but whan ich ete or slepe.
>   (XII. 25–8)

This seems to me to constitute a radical defence of the existence
of one more book (the book of *Piers Plowman*), amongst the
'bokes ynowe' in the world; unlike very many medieval books
which present themselves as passive transmitters of truth, as
simply providing the 'of remembraunce the keye' (Chaucer's
Legend of Good Women, F. 26), Langland (or at the very least Will
as poet) defends his poem as actively recovering the truth. This is
not to say that it is a defence of the poem as creating original

truths, a defence to which Langland as a religious poet would be unwilling to commit himself. The passage does, nevertheless, defend poetry as an irreplaceable way of recovering truth.[29]

CONCLUSION

In conclusion to the whole discussion of the third vision, then, we can say that it is essentially cognitive in its structure, and draws particularly upon the discourse of academia in its style. In exploring its essential theme, however (concerning the value of human works before God), Will exhausts the cognitive powers of reason and the educational faculties which inform them. This exhaustion of the *means* of knowing becomes as much the subject of the vision as its ostensible theme, and provokes Langland both to question his own position as satirist, and to formulate a radical defence of his own poetic 'makynge'. The vision as a whole is not without its inevitable complications, but it remains true that Langland returns to the essential theme at the end of the vision, with a resounding and optimistic affirmation of the value of human works before God. The vision ends with the hardest case for such value being posed: Will asks whether or not pagans can be saved (XII. 275–7); Imaginatif's reply is incisive and affirmative, with his greatest stress being laid on the case of the pure (in both senses) pagan:

> Ac truthe that trespased nevere ne traversed ayeins his lawe,
> But lyveth as his lawe techeth and leveth ther be no bettre,
> (And if ther were, he wolde amende) and in swich wille deieth –
> Ne wolde nevere trewe God but trewe truthe were allowed.
>
> (XII. 285–8)

---

29. See Minnis (1981) for a warning against confusing Will's defence of poetry with 'the Romantic notion of poetry as a medium for the personal discovery of truth' (p. 87). My own argument here might seem to involve this confusion, but my appeal is not to a romantic notion of poetry so much as a strategy common to poems in the *Piers Plowman* tradition: both *Pierce Plowman's Crede* and *Mum and the Sothsegger* generate their search for truth (and therefore justify their existence as new books) out of the inadequacy of institutional spokesmen for truth: the strategy of both these poems is to pretend trust in certain institutional figures (e.g. friars) initially, but to have the reader recognise the inadequacy of these apparently authoritative sources of truth. This is not a romantic notion of poetry, so much as a satirical strategy, which the authors of the two later poems seem to have learned from Langland.

Chapter 5

The Fourth Vision:
Passus XIII–XIV

PASSUS XIII: Will wakes and reflects on the vision he has just had (ll. 1–20); he sleeps, and is bidden by *Conscience* to dine with Clergy. Will accepts; the other guests are an academic *Doctor*, and *Patience*, a mendicant pilgrim. Will sits at a side table with Patience and is served a penitential meal (ll. 21–57a). Will complains to Patience that the Doctor is a hypocrite, but is dissuaded by Patience from attacking the Doctor (ll. 58–97). Will attacks the Doctor nevertheless (ll. 98–110), but is quietened by Conscience, who courteously asks the Doctor what Dowel and Dobet are, to which the Doctor responds (ll. 111–17a). Conscience now asks Clergy, who is unwilling to offer a firm answer, since he recognises the superiority of Piers Plowman's knowledge to his own (ll. 118–29). Patience is now asked about Dowel; Patience responds, but is derided by the Doctor (ll. 130–78). Conscience announces his intention to leave on pilgrimage with Patience. Clergy disputes the wisdom of this decision, until he finally concedes its propriety (ll. 179–214). Conscience and Patience set out on pilgrimage; they meet a minstrel and bread seller, who represents *Activa Vita* (the Active Life), and whose name is *Haukyn* (ll. 215–70). Will notices that Haukyn's coat of Christendom is stained with many sins (ll. 271–408). At the mention of Sloth, the narrator discourses on aspects ·of this sin, in particular on the pleasure the slothful have in listening to minstrels. The narrator declares that lords and ladies should have God's minstrels (by whom he means the poor) before them (ll. 409–59).

PASSUS XIV: Haukyn complains that he could never keep his coat clean (ll. 1–15); Conscience promises to wash it with penitence, and Patience promises to feed Haukyn with man's essential sustenance (ll. 16–47b); Will observes that this essential sustenance is submission to the will of God, a part of the Lord's Prayer ('Thy will be done'); Patience offers this to Haukyn, and refers to examples of humans living without physical sustenance; he also encourages measure (ll. 48–80). Through measure and faith comes penitence, he declares (ll. 81–96). In response to Haukyn's question about the whereabouts of charity, Patience replies that charity is to be found amongst the patient poor. Patience spends the rest of the passus in praise of patiently borne poverty (ll. 97–332).

INTRODUCTION

In the last chapter, I argued that the narrative structure of the third vision (Passus VIII–XII) is shaped out of the structure of the soul as Langland conceived it: as Will questions different rational faculties of his soul, and the educational institutions which train them, so too does the poem take shape. This relation between cognitive and poetic structures also pertains to the fourth vision (Passus XIII–XIV), where Will is also taught to know by parts of his soul. The kind of knowledge which Will seeks has, however, changed: no longer does he learn from the rational faculties of his soul, but rather from those parts and qualities of the soul which direct and condition moral choice – in the fourth vision he is taught especially by Conscience and Patience. The burden of learning is now, in effect, on Will himself, as the human will, since it is the will which must choose, rather than merely be informed of the truth. Whereas the third vision ends with praise of 'wit and wisdom' (XII. 293), the fourth ends with an image of affective choice, of the figure Haukyn, who 'cried mercy faste,/ And wepte and wailede' (XIV. 331–2). And whereas the third vision is largely discursive in its procedures, the fourth vision witnesses a shift to dramatic action.

In moving from rational knowledge of truth to moral willing of that truth, Langland is entirely within standard medieval psychological and moral traditions. For one contemporary

discussion of the reason and the will, we need only recall how the
Cloud author defined these 'two principal worching myghtes' of
the soul; the reason is the 'myght thorou the whiche we departe
the iuel fro the good, the iuel fro the worse, the good fro the
betir, the worse fro the worste, the betir fro the best', whereas
the will is the 'myght thorou the whiche we chese good, after that
it be determinid with reson; and thorow the which we loue God,
we desire God, & resten us with ful likyng & consent eendli in
God' (p. 116).

However much such a movement from the reason to the will
might be intelligible within standard treatments of the relation
between these parts of the soul, Langland's presentation of this
movement is fully alive to its implications. The action of the
poem in these passus focuses on the radical educational, literary
and social concomitants of such a movement. These passus can
be described, in fact, as essentially and self-consciously transitional,
and it is to the elements of this transition (educational, literary,
social), to which I should like now to turn in the body of this
chapter.

EDUCATIONAL TRANSITIONS

The third vision ends with a resounding affirmation of the possibility of good works having validity in God's eyes, and so
answers the question ('What is Dowel?') which had held Will in
'thought' from the end of the second vision. The fourth vision
begins with a waking episode, where for the second time in the
poem, Will ruminates on the previous vision (the first example
of this is at VII. 144–201, where Will is 'ful pencif in herte'
(VII. 146)). In this rumination, described as 'thought' (ll. 4, 21),
Will is strangely unaffected by the positive, optimistic emphases
of the previous vision, and focuses instead on its negative aspects.
In the previous vision, for example, Imaginatif has crisply recognised the positive potential in the statement '*Salvabitur vix iustus
in die iudicii*' ('Scarcely shall the just man be saved at the day of
judgement'), by responding '*Ergo* salvabitur!' ('Therefore he *will*
be saved!') (XII. 278–9); in Will's 'thought' about the vision,
however, he remembers only the minatory aspect: '. . . And
sithen how Imaginatif seide '*Vix iustus salvabitur*' (XIII. 19) (Dove
1986, 116).

This suggests that the resolution of Passus XII has been partial. However much the intellectual problem of the validity of human works in God's eyes has been resolved, it remains to register the force of that resolution in moral terms: if, that is, God is prepared to accept human moral effort into the scales of His justice, it still remains for Will to make that effort. The thematic emphasis of the poem shifts now, as one would expect it to, from the question as to whether or not works are of any value, to the idea of penitence, since the moral effort required of Will can effectively be equated with penitence, with 'paying God back', as it were. It is this which Will must learn in the fourth vision, and to do so he needs moral, rather than rational instructors.

The beginning of the dream offers Will both kinds of instructor – the formal educational institution Clergy, characteristic of the previous vision, and the moral instructor Conscience: Conscience invites Will to a meal to which Clergy has also been invited. After Imaginatif s praise of the value of Clergy in the previous vision, Will is all the more ready to come to this feast: 'And for Conscience of Clergy spak, I com wel the rather' (XIII. 24). But the host is Conscience – Langland pictures Conscience inviting Will to his 'court' (l. 23),[1] and the kind of instruction Will receives here is not of an academic, intellectual kind.

The change in Will's education in the ambience of Conscience is most evident in the 'food' that Will eats. In the previous vision Will had adduced scriptural texts as argumentative counters, particularly in his meeting with Clergy. Here, instead, under the host Conscience, scriptural texts are adduced in a quite different way. Will 'eats' alongside Patience, but his 'food' is made up of penitential, biblical texts. So the sense of Patience as a table companion at such a feast is that Will must read Scripture patiently. The 'dishes' are brought by Scripture, and they are designed to provoke penitence by patient reflection and rumination:

Conscience ful curteisly tho commaunded Scripture

1. Twelfth-century monastic texts which Langland seems to have been influenced by (Wittig 1972) often treat the soul in architectural metaphors, giving Conscience pride of place. One tract is even called *Concerning the Interior House*, (*PL*, 184.507), where the 'house' is the conscience. For the concept of 'conscience', see Potts (1982).

Bifore Pacience breed to brynge and me that was his mette.
He sette a sour loof toforn us and side, '*Agite penitenciam.*'

(XIII. 46–8)

mette: companion; *loof*: loaf; *agite penitenciam*: do penance.

Here is bread which is no (literal) bread at all; the words of Scripture direct Will to penitence, and they 'feed' him in so far as they
nourish the spirit. The words which Scripture brings have a
salutary effect by inviting spiritual rumination, for when we
'chew on' these words, we recognise a web of salutary puns and
scriptural references: the root of '*penitenciam*' is '*poena*', meaning
'punishment'; '*poena*' chimes[2] with French *pain*, the 'loof' Scripture serves to Will; French *pain* also puns with English 'pain',
which reveals the nature of this penitential bread – it is a 'sour
loof'. This series of connections might seem strained and imposed
on the text, but Langland has prepared us for this kind of verbal
resonance at the end of the second vision in Passus VII, when
Piers rejects the literal food produced by his ploughing for the
spiritual food of penitence:

The prophete his payn eet in penaunce and in sorwe,
By that the Sauter seith – so dide othere manye.
That loveth God lelly, his liflode is ful esy:
Fuerunt michi lacrime mee panes die ac nocte.

(VII. 122–4a)

payn: bread; *Sauter*: psalter; *liflode*: sustenance;

fuerunt michi . . . nocte: my tears have been my bread day and night.

Here the scriptural metaphor of tears ('*lacrime*') for bread ('*panes*')
illuminates both the pun in the first line on 'pain' as 'bread'/'pain',
and the phonic presence of 'pain' in 'penaunce'.[3]

Will, and by implication the reader of the poem, are being
invited now to read in a different way, to pass from academic
treatment of scriptural texts (associated with the universities) to
a more inward, reflective consideration of Scripture, drawn from
monastic traditions.[4] As I said in my introduction to this chapter,
Langland is not at all passive to the educational implications of

2. The word 'chime' is taken from Schmidt (1987b, 114), meaning 'words almost
   identical, signifying different things'.
3. See discussion above (Ch. 3, p. 85).
4. For the monastic practice of reading, which often involves metaphors of eating,
   chewing, flavour, etc., see Leclercq (1974), 89–90). See Alford (1977) for the
   ways in which biblical reading informs Langland's compositional procedures.

this transition from one kind of reading to another, and in what follows we can see how the poem definitively places academic learning at a distance now, as it moves into new kinds of knowing, and into new literary modes. Will's question, 'What is Dowel?', is posed again in this passus, for the last time in the poem, as Will is on the verge of leaving academic discourse. At first Will himself asks the question to the representative of the academic establishment in its complacent and well-heeled actuality, the 'maister' introduced at the beginning of the passus. The academic friar is totally unaware of the pressure of Will's question, and he casually glances it aside:

> 'Dowel?' quod this doctour – and drank after –
> 'Do noon yvel to thyn evencristen – nought by thi power.'
>
> (XIII. 103–4)

This is the occasion for a satirical attack on the friar, and Will tries to capitalise on the moment as it is offered to him (XIII. 105–10). But Conscience is the host, or overriding presence, at this meal, and in keeping with the spirit of patience and self-awareness to which the previous vision had pointed, Conscience does not attack the Doctor, but rather defers courteously, if shrewdly, to the Doctor's theological learning:

> . . . Sire doctour, and it be youre wille,
> What is Dowel and Dobet? Ye dyvynours knoweth.
>
> (XIII. 113–14)
> *and*: if; *dyvynours*: theologians.

The Doctor's answer to this courteously posed question reveals the self-protecting, self-aggrandising mentality of the educational institution: 'dowel' is defined as doing as 'clerkes techeth'; 'dobet' as he who teaches; and 'dobest' as he who both teaches and acts according to his own teaching (XIII. 115–17a). In these three steps the Doctor complacently assures himself of both his power and his honour: his power resides in the fact that he controls the unlearned in what they are to regard as 'doing well', while his honour is affirmed in the preservation of the higher stages of moral life to teachers themselves. The inadequacy of this declaration is evident most immediately in the fact that the Doctor does not himself do as he teaches, as Will points out (ll. 105–10).

Conscience does not take issue with this reply, but shrewdly allows its inadequacy to speak for itself beside the discreet answer of Clergy, to whom Conscience now poses the same question. Whereas the Doctor represents the academic institution in its literal actuality, Clergy here seems to me to represent the academic institution in its ideal potentiality. Conscience certainly feels more at ease with Clergy – he addresses him familiarly in the singular, unlike his plural address to the Doctor: '"Now thow, Clergy," quod Conscience, "carpe us what is Dowel"' (XIII. 118). And the answer of Clergy betrays none of the self-protecting assurance of the Doctor:

'I have sevene sones,' he seide, 'serven in a castel
Ther the lord of lif wonyeth, to leren hem what is Dowel.
Til I se tho sevene and myself acorde
I am unhardy,' quod he, 'to any wight to preven it.
For oon Piers the Plowman hath impugned us alle,
And set alle sciences at a sop save love one;
And no text ne taketh to mayntene his cause
But *Dilige Deum* and *Domine quis habitabit*;
And seith that Dowel and Dobet arn two infinites,
Which infinites with a feith fynden out Dobest,
Which shal save mannes soule – thus seith Piers the Plowman.'

(XIII. 119–29)

wonyeth: dwells; *leren*: teach; *unhardy*: lack the confidence; *wight*: person; *impugned*: called into question; *dilige deum*: love God; *domine quis habitabit*: Lord, who shall dwell [in thy tabernacle]?

For the second time in the poem, a figure does not give an answer to Will's question; just as Study in Passus X had deferred to higher learning not by telling Will what Dowel was but by sending him on to Clergy, so too here Clergy is unwilling to give an answer to the question, as *he* defers to higher forms of learning. Study's deference is intelligible, however, within a standard educational progression from the liberal arts to theology. What is remarkable about Clergy's deference in Passus XIII is the fact that Clergy is acknowledging the hesitation of the entire academic establishment (his 'sevene sones' must represent the liberal arts) in the presence of a ploughman's knowledge. Piers, says Clergy, sets each 'science' at nothing, except the 'science' of love; to call love itself a 'science' in this context is to insist that, paradoxically, the essential knowledge is not academic, but moral: we recall Piers's reply to the priest that Abstinence taught him his

ABC, and that 'Conscience cam afterward and kenned me muche moore' (VII. 133–4).

But can Clergy's position be described as anti-intellectual here? Is Clergy taking up a position which Will had occupied against Clergy himself in Passus X, when Will, in despair at the usefulness of learning or any moral action, had argued that the learned are distracted from 'righte bileve', while 'lewed juttes' (including ploughmen) are saved (X. 450–72a)?

It is true that Clergy insists on the simplicity of Piers's learning: it consists in an injunction to love ('*Dilige Deum*'), coupled with a humble question: 'Lord, who shall dwell in thy tabernacle?'. But I think Clergy's position is in fact quite different from that of Will in Passus X; Clergy is not speaking out of despair, but rather out of the proper humility of the learned before the biggest questions. And if we look at the procedure he uses to describe Piers's sense of Dowel, we can see how Clergy's own grammatical knowledge is being drawn upon. Interestingly, Clergy uses a grammatical term, 'infinite', to describe Piers's sense of the Dowel triad (Middleton 1972). In using such a term, Clergy stresses, in a technical way, the active nature of dowel: such a term insists on the fact that the triad is made up of verbs, rather than mere concepts; not only are they verbs, but they are incapable of analysis, since they are infinite verbs. Implicit in this description is the point that the parts of the dowel triad are not easily separable, definable steps, leading one to the other, and that Dowel and Dobet do not stop, when Dobest begins. So however much Clergy might be humbly stating the limitations of analytical, academic knowledge in this speech, it remains true that his procedures are themselves drawn from academic terminology: he manipulates academic terms to point to the inadequacy of academic learning. This suggests not that he is rejecting such learning in its entirety, but rather that he sees a limited place for such learning in pointing towards a knowledge beyond the academic (Simpson 1986c, 63).

It is clear by now that Conscience is quietly conducting a polite, but searching interrogation of his guests, which is what we would expect, after all, from the faculty of the conscience. The last figure to whom the question is put at the dinner party, and in the poem, is Patience. Patience is a totally non-academic, eremitic figure, who has been invited to this feast only as a mendicant pilgrim, and who sits at a side table with Will (ll. 29–36). Middle English 'pacience' bears much more of its Latin root, *patientia* (meaning 'suffering'), than the Modern English word 'patience' (MED sense 1(a)). Langland's Patience will be better understood by referring back for a moment to the words of Imaginatif in Passus XII. In his commendation of clerical and 'kynde' knowledge, Imaginatif had said that grace is, nevertheless, a gift of God, and 'knew nevere clerk how it cometh forth, ne kynde wit the weyes' (XII. 69); he also says there that grace only 'grows' amongst the humble – 'pacience and poverte the place is ther it groweth' (XII. 61). In Passus XIII, Patience is clearly the personification of 'graceful' and wise 'pacience and poverte'; Conscience certainly evokes the distinctions of Imaginatif in his introduction of Patience:

> Pacience hath be in many place, and paraunter knoweth
> That no clerk ne kan, as Crist bereth witnesse:
> *Pacientes vincunt &c,*
>
> (XIII. 133–4a)
>
> *paraunter*: perhaps; *pàcientes vincunt*: the suffering overcome.

and later in Passus XIV it is especially poverty that is praised and expounded by Patience.

Patience's exposition of the dowel triad also points to the importance but limitations of academic learning. For in this academic milieu, his answer suggests a cognitive development which embraces, but transcends the academic culture represented in its potentiality by Clergy:

> '*Disce*,' quod he, '*doce; dilige inimicos.*
> *Disce*, and Dowel; *doce*, and Dobet;
> *Dilige*, and Dobest – [do] thus taughte me ones
> A lemman that I lovede – Love was hir name'.
>
> (XIII. 136–9)
>
> *disce*: learn; *doce*: teach; *dilige inimicos*: love [your] enemies; *lemman*: lover.

Here, too, then, is a figure who is taught, like Piers, by the 'science' of love; but his attitude to academic learning is not hostile: he includes learning and teaching as part of his triad. Unlike the complacent Doctor, though, he does not construct the triad for the self-aggrandisement of the academic institution, but instead opens the dobest element up to a radically Christian concept of love: *dilige inimicos*. This is precisely the concept that the lower reaches, at least, of the academic establishment are incapable of understanding; Study, in Passus X, had pointed to this doctrine of loving one's enemies as being worthy of respect, even if it is unintelligible, and even if it directly contradicts the textbook she can understand, Cato's *Distichs*, which teaches that enemies should be paid back in kind (X. 191–9b).

And at this meal at the court of Conscience, the higher reaches of academic, theological learning are also seen to be impervious to the sense of Patience's paradoxes. Patience's speech, for all its brilliance, is not in the least academic; he exploits two related New Testament paradoxes, of the suffering being victorious (cf. Matt. 10.22), and of loving one'e enemies (Matt. 5.44). He shifts from exposition of the dowel triad to positive exhortation to love one's enemies in this way:

> Cast coles on his heed of alle kynde speche;
> Bothe with werkes and with wordes fonde his love to wynne,
> And leye on him thus with love til he laughe on the.
>
> (XIII. 144–6)

The first line cited here is from scriptural sources (Prov. 25.22; Romans 12.20), but whereas the scriptural text has only the one military image (of casting coals), Patience extends the idea of attacking with love. In the context of 'casting coals', the verbs 'fonde' and 'leye on' assume a specifically military and aggressive sense. They are both used in this way in other contexts: 'fonde' can mean 'to advance in attack' (MED, sense 10), while 'leye on' can mean 'to rain blows or missiles' (MED, sense 5(b), cf. XX. 189). But if these words assume a military meaning from the context, they do so precisely in order to lose it, since the speech is about loving, rather than attacking enemies (Simpson 1986b, 168). The Doctor, however, is quite untouched by the spiritual force of this, and other riddling speeches of Patience: he dismisses the idea of the paradoxical might of suffering as nonsense:

> 'It is but a dido', quod this doctour, 'a disours tale!
> Al the wit of this world and wight mennes strengthe
> Kan noght [par]formen a pees bitwene the Pope and hise enemys.'
>
> (XIII. 172–4)

> *dido*: a trivial tale; *disour*: minstrel.

This reveals the blinkered and uncomprehending view of the Doctor, since it is precisely what Patience has been saying, though with a different intent: it is not 'wit' or 'strengthe' which *can* achieve the peace prophesied by Patience, but 'will' and suffering.[5]

The Doctor's unperceptive and bland remark effectively marks the end of Conscience's discreet examination of his guests; without formally judging the responses given him, Conscience makes clear where his sympathies lie by overturning the etiquette of his role as host in his own 'court'. The Doctor has assumed that Conscience is of his own persuasion, and takes him and Clergy apart as a way of ignoring the mendicant pilgrim Patience, since, as he says, 'pilgrymes konne wel lye' (XIII. 178). Conscience, however, abandons his position as host, and announces that he is leaving to be 'pilgrym with Patience til I have preved moore' (XIII. 182). This is a radical choice from an educational point of view, since it involves abandoning the educational establishment, and entrusting himself to the marginal figure Patience; Conscience wants to 'preve' in the experiential sense (to 'preve . . . in dede', as he says at l. 132 (MED sense 6(a)), rather than in Clergy's academic sense (l. 122) (MED sense 2(a)).

Clergy is not unaware of the threat to his own position in Conscience's choice: he immediately accuses Conscience of wanting to interpret 'redels', and insists on the pedagogic solidity of his own text (which legitimates his discourses), and his own professional expertise:

> I shal brynge yow a Bible, a book of the olde lawe,
> And lere yow, if yow like, the leeste point to knowe,
> That Pacience the pilgrym parfitly knew nevere.
>
> (XIII. 185–7)
>
> *lere*: teach.

I argued in the last chapter that the intellectual faculties of Will's soul, and the educational 'faculties' that train them, are predisposed to emphasise the purely legal aspects of dowel: dowel, it is consistently repeated in different forms, 'is to doon as lawe techeth' (IX. 200). The intellect is predisposed to understand justice, which is rational, rather than forgiveness, which springs

---

5. This situation is similar to that between the priest and Piers in Passus VII: the priest says exactly what Piers wants to say, though without understanding its import.

from love. In Passus XIII Clergy reveals this very limitation, in so far as he insists on his knowledge of the 'olde lawe'; Patience, on the other hand, talks in 'redels' which are all inspired from the New Testament. In moving towards a real, experiential under-standing of the New Law, Langland seems to be saying that it is necessary to move outside formal educational institutions, designed as they are around rational principles. The models of treating Scripture to which the poem now moves are monastic, as distinct from the academic models associated, in the poem, more often than not with friars.

The rest of this scene of leave-taking suggests, however, that the break is not permanent, but part of a continuing process of education. Before he leaves, Conscience whispers in Clergy's ear:

> Me were levere, by Oure Lord, and I lyve sholde,
> Have pacience parfitliche than half thi pak of bokes!
>
> (XIII. 200–1)
>
> *me were levere*: I'd prefer; *and*: of.

Clergy does not see the humour of this remark, and refuses to bid farewell to Conscience. At this point, however, a reconcilia-tion takes place which imaginatively represents the fundamental, ideal relation between formal education and experiential knowl-edge in the poem. Conscience assuages Clergy's hurt pride by saying that 'if Pacience be oure partyng felawe and pryve with us bothe', then Clergy and Conscience will together convert the entire world to the true faith (ll. 205–10). I read 'partyng felawe', in this context, as a revealing pun: on the one hand, it means 'partner', which is the meaning assigned to it in the MED (sense (e)), and this aspect of meaning is extended in the rest of the line – 'and pryve with us bothe'; on the other hand, at this moment of leave-taking, the phrase would seem to be jolted out of its normal meaning to mean something like 'the fellow with whom we take our leave of each other'. This aspect of meaning, which stresses the fact that Conscience and Clergy must separate for the moment, is strengthened by Clergy's reply. He accepts what Conscience says, and agrees to content himself with administering to the formal educational establishment until Conscience returns – until, he says to Conscience, 'Pacience have preved thee and parfit thee maked' (XIII. 214). These two senses of 'partyng felawe', then, suggest that if Clergy patiently parts from

Conscience for the moment, then both Clergy and Conscience will be partners in the conversion of the world. The full power of formal education is only revealed after Conscience has been 'preved' experientially; a perfected formal education is not felt to lead to a perfect conscience, but is, rather, subsequent on the perfection of the conscience.

POETIC TRANSITIONS

One critic has remarked that Conscience's leave-taking of Clergy is the 'nearest equivalent' to the leave-taking of Dante from Virgil in the *Divine Comedy*, where Dante bids farewell to a culture as much as to a man (Murtaugh 1978, 96). Of course Virgil represents a quite different (and broader) culture from that of Clergy, but the comparison seems to me to point us in the right direction: this is a leave-taking which represents a transition of intellectual and emotional allegiance, a moment when sympathies for a culture are expressed, but, in leaving it, judgement is made about its limitations. And just as Dante farewells both a philo-sophic and a poetic culture in parting from Virgil, so too does Conscience leave not only a pedagogic institution, but also a certain kind of poetry. In this section, I would like to consider the ways in which Langland is clearly revaluing the role of poetry and minstrelsy as Conscience goes on pilgrimage with patience.

Patience as Minstrel

At the end of Passus XIII Langland breaks the fiction of his poem to define and denounce sloth, from l. 409. The feature of sloth to which he particularly objects is the predisposition of the slothful to listen to 'an harlotes tonge', and 'wordes of murthe', when all who tell of 'penaunce and povere men and the passion of seintes' are despised (ll. 418–19). This provokes Langland to encourage lords to transform the practice whereby they receive minstrels at feasts: just as 'clerkes and knyghtes' welcome the king's minstrels, so too, he says, should the rich receive beggars, who are 'Goddes minstrales' (ll. 436–40a). Instead of simply rejecting the practice of listening to minstrels at feasts, Langland characteristically transforms it. He says that the rich should have

the poor 'for a fool sage', and a lerned man to 'fithele thee . . .
of Good Friday the storye', and 'a blynd man for a bourdeour':

> Thise thre maner minstrales maketh a man to laughe,
> And in his deeth deyinge thei don hym gret confort
> . . .
> Thise solaceth the soule til hymself be falle
> In a welhope . . .
>
> (XIII. 449–53)

maner: kinds; *solaceth*: delight/comfort; *welhope*: good hope.

The words which apply to the normal practice of minstrelsy are
here transformed and spiritualised: 'laughe', 'confort' and 'solace'
are all often used in contexts of amusement and relaxed entertainment, whereas here those senses are evoked in order to be
excluded by spiritual senses of the words;[6] 'comfort', for example,
can mean 'pleasure, delight, gratification' (MED sense 3(a)) in a
literary sense, as in Chaucer's Host's comment that 'comfort ne
myrthe is noon,/ To ryde by the weye domb as a stone' (A. 773).
MED gives sense 3(b), however, as 'spiritual gratification, joy',
which is the 'comfort' produced by the minstrels Langland has
in mind.

The subject of this 'digression' is not in the least eccentric to
the concerns of the fourth vision, one of which is to revalue the
status of minstrelsy and poetry. It is significant, for example, that
Langland does not reject minstrelsy; instead, he preserves the idea
of a public poetry, addressed to the powerful, designed to move
and convert them.

The feast scene at the beginning of Passus XIII offers, in fact,
a model of the kind of poetry Langland might have in mind.
Conscience is said to provide 'murye tales' for Patience and Will,
with a quotation from one of the penitential psalms (ll. 57–57a).
But the best example of the kind of poetry Langland might have
in mind is offered by the mendicant pilgrim Patience, whom the
lord Conscience has taken into his feast to eat at a side table.
When he is asked to speak, he uses paradoxes and riddles, based
on New Testament passages. Unlike all the rational figures who
have so far been asked the question 'what is dowel', Patience's
speech does not dwell on the legal requirements of meeting God's

6. This effect is called the 'anti-pun' in Schmidt (1987b, 116), 'by which another
   sense of a word is called up only to be fended off'.

justice, and instead focuses on the paradoxical, apparently sense-
less injunctions of his teacher Love. I have already pointed to his
overturning of linguistic convention in his speech about loving
one's enemies by attacking them; he takes this play at the borders
of sense to its limit in his riddle:

> Kynde love coveiteth noght no catel but speche.
> With half a laumpe lyne in Latyn, *Ex vi transicionis*,
> I bere ther, in a bou[s]te, faste ybounde Dowel,
> In a signe of the Saterday that sette first the kalender,
> And al the wit of the Wodnesday of the nexte wike after;
> The myddel of the moone is the myght of bothe.
>
> (XIII. 150–5)
>
> *catel*: property; *laumpe*: lamp; *ex vi transicionis*: by the power of transivity;
> *bouste*: box (for Host).

This is clearly a speech of deliberate opacity, a 'redels' as Patience
himself calls it (l. 167). The best interpretation of it which has so
far been offered is, in my view, that of E. C. Schweitzer (1974);
he argues that '*ex vi transicionis*' is a grammatical term, meaning
'by the power of transivity', referring to the power of a transitive
verb over the noun it governs. In the context of this academic
feast, it is appropriate that Patience should play on the terminology of formal education; but given Patience's interest in
transcending that academic milieu, it is equally appropriate that
he should open that limited grammatical sense to a much wider
field of meaning, by punning on the word '*transitio*': for the
'Saterday that sette first the kalender' is a reference to the Jewish
Passover, or *transitus*, from which the Jewish year begins. The
transitus, or passing over referred to here is, I think, the passing
from the Old to the New Testament, from Jewish to the Christian
culture, since Holy Saturday is also the day from which the
movable feasts of the Christian Church are dated. What gives this
transition 'might' is the 'myddel of the moone', an enigmatic
reference to the Easter moon.

Such an interpretation sits well with this essentially transitional
moment in the poem, and particularly a moment of transition
from questions of justice and the 'olde lawe' which have characterised the poem from the beginning of the third vision, to the
specifically New Testament spirit introduced by Patience. But
whatever the exact interpretation of this deliberately recalcitrant

passage, it is Patience's specifically poetic mode here which is itself significant at this moment, when the limit of academic institutions and analytical discourses is being registered.[7]

I am not appealing to a romantic notion in saying that Patience's mode is 'specifically poetic'. Thirteenth-century scholars defined the kinds of literary modes (what they called *formae tractandi*), found in the Bible, which were designed to appeal to the will rather than the intellect; the general term they gave to these modes was the 'symbolic', or 'poetic' mode, and among the 'poetic' modes they included, for example, the 'prophetic mode' (*modus prophetalis*). This is the mode which Patience adopts, in so far as it is certainly symbolic, prophetic, and, beyond that, designed to appeal to the will. Patience himself points to the prophetic mode he uses, in his statement, 'Kynde love coveiteth noght no catel but speche' (l. 150); this picks up on I Corinthians 13.4–7: 'Charity suffreth long (*patiens est*), and is kind; charity envieth not . . .'. The idea of charity being 'patient' clarifies why it should be Patience who discusses 'kynde love'; and the continuation of the biblical passage also points to the mode Patience uses: 'Follow after charity, and desire spiritual gifts, but rather that ye may prophesy' (I Cor. 14.1). So the one thing charity does 'desire' is prophecy: this is the 'speche' which 'kynde love' covets.

And just as Patience's speech conforms to a prophetic mode, so too does it appeal to the will, rather than the intellect (as we would expect in this vision, representing as it does the conversion of the will). It is Patience's appeal to the will which persuades Conscience that he will go on pilgrimage. When Clergy taunts Conscience by asking him whether or not he wants to 'rede redels' in going off with Patience, Conscience disowns interpretative skill, and states instead that Patience's will has moved his own will (by which we must understand, I think, Will himself):

> For al that Pacience me profreth, proud am I litel;
> Ac the wil of the wye and the wil of folk here
> Hath meved my mood to moorne for my synnes.
>
> (XIII. 189–91)
>
> *profreth*: offers; *wye*: man; *mood*: spirit.

7. The following three paragraphs are based on Simpson (1986a). For a fuller discussion of the modes (*formae tractandi*) of Scripture, see the same article, but more especially Minnis (1979; 1984).

It is not as if Patience's kind of poetry is without intellectual stimulation; on the contrary, it is intellectually demanding, but its intellectual force is designed to move the will, unlike, say, the argumentative modes of the third vision.

So Conscience's choice to leave with Patience is not only a choice concerning educational institutions, but it is also a literary choice, and an adventurous literary choice: Conscience is impressed by the tale of a pilgrim, despite the not absurd charge of the doctor that 'pilgrymes konne wel lye' (l. 178). That the doctor's charge has force in the poem as a whole is clear from Will's (or Langland's) own comments about lying, tale-telling pilgrims in the Prologue. There he observes that these pilgrims

> Wenten forth in hire wey with many wise tales,
> And hadden leve to lyen al hire lif after.
>
> (Prol. 48–9)

However much Chaucer does commit himself as a poet, at least provisionally, to such 'wise tales', Langland's position, as I argued in Chapter 1, is initially hostile to fiction, to fables 'that weyven soothfastnesse', as Chaucer's Parson says. Here, however, he sees his way through to committing the highest moral faculty, the Conscience, to what the doctor dismissively calls a 'disours tale' (l. 172).

Patience, then, is the model of the ideal minstrel described at different points in the poem: in Passus IX, Wit points to the minstrel who uses speech as 'Goddes gleman and a game of hevene' (IX. 102); in Passus X Study refers to the spiritual entertainer who, is 'litel . . . loved' for his scriptural entertainment (X. 30–50); and at the end of Passus XIII the narrator praises the mendicant 'jester of God', who can 'solace' the souls of lords at feasts with his 'ministrelsy'.[8] In presenting Patience as such a figure, Langland preserves the model of a minstrelsy associated with feasting, but transforms it into the idea of a spiritual feast. But if Patience represents the ideal of minstrelsy, the first figure Patience and Conscience meet represents its earthly standard, Haukyn.

---

8. The term 'Goddes minstrales' (cf. 'Goddes gleman', IX. 102) may well be a translation of the term *ioculatores dei*, as used by Franciscans. See Fleming (1977).

Haukyn as Minstrel

When Patience and Conscience leave on pilgrimage together, the association of minstrelsy and feasting, words and food, is again made at the outset: Patience has 'vitailles' in his pilgrim's bag, of 'sobretee and symple speche and soothfast bileve', to 'comfort' himself and Conscience in the 'hungry contrees' of unkindness and covetousness (XIII. 215–19). The first (and only) figure they meet is also intimately linked with both food and words, with feasting and with minstrelsy (Mann 1979). Haukyn is a minstrel concerned with words, and at the same time a waferer (a seller of flour-based snacks), concerned with food. The two professions are in fact related: at any great feast, a lord would employ many kinds of minstrels, as well as waferers (Bullock-Davies 1978, 15–50). Records of such employment exist for great, royal feasts, but it is clear that the two professions are associated at a much lower end of the social scale as well, as part of the 'pub scene', as it were. Chaucer's *Pardoner's Tale*, for example, opens with a description of a tavern, where

> . . . right anon thanne comen tombesteres
> Fetys and smale, and yonge frutesteres,
> Syngeres with harpes, baudes, wafereres,
> Whiche been the verray develes officeres
> To kyndle and blowe the fyr of lecherye,
> That is annexed unto glotonye.
>   (ll. 447–82)
> *fetys*: elegantly shaped; *smale*: slender; *frutesteres*: girls who sell fruit.

Haukyn declares himself to be on the very margins of the entertainment world, since he is a failure as a minstrel. He works for both secular and ecclesiastical lords, but receives no satisfying payment from either: few 'robes . . . or furrede gownes' from lords (l. 227), and a cheap document of pardon from the Pope (l. 246).

Coats were, in fact, one of the standard gifts given by lords to minstrels (Bullock–Davies 1978, 17), and in the same way that he preserves the idea of minstrelsy, so too does Langland preserve, in the Haukyn scene, the standard gift to the minstrel, of a coat. But Haukyn's receiving of this coat is possible only after a searching revaluation of the elements of his trade, his words and the bread he sells.

Haukyn is already wearing a coat when he meets Patience and Conscience:

> He hadde a cote of Cristendom as Holy Kirke bileveth;
> Ac it was moled in many places with manye sondry plottes.
>
> (XIII. 273–4)
>
> *moled*: stained; *plottes*: stains.

The range of stains on this coat reveal Haukyn to be representative of a much wider range of humanity than simply waferers and minstrels: it is marked by all the deadly sins, and includes the professional failings of a wide range of trades, representing more widely the 'active' life – that level of life which involves activity in the world, as distinct from the contemplative life of eremitic withdrawal. But even if Haukyn does represent a wide range of occupations, Langland holds the image of Haukyn within the frame of minstrelsy and feasting, of words and food, in the vision as a whole. At the beginning of Passus XIV, for example, Haukyn explains to Conscience why he is unable to clean his coat:

> And also I have an houswif, hewen and children –
> *Uxorem duxi, et ideo non possum venire*
>
> (XIV. 3–3a)
>
> *hewen*: servants; *uxorem duxi . . . venire*: I have a wife, and am not therefore able to come.

Given Haukyn's filthy coat, the reference here to Luke 14.20 (the Parable of the Wedding Feast to which the lord's invited guests refuse to come) evokes another biblical parable used in Passus XI (discussed above, p. 121) – that of Matthew 22, the feast to which many are called, where the guest is violently ejected because of his improper garment. If we are permitted to make this connection, Haukyn is both the figure of Luke 14.20 who declines the invitation because he has a wife (traditionally interpreted as the flesh) (Alford 1974, 136), and the figure of Matthew 22 who does go to the feast, but is thrown out because of his dress. In the sequence which follows, Conscience and Patience offer both to clean his coat, and to give him food. Conscience promises to teach Haukyn how to wash his coat with the three steps of penitence (contrition, confession, and satisfaction). When it is clean, Haukyn the minstrel will be admitted to any company:

> Shal noon heraud ne harpour have a fairer garnement

Then Haukyn the Actif man, and thow do by my techyng,
Ne no mynstrall be moore worth amonges povere and riche
Than Haukyn wil[l] the wafrer, which is *Activa Vita*.

(XIV 25–8)

heraud: herald; *and if*; *wafrer*: wafer seller; *activa vita*: active life.

And if Conscience will clean Haukyn's coat, Patience will
provide him with both bread and words, the two elements of his
trade as waferer/minstrel. He tells Haukyn that he will provide
him with 'paast', 'and flour to fede folk with as best be for the
soule' (ll. 29–30). This bread, however, can be provided even if
no grain grows, says Patience, recalling Piers's rejection of
ploughing in favour of the 'payn' of penitence (he even cites the
same biblical text as Piers, *Ne soliciti sitis* (l. 34b)). Like most of
Patience's statements, this is paradoxical, offering bread at the
same time as he discourages attachment to bread. Haukyn, for
one, is not impressed – he laughs and says that who ever believes
Patience will not be 'blessed' (l. 36), where he uses the word
'blessed' in a casual, secular sense.

Once again, Patience seems to be at the borders of sense. In
what follows, however, we can see that his sense is a profound
and religious one: he argues that God provided sustenance for all
his creation; as each animal can live in its essential element, so too
can man nourish his essential nature through 'leel bileve and love'
(l. 47). This 'vitaille of grete vertue' (l. 38) is implicitly equated
here with Holy Church's 'plante of pees, moost precious of
vertues' (I. 152), where the biological sense of 'vertue' (the 'life-
giving force of a plant') combines with its cosmic sense of
'power', and with its moral sense of Modern English 'virtue'.
Patience moves to the essence of his idea in his citation of
Matthew 4.4, and his offer of his bread to Haukyn:

Non in solo pane vivit homo, set in omni verbo, qoud procedit de ore Dei
But I lokede what liflode it was that Pacience so preisede;
And thanne was it a pece of the Paternoster – *Fiat voluntas tua*.

(XIV. 47b–49)

liflode: sustenance; *paternoster*: the Lord's Prayer; *fiat voluntas tua*: Thy will be
done.

The biblical text here ('Man shall not live by bread alone, but by
every word that proceedeth out of the mouth of God') poses two
kinds of essential nourishment for man: bread and divine words;
Patience's point is more radical than the biblical text, since he

equates bread with words. The words he chooses for Haukyn's nourishment are especially appropriate from Patience, accepting as they do an attitude of suffering and patience. But precisely as such, they involve a rejection of earthly food, or at least of any conscious care about such food, in favour of essential human sustenance, which is the divine Word.

In the nexus of images of minstrelsy/feasting, words/food within which the poem has been moving, then, Patience's position is the most radical: for Patience the divine Word *is* man's food. Scriptural texts are now being invoked in the poem in a profoundly different way from the moralising use of such texts by Holy Church, or the argumentative use by Will. Patience's characteristic rhetorical figure is paradox, deriving from repeated use of the proverb '*Patientes vincunt*' – 'Those who suffer will be victorious'. He consistently evokes the sense of a word only to dislodge and spiritualise it. One further example of this procedure must suffice. Haukyn says that he has been given pardons by the Pope which are of no use. In his penitential exhortation, Patience, too, promises Haukyn a pardon, but he sets up the idea of a documentary pardon, with literal words, only to subvert such an idea. He says that Haukyn can have confidence in the pardon gained through proper penance, and that if the Devil should raise legal objections,

> We sholde take the acquitaunce as quyk and to the queed shewen it –
> *Pateat &c: Per passionem Domini* –
> And putten of so the pouke, and preven us under borwe.
>
> (XIV. 189–90)
>
> *acquitaunce*: document in evidence of a transaction; *queed*: evil one; *pateat . . . Domini*: 'let it be manifest' (the opening words of a deed) . . 'through the passion of our Lord'; *pouke*: devil; *borwe*: surety.

So far Patience has set up the idea of a formal legal document, by imitating the form of a king's letter patent, by which a king publicly grants rights to the addressee. But in ostensibly elaborating the idea of this legal document, he explodes its purely legal, documentary status by insisting on the necessary spirit behind the words of the document:

> Ac the parchemyn of this patente of poverte be moste,
> And of pure pacience and parfit bileve.
>
> (XIV. 191–2)
>
> *parchemyn*: parchment; *patente*: letter patent.

The homophony between 'patente' and 'patience' here insists on the fact that this 'document' is no document at all, though through the spirit of suffering which is its 'parchemyn' it is more potent than any mere paper pardon 'with a peis of leed and two polles amyddes' (XIII. 246).

Patience, then, seems to me to practise a specifically New Testament poetics, a poetics of paradox whereby the spirit of a statement consistently threatens to unsettle the normal senses of its words. And the effect of this procedure, however intellectually stimulating it is, is affective and emotional. Patience does not practise the judgemental satire commended by Lewtee in Passus XI (91–105a). Not only does he restrain Will from attacking the friar at the feast scene (although Will does anyway), but he also refrains from any kind of satirical blaming of Haukyn. Instead, the approach of Patience and Conscience is consistently 'in a curteis manere' (XIII. 458); they instinctively understand the admonition of Imaginatif at the end of Passus XI, who warns Will against judgemental blaming, since

> . . . shal nevere chalangynge ne chidynge chaste a man so soone
> As shal shame, and shenden hym, and shape hym to amende.'
>
> (XI. 423–4)
>
> *shenden*: mortify.

And the effect of their speech on Haukyn is precisely this, to provoke shame in him, and to affect his will; the vision ends with a moving image of a contrite Haukyn, who declares that he deserves to wear the covering of 'shame one / To covere my careyne' [body] (ll. 330–1), which, paradoxically, is exactly the covering which will restore his 'coat of Cristendom'.

SOCIAL TRANSITIONS

In the fourth vision, then, we can see a transition from both the educational and literary premises of all that has preceded these passus. In particular, we can see a change from the authoritarian educational and discursive modes of Holy Church in Passus I, since here Langland is moving to an inward knowledge, which cannot simply be taught by external institutional sources, and which involves new, affective, more specifically poetic modes of apprehension. Does this moment of conversion and transition in the poem also involve changes in the way Langland imagines a Christian in society?

In the Prologue, the Commons organise themselves under the ultimate direction of the King, who is himself aided by 'Knyghthod and Clergie' (l. 116). Under this superior direction, the Commons are said to develop 'craftes',

> And for profit of al the peple plowmen ordeyned
> To tilie and to travaille as trewe lif asketh.
> (Prol. 119–20)

This statement of standard feudal ideology identifies the life of 'truthe' with that of work, and particularly, in this case, the work of producing food. As I argued in Chapter 1, 'truthe' is for Langland essentially a divine principle, a name used to indicate God Himself in His judgemental aspect. The divine sanction of productive labour implicit in this passage from the Prologue is restated in explicit terms in the Pardon from Truthe in Passus VII:

> Alle libbynge laborers that lyven with hir hondes,
> That treweliche taken and treweliche wynnen,
> And lyven in love and in lawe, for hir lowe herte
> Haveth the same absolucion that sent was to Piers.
> (VII. 60–3)

Everything in the poem up to this points suggests, as I argued in Chapters 1 and 2, a congruence of 'truthe' in its earthly and divine senses: by working faithfully in the world, one meets the standards of divine justice. This squaring of earthly and spiritual responsibility is broken, though, at the moment the 'pardon' arrives, since we realise there that 'doing well' is impossible before God. 'Truthe's 'pardon' does declare that doing well will be rewarded in heaven, but at the same time we realise that this is an impossible demand for men to meet. Given man's natural propensity to sin, he requires a genuine pardon rather than a statement of strict justice from God. Piers instinctively realises the inadequacy of works themselves before God, and renounces his ploughing:

> 'I shal cessen of my sowyng,' quod Piers, 'and swynke noght so
>   harde,

Ne aboute my bely joye so bisy be na moore;
Of preieres and of penaunce my plough shal ben herafter,
And wepen whan I sholde slepe, though whete breed me faille'.

(VII. 118–21)

swynke: work.

Whether or not Piers renounces ploughing altogether here (there are indications either way), it is certain that he gives absolute primacy to penance as a kind of labour, regardless of whether or not food will be produced. He does not reject labour itself as such, but he does transform it: his prayers will be his 'plough'.

Piers, then, as the uneducated 'lewed jutte' (Schmidt 1987b, 86) realises instinctively what Will takes a long and intellectual route to understand: that God will accept human effort into the scales of his justice, but also that moral effort essentially consists of trying to pay God back, as it were, for the debt of sin into which man has inevitably fallen. In Passus VII Piers moves immediately to the position of penitential poverty which Patience advocates in Passus XIII.

And as Will reaches the same point as Piers, then we should not be surprised to find the same primacy being given to the life of penitential 'payn' in the fourth vision as Piers had given it in the second. We have already observed that Patience cites the same text as Piers. 'Ne solliciti sitis' – 'take no thought for your life, what ye shall eat . . .' (Matt.6.25), and that Patience enjoins complete confidence in God as a provider of earthly food. Patience extends this idea by citing other biblical and legendary examples of God's feeding of his creatures (XIV. 60–9). And he goes on to identify a truly spiritual life of penance, and of charity, with a life of 'patiente poverte'. The rich, paradoxically, are inevitably 'in debt' (spiritually) at the final 'rekenyng' (ll. 103–7), whereas the poor can claim entry into heaven by legal right (ll. 108–20).

The rest of Patience's speech (XIV. 121–319) develops this opposition between patient poverty and complacent wealth; his examples of the poor are not those of poor labourers, but rather those of mendicant beggars:

Ac beggeris aboute Midsomer bredlees thei soupe,
And yet is wynter for hem worse, for wetshoed thei gange,

Afurst soore and afyngred, and foule yrebuked
And arated of riche men, that ruthe is to here.

(XIV. 159–62)

soupe: sup; gange: go; afurst: thirsty; afyngred: hungry; arated: rebuked; ruthe: pitiful.

He also transforms images of beggary into images of spiritual possession. Using the Beatitudes (Matt. 5.3–12) as his base text, Patience develops the paradoxes of the New Testament passage by arguing that it is almost impossible for a rich man to enter heaven, whereas

. . . the poore preesseth bifore, with a pak at his rugge –
Opera enim illorum sequuntur illos –
Batauntliche, as beggeris doon, and boldeliche he craveth
For his poverte and his pacience a perpetuel blisse:
Beati pauperes: quoniam ipsorum est regnum celorum

(XIV. 212–14)

rugge: back; opera enim . . . illos for their works follow them; batauntliche: eagerly; beati pauperes . . . celorum: blessed are the poor [in spirit], for theirs is the kingdom of heavan.

Here the anxious and competitive pleading of beggars is transformed into a gesture of confident, energetic request.

What Patience is proposing, then, is an abandonment of the Active Life. Malcolm Godden has recently argued convincingly that for Langland the Active Life is 'pre-eminently the life of honest toil represented by the plowmen', arguing from such passages as B. VI. 247–9 and A. XI. 179–84 (Godden 1984, 138–40). He goes on to say that '. . . Haukyn is in the end offered a reformation which . . . would change his very identity. At the heart of the Haukyn episode is a rejection of the values associated with the Active Life in the Langlandian sense of honest toil, in favour of those associated with 'pouerte', in the Langlandian sense of an eremitic life of voluntary hardship' (Godden 1984, 148–9). The final image of Haukyn suggests the difficulty, even the impossibility of living in the world without falling into sin: he laments that it is very 'hard' (meaning 'wretched') 'to lyve and to do synne', but goes on to suggest that 'living' has meant 'living in the world' – he regrets

That evere he hadde lond or lordshipe, lasse other moore,
Or maistrie over any man mo than of hymselve.

(XIV. 327–8)

maistrie: power.

Piers Plowman as a whole is clearly written for a general audience; in its overall concerns it is not remotely like the works written or translated for a 'special', contemplative audience in the late fourteenth century, like the *Cloud of Unknowing*, or the *Book of Privy Counselling* – it is profoundly embedded in the problems of living a spiritual life in the world. Part of its popularity might be explained in terms of the growing audience of lay people who were nevertheless spiritually sophisticated – the audience for whom works like the *Abbey of the Holy Ghost*, or Walter Hiltons's 'Epistle on the Mixed Life' were written, designed as these works are to teach lay readers how they can approximate to a formally religious life while remaining in the world. Here, however, at the end of Passus XIV, we are presented with an image of the 'Actif Man' weeping not only for his sins, but also for the inevitability of sinning while he remains in the world. If sin is inevitable, then man simply cannot meet the standards of God's strict justice – man cannot 'dowel' absolutely. Patience perceives in penance a way of meeting a statuted pact with God, and, thereby, a way of 'doing well' which might not be absolute, but which is nevertheless satisfactory; but this spiritual solution is nothing if not radical in its demand that Haukyn abandon active concerns. In pointing to such a solution, Patience puts into relief the crisis of the Active Life in general.

CONCLUSION

In conclusion to this whole discussion of the fourth vision, then, we can say that it too represents a *transitus*, a Passover from the Old Law to the New. Will had been preoccupied with the problem of whether or not human action, or 'dowel', is of any value in the scales of God's justice throughout the third vision. With the limited help of rational psychological and educational faculties, Will comes to a personal realisation in that vision that God will take into account man's best efforts. But the effort man must make is to repay God for the sin into which he inevitably falls, and if the third vision points to this fact in an intellectual way, the fourth vision is designed to persuade Will in an affective, moral way to choose a life of penitential effort. But this movement involves a shift to more marginal educational, discursive, and social positions which have no immediately obvious, or represented institutional grounding. It involves a shift, that is, from the legalistic teachers of the intellect to the charitable teachers of the will, and as such a departure from formal educational institutions. It also involves, for Langland, the radical revaluation of his own kind of poetry, as it must change from the analytic and satiric procedures of the previous vision to the affective, intuitive procedures appropriate to Patience, as it seeks to accept and transmit the text of the New Testament without reserve. And finally, this unreserved acceptance of the Word of the scriptural text as the essential sustenance of man involves a recognition of the impossibility of combining 'paciente pouerte' with the Active Life. That is the way it appears at the end of this vision, at any rate; but the poem does not become, from this point on, a rule for anchorites – Langland will return to this fundamental problem in further visions.

Chapter 6

The Fifth Vision:
Passus XV–XVII

PASSUS XV: Will recounts his waking life, in which he has become a marginalised 'fool' (ll. 1–10); he falls asleep and meets *Anima*, who explains his various names, and chastises Will for wanting to know the 'cause' of all these names. Anima makes this the occasion for praising simplicity of knowledge, and attacking clerical abuses (ll. 11–91). The Church, he says, is like a tree, whose inner health or sickness determines the health of its fruit and leaves (ll. 92–102); the clergy are particularly given to avarice, and ignore charity (ll. 103–48). Here Will asks what charity is; Anima replies by saying what charity does, how charity may be known, and the historical manifestations and contemporary institutions in which charity can be found (ll. 149–297); he goes on to argue that these historical models of charitable living offer a model of how religious should gain their sustenance in a charitable way, unlike the avaricious practices of the contemporary Church (ll. 298–342e). All Christians should be charitable; because they are avaricious instead, all human skills and practices fail and degenerate (ll. 343–82). Anima's stress on simplicity leads him to argue that even Moslems and Jews can be saved through faith; he digresses to recount the division of Islam from Christianity (ll. 383–409); he then returns to his theme of avarice, pointing to the simplicity of life of many founders of church orders (ll. 410–26a), and exhorting priests to teach by example, and turn their energy to the conversion not only of Christendom, but also of Muslims and Jews (ll. 427–535a); the present state of an avaricious clergy leads Anima to prophesy, and actively to exhort, the dispossession of the Church by the secular order (ll. 536–67). He ends by addressing bishops, exhorting them to convert both their own flock, and all the world (ll. 568–610a).

PASSUS XVI (containing an inner-dream): Will thanks Anima on Haukyn's behalf, but goes on to ask Anima what charity means; Anima replies that charity is a tree, that it grows in man's heart, and that it is tended by *Liberum Arbitrium*, under the direction of Piers Plowman (ll. 1–17). At the mention of Piers, Will falls asleep (from within his dream), and sees the tree; Piers explains the supports of the tree as being the three persons of the Trinity (ll. 18–65); Will asks about the levels of fruit on the tree, and is answered that they represent three levels of Christian life – matrimony, widowhood, and virginity (ll. 66–72). Will asks Piers to pick an apple, that he [Will] might taste it; Piers tries to pick an apple, but as soon as he shakes the tree, the apples, now named as biblical figures from the Old Testament, fall down into the Devil's power (ll. 73–85). Piers is powerless to prevent the Devil taking the apples, at which point Langland relates the scene of the Annunciation, and some events from the life of Christ, leading up to the crucifixion and Christ's victory over death (ll. 86–166). Will wakes from this inner-dream, and meets *Abraham/Faith*, who is looking for Christ; Abraham speaks about the Trinity, and about God's promise to release human souls from the Devil's power (ll. 167–271); the passus ends with Will meeting another figure moving in the same direction as Abraham (ll. 272–5).

PASSUS XVII: This new figure announces himself as *Spes* (*Hope*), and is clearly identifiable with *Moses*. He shows Will the King's letter (the tables of the law) where Will reads the gloss 'Love God and thy neighbour' (ll. 1–15); Will asks Moses who should be believed most – Abraham, who directed Will to faith in the Trinity, or Moses, whose message is love. (ll. 16–48). Before Moses

can reply, they see a Samaritan going in the same direction as themselves, on his way to a joust in Jerusalem.
The Parable of the Good Samaritan (Luke 10.30–6) is
played out, with Faith and Hope acting the parts of the
priest and the Levite (ll. 49–84). The Samaritan explains
to Will why Faith and Hope are insufficient without
Christ; he goes on to answer Will's question to Moses
about the relative worth of Abraham's and Moses's
teaching. He says Will should believe both, and offers
two images of the Trinity (a hand and a candle) which
clarify the relation of Abraham's doctrine of the Trinity
with Moses's exhortation to love (ll. 85–295). The passus
and the vision end with the Samaritan's confident affirmation that salvation is possible even for the repentant
murderer (ll. 296–353).

INTRODUCTION

At the end of the fifth vision (Passus XV–XVII), Will poses a
hardest case question to his interlocutor, the Good Samaritan,
concerning salvation. After the Samaritan has condemned murder
as the act which most offends the Holy Spirit, Will asks this
question:

> I pose I hadde synned so, and sholde now deye,
> And now am sory that I so the Seint Spirit agulte,
> Confesse me and crye his grace, God that al made,
> And myldeliche his mercy aske – myghte I noght be saved?
>
> (XVII. 296–9)
>
> *pose*: put it that; *agulte*: sinned against.

The Samaritan's answer is unequivocal:

> 'Yis,' seide the Samaritan, 'so thow myghte repente
> That rightwisnesse thorugh repentaunce to ruthe myghte turne'.
>
> (XVII. 300–1)
>
> *rightwisnesse*: justice; *ruthe*: compassion.

In this last line the three full staves (i.e. the alliterating stressed
syllables) encapsulate the central focuses of Langland's poem:
justice, repentance and compassion, where the first, justice, is
turned into the third, compassion, by the second, repentance. The
Samaritan concludes the vision as a whole with a development of

the same idea – here the act of repenting (in order to gain mercy) is itself an act of mercy:

> For ther nys sik ne sory, ne noon so muche wrecche
> That he ne may lovye, and hym like, and lene of his herte
> Good wille, good word – bothe wisshen and wilnen
> Alle manere men mercy and foryifnesse,
> And lovye hem lik hymself, and his lif amende.
>
> (XVII. 347–51)
>
> lene: give.

The Samaritan's clear affirmation of the possibility of salvation through repentance answers to what I have defined as the central problematic of Langland's poem – the question, that is, of how Dowel, or the demands of justice, can be met, when man inevitably falls short of such standards, and when pure mercy is itself unjust. As I have argued in the previous two chapters, the poem increasingly emphasises the possibility of salvation, given God's free decision to accept repentance as a kind of repayment for sin, even if that repayment does not match the degree to which man has fallen. The Samaritan himself concludes his answer to Will's hardest case by stressing how repayment, even if it is inadequate, is necessary:

> Ac er his rightwisnesse to ruthe torne, som restitucion bihoveth:
> His sorwe is satisfaccion for [swich] that may noght paie.
>
> (XVII. 316–17)
>
> torne: be converted; bihoveth: is necessary.

This optimistic emphasis at the end of the vision recaps the endings of Passus XIV (the end of the fourth vision) and Passus XVI: just as Haukyn weeps at the end of Passus XIV, 'and cride mercy faste' (XIV. 331), so too does Will himself weep at the words of Abraham at the end of Passus XVI, as he laments 'that synne so longe shal lette / The myght of Goddes mercy, that myghte us alle amende!' (XVI. 270–1). And the emphasis on willing mercy, to 'bothe wisshen and wilnen . . . mercy and foryifnesse', is also, as we have seen, characteristic of the repentance scene of Haukyn at the end of Passus XIV; it is, moreover, consistent with the broad psychological movement in the poem, from the reason, which comprehends justice, to the will, through which man is both able to solicit and in some measure to comprehend God's mercy.

If, then, the intellectual and emotional quality of the Samaritan's speech at the end of this vision might seem simply to recap the essential emphases of earlier visions, then what, it might be asked, is new in the fifth vision? In what ways is this fundamental theme of the poem developed? And if, as it seems, the essential question of the poem concerning salvation hás been resolved, then what new directions does the poem take in this vision?

One early reader of the poem clearly thought that a large new development in the poem does occur at the beginning of the fifth vision, since Passus XV is marked in some manuscripts with an apparently non-authorial rubric (Adams 1985): '*finit dowel & incipit dobet*' ('dowel ends and dobet begins'). When we look to the body of the vision, I think we can see that the reader responsible for these rubrics was not unperceptive: Langland broaches large new subjects in this vision, in particular those of the Church and of charity, and he calls upon new discourses to express these subjects, in particular ecclesiology and typological allegory. The fourth vision had ended with an image of the penitent Haukyn, whose penitence had seemed to imply a withdrawl from the Active Life into an eremitic life of penitential contrition. The discourses we might have expected in the fifth vision, then, are those of the individual, eremitic life. Instead, the reverse is true: Langland moves on to historical and institutional discourses which set the individual Christian in the context of salvation history and of the Church.

I will discuss each of these subjects (the Church and charity) and the modes by which they are expressed in the body of this chapter. But before we look to the content of the fifth vision, it is important that we should consider the psychological perspective which allows Langland to move on to such important subject matter with the authority he does.

ANIMA – THE WHOLE SOUL

From the moment Will dreams near the beginning of Passus Eight, Langland practises, as we have seen, a kind of psychoanalysis, or psychological allegory: that is to say that Will interrogates first different parts of his reason, and the educational institutions which train the reason (in the third vision); in the fourth vision the poem turns more towards reformation of the will, and we realise that Will himself represents that emotional faculty of the soul which is capable of loving and of contrition. The actual subject matter and style of these visions is a function of the psychological faculties in operation: in the third vision the matter and style of the poem are rational and academic, whereas in the fourth vision the main thematic emphasis is on penitence, while the style is, accordingly, affective. The form of the poem takes its shape, that is, as Langland addresses different capacities of the soul.

Langland does not abandon this psychological structure which determines both his matter and his style in the fifth vision; on the contrary, the opening of the dream invokes a reintegrated psyche – the whole soul. Will's interlocutor, 'a sotil thyng withalle – / Oon withouten tonge and teeth' (ll. 12–13),[1] is certainly a figure of authority – he announces (unlike any of the psychological faculties thus far encountered) that he is 'In Cristes court yknowe wel, and of his kyn a party' (l. 17). And his self-description clarifies why he is authoritative, since he[2] represents the deepest principle of the self, the soul in its unity and most profound coherence; under the name 'Anima' (the animating principle which 'quickens' the body), are contained many other names which represent all aspects of human being – sensitive (*Sensus*), emotional (*Animus*), intellectual (*Mens, Memoria, Racio*), moral (Conscience), and charitable (*Amor*) (XV. 23–39e).

This description of the soul is taken by Langland from standard sources (the passage just referred to is from Isidore of Seville's (sixth century) *Etymologies* – a standard, if limited, source of encyclopedic information in the Middle Ages. Here the rational part of the soul which has been interrogated in the third vision, and the will, which has been reformed in the fourth vision, are present in the one figure: Anima says about himself both that 'I deme domes and do as truthe techeth' (l. 27), and that 'I wilne and wolde' (l. 24). In the C-Text, Langland underlines the

---

1. 'sotil' translates '*subtilis*' we find in the psychological treatises: e.g. '. . . cum [anima] sit subtilis et invisibilis, videri non potest, sed per potentias suas se extendit et ostendit' ('. . . since the soul is fine and invisible, it is not able to be seen, but extends itself, and shows itself through its powers' [my translation] (*De Spiritu et Anima*, PL 40.789). The fact that the soul is invisible explains why Will should see him 'as it sorcerie were' (l. 12).

2. Despite the Latin feminine ending 'a' of Anima, the pronouns used indicate a masculine figure.

combination of these faculties which have been previously separate, by calling the speaker *Liberum Arbitrium* (Free Judgement).

Such a faculty brings together the two fundamental acts of the soul for Langland, reasoning and desiring. This is exactly how *liberum arbitrium* is described in psychological treatises: in, for example, the important compilation of psychological theories by the Franciscan John de la Rochelle, the *Tractatus de divisione multiplici potentiarum animae* (*The Treatise concerning the Multiple Division of the Soul's Powers* (1230)), the author cites the opinions of the Greek theologian John Damascene on the *liberum arbitrium*, by saying that 'free judgement . . . is as much as to say a conflation of the will and the reason' (Michaud–Quantin 1964, 122), and that the free judgement 'has the movement of the will and the judgement of the reason: for free judgement, insofar as it is judgement, recognises and discerns, and insofar as it is free, it desires and chooses freely' (p. 122).[3]

If the figure Anima represents the achievement of a reintegrated soul, and if the matter and style of these psychological, or noetic visions are consistently a function of psychological faculties, then what thematic and discursive possibilities does Anima open up for Langland as a poet? As I said in my introduction to this chapter, the two main subject matters Anima broaches are the Church on the one hand, and the nature of charity on the other. These two subject matters might seem entirely disparate, the one being concerned with an external institution, the other with the most profound source of the self. And if it is reasonably the business of Anima to treat charity (one of his names, after all, is *Amor*), we might want to ask why Anima should treat of the Church. But in the texture of Anima's speech as a whole, we can see that a treatment of charity is inseparable from a treatment of the Church for Langland. The two subjects are intimately related, and we can see their interrelation in the two tree images that Anima uses, near the beginning of Passus XV, and at the beginning of Passus XVI.

3. '. . . liberum arbitrium . . . quod est potentia conflata, habens motum voluntatis et iudicium rationis: liberum enim arbitrium, in quantum arbitrium cognoscit et discernit, inquantum vero liberum libere appetit et libere eligit' [my translation]. For a discussion of '*liberum arbitrium*', and of the Franciscan, voluntarist tradition from which Langland's voluntarism derives, see Korolec (1982).

Near the beginning of Passus XV, Anima compares the Church to a tree. He says that just as holiness and honesty 'spread' from the Church through honest men who teach the law, so too all evils spread from the Church when the priesthood is imperfect. He then elaborates this argument through the image of a tree:

> And se it by ensaumple in somer tyme on trowes:
> Ther some bowes ben leved and some bereth none,
> Ther is a meschief in the more of swiche manere bowes.
> Right so persons and preestes and prechours of Holi Chirche
> Is the roote of the right feith to rule the peple;
> Ac ther the roote is roten, reson woot the sothe.
> Shal nevere flour ne fruyt, ne fair leef be grene.
>
> (XV. 96–102)

more: root; *woot*: knows.

This image suggests that the moral health of individual Christians ('fruyt' and 'fair leef') is dependent on the moral health of their root, which is the institution of the Church. The source of individual health, according to this image, is the institution itself. At the beginning of Passus XVI, Anima offers another tree image, whose logic runs in a contrary direction. Will says at the beginning of that passus that he is 'in a weer what charite is to mene' (l. 3). Anima replies with the image of a tree:

> 'It is a ful trie tree,' quod he, 'trewely to telle.
> Mercy is the more therof; the myddul stok is ruthe;
> The leves ben lele wordes, the lawe of Holy Chirche;
> The blosmes beth buxom speche and benigne lokynge;
> Pacience hatte the pure tree, and pore symple of herte,
> And so thorugh God and thorugh goode men groweth
>   the fruyt Charite'.
>
> (XVI. 4–9)

trie: choice; *more*: root; *myddul stok*: trunk; *buxom*: humble; *hatte*: is called; *pore symple*: humble simplicity.

According to the logic of this second image, the source of moral health lies in individuals themselves (Anima says a few lines further on that this tree grows in man's heart); and the institution of the Church is the product of this tree – the 'leves', which are glossed as 'the lawe of Holy Chirche' (l. 6).

These two images are not contradictory: charity is both the source and the product of the Church as it is conceived by Langland. If he is to treat charity, then he must necessarily treat the subject of the Church also. And treat charity he must: this is the question asked by Haukyn at XIV. 97 ('Where wonyeth Charite?'), and the question that must be answered completely if Will is to understand how the demands of justice can be met through God's mercy. It might also be noticed that a very important discussion of charity comes *within* Anima's discussion of the Church, at XV. 149–258.[4] So for Langland, ecclesiology, i.e. discussion of the Church as an institution (Lat. and Grk. *ecclesia*), is naturally bound up with discussion of charity, and naturally follows on from the penitential discourse of Passus XIV, especially given the inadequate ways in which the official Church has met Haukyn's plight, with nothing but 'a pardon with a peis of leed and two polles amyddes' (XII. 246). And it is these two subjects, the institutional question of the Church and the personal question of charity, which can be treated by the totality of the soul, by virtue of its integrated judging and loving powers. I shall turn to the subject of ecclesiology, before considering the presentation of charity.

ANIMA AND THE CHURCH

In Passus I, the figure Holy Church had confidently instructed the individual Christian, Will, teaching him in particular to obey the commandments of 'truthe', with its range of religious, social and verbal senses. As we have seen, it is Will's investigation of the idea of 'truthe' that provokes a crisis of the poem, in recognising the impossibility of individual Christians to meet the standards of God's truth. The third and fourth visions, with their movement towards an understanding of God's mercy, lead Will out of this crisis, and lead him towards an understanding of charity. But in precisely so doing, they lead the poem into a radical critique of the institution of the Church; whereas it had been the personified (though certainly idealised) institution confidently instructing the individual soul in Passus I, in Passus XV it is instead the rein-

---

4. The intimacy of connection between charity and the Church is affirmed as an identity in the C-Text. In answer to Will's question 'What is holy churche, chere frende?', *Liberum Arbitrium* replies, in the same line, 'Charite' (XVII. 125).

tegrated soul confidently and radically questioning the Church in
its contemporary actuality.

Themes

The essential attack on the contemporary Church projected by
Anima is that it is infected and debilitated by avarice. In the
discu*s*sion of charity which Anima sets into his larger discussion
of the Church, he describes various institutions where Charity is
likely to come; he says that Charity comes often to the king's
court, at least 'ther the counseil is trewe', and not avaricious
(ll. 235–6); he does not come 'ful ofte' (surely an overstatement)
into the consistory court (ecclesiastical court), since the law takes
too long there unless money is had (ll. 239–43). Finally, he says,

> Amonges erchebisshopes and other bisshopes and prelates of Holy
>   Chirche,
> For to wonye with hem his wone was som tyme,
> And Cristes patrimonye to the poore parcelmele dele.
> Ac avarice hath the keyes now and kepeth for his kynnesmen
> And for his seketoures and his servaunts, and som for hir children.
>   (XV. 244–8)
>
> *wonye*: dwell; *wone*: custom; *parcelmele*: by portions; *seketoures*: executors.

The Church, in Anima's view, has become another self-defending
institution, itself modelled on the systems of client patronage and
exclusive familial loyalties characteristic of noble households in
the fourteenth century; the papal keys have become the keys of
Avarice. Satire of the venality of the Church and its officers is a
well represented genre of medieval writing, and Langland's satire
in this passus draws on, as one would expect, many standard
topoi of the genre, as of satire more generally, as in the 'now-a-
days (everything is going badly)' topos (XV. 355–88) (Peter 1956,
68), or the topos of idolatrous worship of the cross which is
imprinted on the coin, the 'rede noble' (XV. 537–45) (Yunck
1963, 173). But Langland's satire is not restricted to satire of
individual groups or practices within the Church, but rather
directed to the conception of the institution as a whole, and aimed
at root distortions in its organisation. The discourse is rather
ecclesiology than ecclesiastical satire.

With regard to the first point, that the satire is directed at the
whole conception of the institution, it is characteristic of Anima's

speech to put the contemporary institution of the Church into relief by broad comparisons with either its historical beginnings or its contemporary limits. The ideal of charity is essentially located in the past, 'fern ago'. As examples of those who lived charitably in poverty, Anima cites the early hermits Antony, to whom the origins of monasticism are drawn, Egidius, and Paul (claimed as the founder of the Austin Friars) (XV. 269–89); or some great figures of the primitive Church, Paul the Apostle, the disciples Peter and Andrew, and Mary Magdalen (XV. 290–306). Or he says, in making the same point, that religious should not take alms from unjust rulers, but act

> . . . as Antony dide, Dominyk and Fraunceys
> Beneit and Bernard [bo]the, whiche hem first taughte
> To lyve by litel and in lowe houses by lele mennes almesse,
>
> (XV. 419–21)

where each of these figures is associated with the idealistic founding of an order (apart from Antony, who has already been mentioned, the orders are as follows, respectively: Dominican friars (1216); Franciscan friars (1223); Benedictine monasticism (c. 530); and Cistercian monasticism (1098)). Closer to home, but still in the historical frame of Christianity, Anima also refers to the conversion of England:

> Al was hethynesse som tyme Engelond and Walis,
> Til Gregory garte clerkes to go here and preche.
> Austyn [cristnede the kyng at Caunterbury],
> And thorugh miracles, as men mow rede, al that marche he tornede
> To Crist and to Cristendom . . .
>
> (XV. 441–5)

tornede: converted.

This reference to the initial historical conversion of England is part of a larger polemic in Anima's speech designed to incite religious to the challenge of converting Islam to Christianity. It is this motive which brings into focus not only the historical frames of Christendom, but also its contemporary limits. Langland does not draw what is effectively a map of Christendom in the way Chaucer does in the account of the Knight's campaigns in the General Prologue to the *Canterbury Tales*, but he does focus on the two major rivals to Christianity as he sees it, Islam and Judaism. Thus Anima states the basic similarity of monotheistic belief between Christians and Muslims, and goes on to mark the historical point at which Islam parted from what Anima posits as its Christian origins (XV. 391–409). And by way of attacking the contemporary practice whereby bishops were appointed to sees which were in fact in Muslim-held territories, Anima urges religious to go and convert those sees to Christianity (XV. 490–509). Likewise he turns his attention to the Jews, both to the point at which Jesus paradoxically defeats the Jews through patience (XV. 580–602), marking the historical limit of Christendom, and to the necessity of converting the Jews, marking the contemporary limits of Christendom; the passus ends, in fact, with an exhortation to religious to convert both Jews and Muslims:

> . . . sithen that the Sarsens and also the Jewes
> Konne the firste clause of oure bileve, *Credo in Deum patrem*
>   *omnipotentem,*
> Prelates of Cristene provinces sholde preve, if thei myghte,
> Lere hem litlum and litlum *Et in Jesum Christum filium* . . .
> 　　　　　　　　　　　　　　　　　　　　(XV. 605–8)
>   *credo . . . omnipotentem*: I believe in God the Father Almighty; *litlum*: by little;
>   *et in . . . filium*: and in the Son Jesus Christ.

So Anima evokes Christendom as a whole unit by fundamental historical and cultural oppositions. And not only is his speech addressed to the whole institution, but it also aims, as I said, to diagnose radical distortions in its organisation. The Church is seen by Anima to exclude its essential animating principle, charity, through its avarice. The point of the local satire is that religious should neither receive endowments from temporal lords, nor beg for their living, but 'lyve by litel and in lowe houses by lele mennes almesse' (l. 421) (e.g. XV. 272–340). But this specific point about avarice has its roots in what was seen as a critical historical turning point in the Middle Ages, the so-called 'Donation of Constantine'. According to this legend the first Christian Emperor Constantine (emp. 306–37) endowed the Church with the Lateran palace in Rome, thus establishing a precedent for secular endowment of the Church. Anima refers explicitly to this donation as the source of the contemporary corruption of religious through avarice:

> Whan Costantyn of curteisie Holy Kirke dowed
> With londes and ledes, lordshipes and rentes,

An aungel men herden an heigh at Rome crye,
'*Dos ecclesie* this day hath ydronke venym,
And tho that han Petres power arn apoisoned alle!'
(XV. 555–9)

dowed: endowed; ledes: property; dos ecclesie: the endowment of the Church.

Anima, then, is concerned not only to address the whole of Christendom, but also to diagnose a radical disease at the heart of the Church, which excludes charity from the company of its prelates, now that 'avarice hath the keyes' (l. 247).

It is this diagnosis which prompts Anima to propose specific, concrete political measures to reform the Church. The reference to the Donation of Constantine is enclosed, in fact, in the programme of such a reform: before he mentions the donation, Anima says that bishops would lose their 'lordship of londes', and live instead on tithes ('dymes'), if only the secular powers were committed to such action (XV. 551–4); and immediately after his comments about Constantine, he directly addresses the secular powers in an exhortation to dispossess the prelates of the Church:

Taketh hire landes, ye lordes, and leteth hem lyve by dymes;
If possession be poison, and inparfite hem make,
Good were to deschargen hem for Holy Chirches sake,
And purgen hem of poison, er moore peril falle.
(XV. 562–5)

dymes: tythes.

This radical proposal for reform, the most concrete in *Piers Plowman*,[5] is not isolated in the period; at precisely the time the B-Text is being written (around 1378), John Wyclif argued in his *De civili dominio* (published between 1376 and 1378) and in his *De officio regis* (1379) that the Church should be disendowed. In the second of these tracts, he argued that the King had supremacy over all men, including the priesthood, and he looked to the King to reform the Church by disendowment. Such a programme was obviously not without its attractions for a secular power in constant need of money, and Wyclif was initially supported by powerful nobles, such as John of Gaunt, Richard II's uncle. The Church reacted swiftly against this and other Wycliffite doctrines, with Wyclif having to face two prosecutions and three condem-

5. The speech at X. 314–27, which looks forward to disendowment, is more a prophecy than a proposal for reform.

nations between 1377 and 1382.[6] Langland is not a Wycliffite: his repeated affirmation of the 'semi-Pelagian' idea that men can be saved through full repentance (developed *against* the idea, posed by Will in Passus X, that men are saved by predestination, regardless of their individual efforts), is, for example, diametrically at odds with Wyclif's doctrine of predestination;[7] nonetheless, Langland's own diagnosis of the 'poison' in the Church, which excludes charity, leads him, like Wyclif, to propose the disendowment of the Church. As we shall see in Chapter 7 (dealing with Passus XIX and XX), the powerful imaginative development of Langland's ecclesiology brings him into territory shared with the popular dissenting movement which sprang from Wyclif's doctrines, Lollardy.

Genre

The main subject, then, of Anima's speech in Passus XV is the Church; the genre he uses to discuss this subject is satire. The speech is characterised by the estates address of satire, in this case either to the 'lordes' who should dispossess the Church, or to the 'preestes, prechours and prelates' who need reforming; and it is generally declamatory in style. But if the import of the speech is directed against priests, its *invitation* is to secular readers; thus immediately after he cites the tree image from an authoritative Latin text (in Latin), Anima makes this remark:

> If lewed men wiste what this Latyn meneth,
> And who was myn auctour, muche wonder me thinketh
> But if many preest beere, for hir baselardes and hir broches,
> A peire of bedes in hir hand and a book under hir arme.
>
> (XV. 119–22)
>
> *lewed*: ignorant; *baselardes*: daggers; *broches*: brooch ornaments.

This remark is disingenuous, since the entire passage preceding the Latin citation (XV. 92–116) is in fact an English version and elaboration of precisely the Latin text, which is prefaced by a reference to its author ('Johannes Crisostomus' – an authoritative doctor of

---

6. For Wyclif's proposals to disendow the Church, see Leff (1967), Vol. II, pp. 542–5.
7. For accounts of Langland's relation to Lollardy, see Gradon (1980) and Hudson (1988).

the Greek Church); so although the remarks cited here pretend that the Latin is unintelligible to the layman, and that priests who can read it are protected by that unintelligibility, the evident truth is that 'lewed men' *can* now read it, and that they *do* know who was Anima's 'auctour'.

And twice during this speech, Anima makes it clear that he aims the burden of his satire, regardless of the dangers, at priests: he introduces the image of the rotten tree (effectively the introduction to the whole speech) by saying that he will speak of 'curatours of Cristen peple . . . for truthes sake' (ll. 90–1), and at l. 487 he remarks that 'persons and priests' 'wol be wrooth for I write thus'.

But if the genre of Anima's speech is satire, and the style, accordingly, declamatory, how does this stand with what was said in Chapter 4 about the 'deconstruction' of the genre of satire? In that chapter, it will be remembered, I argued that for Langland the question of his own use of satire becomes intimately bound up with his own sense of how salvation is possible: if, that is, salvation is possible only by recognising one's personal failure to meet the standards of God's justice, and by making amends, or repayment for this failure, then how can one stand in judgement on others, which one necessarily does in being a satirist? The figure Lewtee defends Will's right to '[l]egge the sothe' in Passus XI (ll. 87–106a), but, as I argued earlier, it is precisely God's 'lewtee', or 'truthe', which Will is unable to meet, and it is immediately after Lewtee's speech that Scripture precipitates the crisis of justice with the Parable of the Wedding Feast to which many are called but few chosen (XI. 107–14). The theme of patient poverty which develops in response to this crisis consistently discourages satirical blaming – 'poverte and poore men parfournen the comaundement – *Nolite iudicare quemquam*' ('Judge not [that ye be not judged]') (XIV. 290–290a).

Here, however, in Passus XV, Anima engages in a sustained and uninhibited satire against the institution of the Church, 'for truthes sake' (l. 91). Is Langland being inconsistent, or can Anima's use of satire be reconciled with the critique of this genre made in the latter part of the third, and in the fourth visions? Langland himself does not answer this question directly, and so we must fall back on conjecture. My own answer to this question is that satire becomes justified again under the auspices of the integrated soul. The critique of satire, profound as it is, is restricted, it seems from the perspective of Passus XV, to that part of the poem dealing with the reformation of the will, in the third and fourth visions. Anima, as the whole soul, includes not only the will, but as I mentioned earlier, that part of the soul which judges, both intellectually and morally: Anima says that he is called *Ratio* 'whan I deme domes and do as truthe techeth' (l. 27), and that he is called Conscience 'whan I chalange or chalange noght, chepe or refuse' (l. 31). So Anima includes both active, judgemental qualities, and passive, charitable qualities – in the C-Text *Liberum Arbitrium* (the C-Text substitute for Anima) expresses this neatly by saying that sometimes he fights, 'falsness to destruye', while other times he suffers 'bothe tene and sorwe' (C. XVI. 173–4). If Langland engages in satire here, he does so only after searching examination of its justification and moment. The 'reasonable' side of Anima is justified in, and predisposed towards, satire; the 'loving' side treats of charity.

The particular (radical) emphases of Langland's ecclesiology in Passus XV indicate that he is no longer working within established authoritative discourses of the Church, but rather that the poem has now arrived at a point where the integrated soul takes issue with the institution which should be nourishing it. It is true that Langland's satire here is not particularly easy reading (Passus XV seems to me unworked and sometimes turgid), but the fruit of this passus will be produced especially in the last two passus, where Langland imaginatively projects a reformed, renewed Church with great poetic power.

ANIMA AND CHARITY

At the beginning of Passus XVI, Will thanks Anima for his 'faire shewyng'; the effect of the exposition on Will has been positive – he says he will always love Anima 'For Haukyns love the Actif Man' (l. 2). While Haukyn was felt to be totally isolated from both secular and ecclesiastical institutions at the end of Passus XIV, Anima's speech about the reformation of the Church is understood by Will to answer Haukyn's situation. But, as I mentioned earlier, there are two, interrelated subjects in Anima's speech – on the one hand, the Church, and on the other, charity.

It is this second question that Will now asks Anima to broach: 'Ac yit am I in a weer what charite is to mene' (l. 3). This is the third time in the poem that this question has been asked (cf. XIV. 97, by Haukyn, and XV. 149, by Will), and the response here is the fullest and most imaginatively powerful. But before we consider it, it is necessary to look to the answer given by Anima to this same question when Will asks it for the first time, at XV. 149.

Will's first encounter with Anima in Passus XV is essentially a naming sequence (XV. 14–46), a topos frequent in medieval literature. This naming sequence is particularly complex, however, given the multiplicity of Anima's names, and Anima, in fact, chides Will for wanting to know the cause of all his names (ll. 44–6). Naming sequences are very often important in medieval literature, but Langland gives the topos a cognitive resonance here, since to know the 'causes' of Anima's names is to have complete self-knowledge. This is particularly true concerning Anima's name 'Lele Love', or Latin '*Amor*', which Anima says he is called when 'I love lelly Oure Lord and alle othere' (l. 33). For to know the 'cause' of this name 'lele Love' is to have knowledge of the deepest spiritual sources of the self.

Knowledge of 'lele Love' is self-knowledge of a profound kind. This is evident when Will soon asks Anima the simple question 'What is charite?' (XV. 149).[8] For Anima's response, simple and direct, points directly to the identification of charity and Will himself:

> 'A childissh thyng,' he seide
> . . .
> 'Withouten fauntelte or folie a fre liberal wille'.
>
> (XV. 149–50)

Will, however, misses the point of the simple truth expressed by Anima (i.e. that charity is the will/Will himself), and sees in it, instead, the occasion for further enquiry:

> 'Where sholde men fynde swich a frend with so fre an herte?
> I have lyved in londe,' quod I, 'my name is Longe Wille –
> And fond I nevere ful charite, bifore ne bihynde'.
>
> (XV. 151–3)

8. The following five paragraphs are based on Simpson (1986d).

Line 152 has given us the strongest internal evidence for calling
the poet of *Piers Plowman* 'William Langland' (Kane 1965, 65–70);
but here Will himself is blinded by the proper meaning of his
name, without seeing its common force: for if Will has never seen
charity (which Anima defines as 'a fre liberal wille') 'bifore ne
bihynde', this is surely because he is himself, as the will, the locus
of charity; to look for charity 'bifore' or 'bihynde' is simply to
miss the obvious by looking in front of one's nose.

The way Will formulates his incapacity to see charity poses
itself as a kind of riddle; in the continuation of his speech, he says
exactly this, in fact – that he has seen charity (which Will calls
'Crist') only in himself, in a kind of riddle, or enigma. Will says
that he has never found the radical, unselfseeking charity
described by Paul in I Corinthians 13: 4–5; despite the fact that
priests say that 'Crist is in alle places', Will says that he has never
seen him truly

> . . . but as myself in a mirour:
>   *Hic in enigmate, tunc facie ad faciem.*
>   (XV. 162–162a)

The translation of 'enigma' here, so familiar to readers of the
Authorised Version of the Bible as 'in a glass, darkly' (rendered
by Langland's 'mirour'), can also be rendered by a rhetorical sense
of the word. This is given by classical and medieval rhetoricians
as 'allegory, of an obscure kind' (including, it might be added,
riddles). Will's assertion that he has never seen Christ/charity 'but
as myself' suggests that the knowledge of charity is strangely
close; but the technical meaning of '*aenigma*' (i.e. 'allegory, of an
obscure kind') suggests at the same time that knowledge of
Christ/charity will not be immediate and transparent.

The hint that this knowledge of Christ, or charity, in the self
is not directly perceptible is strengthened in the development of
this encounter; after Anima's moving description of Charity's
activity (XV. 165–94a), Will again expresses his desire to know
charity in a formulaic yet revealing expression: 'By Crist! I wolde
that I knewe hym,' quod I, 'no creature levere' (l. 195). Anima
offers Will specific directions now, as to how he might know
charity: the *sine qua non* of such knowledge is Piers the Plowman;
whereas Anima's speech about the Church was felt to answer to

the situation of the Active Man Haukyn (XVI. 1–2), the other main subject of his speech, charity, attaches itself especially to Piers. Anima says that without the help of Piers Will will never see charity's 'persone', and in response to Will's question as to whether or not the clergy know charity, Anima distinguishes the penetration of Piers's perception from the more limited understanding of the clergy:

> 'Clerkes have no knowyng,' quod he, 'but by werkes and by wordes.
> Ac Piers the Plowman parceyveth moore depper
> What is the wille, and wherfore that many wight suffreth:
> Et vidit Deus cogitaciones eorum'.
>
> (XV. 198–200a)
>   wight: person; Et vidit . . . corum: And God saw their thoughts.

This reference to the limitations of clerical learning recalls Clergy's speech in Passus XIII, in which he disowns cognitive perception before the understanding of the unlearned layman Piers Plowman, who 'set alle sciences at a sop save love one' (XIII. 124). More surprisingly, and more daringly, it implicitly links the perception of this unlettered lay figure with Christ Himself, since the biblical citation here refers to Christ seeing the thoughts of His tempters (cf. Luke 11.17).

The logic of the passage is strangely circular, however: Will can know charity (which Anima has defined as 'a fre liberal wille'), only by knowing Piers, since Piers knows the will. Will, that is, can know charity only by knowing the figure who knows him. Has Langland simply lost his way? Not at all: the biblical text from which Langland takes his inspiration here, I Corinthians 13, is as much concerned to define what charity is as to define how one might know it; Paul defines full understanding in terms of knowing to the degre that one is known by a principle outside the self ('Now I know in part; but then I shall know even as also I am known' (I Cor. 13.12)); in another epistle which was important for Langland, Galatians, he makes the same kind of point: '. . . but now, after that ye have known God, or rather are known of God . . .' (Gal. 4.9). Just as Paul, then, defines perfect knowing as knowing to the degree that one is known, so too does Anima define the knowing of charity as being both active and passive, or as active in being passive. This peculiar quality of knowing is reflected in the syntax of Anima's concluding sentence, where the subjects of the verb 'to knowe' change in this way:

> Therfore by colour ne by clergie knowe shaltow hym nevere,
> Neither thorugh wordes ne werkes, but thorugh wil oone,
> And that knoweth no clerk ne creature on erthe
> But Piers the Plowman – *Petrus, id est, Christus*.
>
> (XV. 209–12)
>
> *colour*: outward appearances; *Petrus, id est Christus*: Peter, that is, Christ.

Will will only know charity, or Christ, by seeking out the principle by which he, as the human will, is known. This principle is provisionally Piers, and ultimately Christ.

Petrus, id est, Christus: this formulation is also riddle like, or an enigma – 'Peter, that is, Christ'. It is this apparently obscure, and certainly daring allegory which determines the shape of the poem from Passus XVI up to and including Passus XVIII. It is to these passus of the fifth vision that I shall now turn, focusing first on Langland's historical sense of the self and of charity, then on the mode by which he expresses that historical sense (typological allegory), and finally on the subject matter of the Samaritan's speech in Passus XVII.

Langland's Historical Sense of the Self and of Charity – the Inner-Dream

As I mentioned earlier, Anima introduces the large themes of Passus XV with the image of Holy Church as a tree whose roots are the clergy, and whose leaves and fruit are an informed laity; so too does he begin Passus XVI with the image of a tree, though this image suggests a much more intimate perception of the self, which then branches out into institutional forms: the tree is the tree of charity, whose root is mercy, and whose trunk is pity, while the leaves are the faithful words which constitute the law of the Church. The fruit of the tree is itself called charity (XVI. 4–9). This image is essentially a psychological one, giving a local habitation to that aspect of the soul by which Anima says he is called 'lele Love'; the place where it grows, says Anima is 'in a gardyn'

> . . . that God made hymselve;
> Amyddes mannes body the more is of that stokke.

Herte highte the herber that it inne groweth,
And *Liberum Arbitrium* hath the lond to ferme,
Under Piers the Plowman to piken it and to weden it.

(XVI. 13–17)

more: root; *stokke*: trunk; *herber*: garden; *liberum arbitrium*: free judgement;
ferme: tend; *piken*: hoe.

The tree of charity and its fruit, then, are the special preserve of
Liberum Arbitrium, that conflation of the soul's main faculties, the
will and the reason: for Langland the soul is clearly not merely
a functional principle, animating the body, but also religious in
conception, since its prize fruit is charity.

But if the idea of charity is essentially a *psychological* one for
Langland, to be found in the inmost recesses of the self, it is at
the same time a *historical* idea; charity, as Will has already
assumed (XV. 161–62a), can be identified with Christ, and, as is
clear from the inner-dream which follows, to know Christ, Will
must proceed through Old Testament history. Understanding, or
even experience of the passage from the Old to the New Covenants is as much a part of self-hood in Langland's view, as are
the functional aspects of the soul (e.g. thinking, desiring). The
self, that is, is in its most profound realisation a historical entity,
and to know the springs of the self, one must know one's history.
This might sound complex, but the action of the inner-dream
clarifies what I mean.

At the mention of Piers Plowman by Anima, Will is taken by
joy (as Anima has told him already, Will's point of entry to
charity will necessarily be Piers), and falls into a love/lone dream
(l. 20).[9] He sees the tree itself, with Piers as his guide. This is the
second inner-dream of the poem, and it will be remembered that
the first (XI. 4–402) was a point of crisis and resolution for Will,
where issues that had been debated in a schematic way suddenly
took on an intensely personal pressure;[10] this inner-dream is also
intensely personal, in the sense that Will is observing the most
profound action of his own soul, and this dream, too, opens the

9. The readings 'lone' or 'love' are identical in the script of the manuscripts;
   Schmidt (1987a) reads 'lone', Kane and Donaldson (1975) 'love'. Strong
   arguments can be made for either, but in the context of the search for charity,
   I prefer 'love'.
10. The verbs which designate the entry of Will into these inner-dreams seem to
    indicate their intensity: compare 'ravysshed' (XI. 7) with 'swowned' (XVI. 19)
    (Schmidt 1987a, 346).

way to resolution of the deepest question of the poem, concerning the relations of justice and charity.

At first, however, the action of the inner-dream seems static and diagrammatic rather than imaginative and dynamic.[11] Will sees a tree held up by three props. Piers serves the reader as much as Will as an exegete, or interpreter, within the poem: the three props 'stand for' the Trinity; against the moral dangers (or 'winds') of the world, the flesh and the Devil,[12] Piers says that he strikes with the Father, the Son and the Holy Spirit respectively (XVI. 25–52). This diagram allegory is based on an important Augustinian notion that the soul of man is made in the trinitarian image of God,[13] but at this point Langland does not want to develop the image: as if in interdiction to Langland's readers as well as to Will, Piers makes it clear that no more questions are to be asked about the pillars (ll. 53–65). So instead, Will asks Piers about the fruit of the tree. Again, Piers's answer provides us with a diagrammatic moral allegory: the three fruits represent the Christian life divided according to a frequent sexual typology: marriage, chaste widowhood, and virginity (Bloomfield 1958), conceived in a hierarchical order represented by their respective levels on the tree (i.e. marriage lowest, etc.) (ll. 67–72).

After these two static diagrams, the scene suddenly begins to move, and as it moves, the picture becomes historical: Will asks Piers to pull an apple down, 'to assaien what savour it hadde' (l. 74), and in response to this apparently domestic question, a vision of human, Old Testament history opens. Each level of the tree cries as Piers attempts to claim the apples as they fall, but

> . . . evere as thei dropped adoun the devel was redy,
> And gadrede hem alle togideres, bothe grete and smale –
> Adam and Abraham and Ysaye the prophete,
> Sampson and Samuel, and Seint Johan the Baptist;
> Bar hem forth boldely – no body hym letted –
> And made of holy men his hoord *in Limbo Inferni*,
> There is derknesse and drede and the devel maister.
>
> (XVI. 79–85)

letted: hindered; *in Limbo Inferni*: in the verge of Hell.

---

11. The best discussions of this scene, and in particular the shift from static to dynamic models, are Aers (1975, Ch. 5) and Dronke (1981).
12. A standard triad of enemies to the soul. See Pearsall (1978, 44).
13. *De Trinitate*, 10.11.17–18.

According to Christian doctrine, all men are wounded with original sin; even the virtuous Old Testament figures who did believe
in God are nevertheless doomed to remain in the Devil's power
until Christ should liberate them. The scene discussed here
dramatically re-presents Old Testament history from an essentially Christian view of it, emphasising its powerlessness against
the rights of the Devil; Piers himself seems to be equally debilitated by this Old Testament status, since he fails to beat off the
Devil with the prop of the Trinity he chooses (the Son, with the
participation of the Father and the Spirit), which he takes up 'for
pure tene' (l. 86). This formula recalls two other instances of
'tene' in the face of a strict and menacing justice: immediately after
the 'pardon' from Truthe in Passus VII has proclaimed that those
who sin need not hope for anything else than that the 'devel shal
have thi soule', Piers 'for pure tene pulled it atweyne' (VII. 115);
and in Passus XI, in the first inner dream, Will trembles in
anxious 'tene' at Scripture's austere text 'Many are called but few
are chosen' (XI. 115). The 'tene' of Piers in Passus XVI, again
expressing anxiety and helplessness before Truthe, or the inex-
orability of the Law, has a miraculous effect, however, as Christ
is born into the poem; without registering any change in the
narrative scene, Langland continues in this way:

> And thanne spak *Spiritus Sanctus* in Gabrielis mouthe
> To a maide that highte Marie, a meke thyng withalle,
> That oon Jesus, a justices sone, moste jouke in hir chambre
> Til *plenitudo temporis* tyme comen were
> That Piers fruyt floured and felle to be rype.
>
> (XVI. 90–4)
>
> *Spiritus Sanctus*: the Holy Spirit; *jouke*: rest; *plenitudo temporis*: the fullness of
> time.

At this point, Langland gives a brief resumé of the life of Christ,
focusing on his healing miracles, his prophecies about the reno-
vation of the temple, and his betrayal and victory on the cross
(ll. 95–166), where the inner-dream ends. The account is based
on the Gospels, except for the reference to Piers teaching Christ
'lechecraft' (ll. 103–110a, where there is, incidentally, a syntactic
blurring of subjects between Christ and Piers – Piers begins as the
subject of the sentence, but before the sentence has finished, the
subject is Christ).

The central problem of the poem, then, is now being broached from an *historical* perspective: the incarnation of Christ is represented by Langland as satisfying the demands of justice: Jesus is 'a justices sone' who comes to relieve the Old Law from the strict justice of Truthe. But for Langland the incarnation is not simply an historical event, but one which happens in the moral lives of individuals; it is for this reason that the tree from which the apples fall is not only historical in meaning, but also *moral*. Matrimony, it will be remembered, was used by Wit in Passus IX as an example of the basic moral life, representing the basic life of the Law: '[In this world is Dowel trewe wedded libbynge folk]' (IX. 108). Thus Christ is represented as coming into the life of Dowel (represented by matrimony), answering to its insufficiencies.

So Langland's representation of the incarnation answers to the problem of justice from both an historical and a moral perspective. Beyond these frames, the incarnation is also represented as a *psychological* act: the whole scene is provoked by Will's desire to taste the fruit charity, 'to assaien what savour it hadde' (l. 74). Some critics have seen this as a reference to Eve's eating of the apple (e.g. Kaske 1963, 202; Carruthers 1973, 132; Goldsmith 1981, 67); this seems to me to blur the noetic, psychological frame in which Langland represents the incarnation – Will now wants knowledge of a sapiential, 'tasty' kind, identified with the term *sapientia* ('wisdom') by an influential metaphorical tradition which understood the etymology of the word *sapientia* to be *sapere*, 'to taste'. This tradition saw theology as essentially an affective discipline, understood by the will (rather than the reason), and apprehended *'per modum gustus'* – 'through means of taste' (Simpson 1986a). It is this psychological tradition which we see enacted in Will's desire to taste the fruit of charity – as he wants to *know* charity, so he asks to *taste* it. So we can see that the incarnation is represented by Langland not only as a historical and moral event, but also as a psychic event: for Langland, the incarnation happens as much in 'a gardyn' which 'herte highte', as it happens in history. It certainly is an historical event, but it needs to be understood in the soul of each individual Christian; it is for this reason that Langland pictures the incarnation as occurring in the tree of charity, which is situated in Will's heart.

Typological Allegory

The inner-dream of Passus XI is a kind of 'replay' of arguments produced earlier in the third vision, from a more intense and personal point of view. So too is the inner-dream of Passus XVI a compressed version of action found in the larger vision in which it is enclosed, though this time the inner-dream is a 'preplay', as it were, of action to come. For just as the inner-dream of Passus XVI realises the movement from justice to mercy as an historical movement from the Old to the New Covenants, the rest of the fifth vision likewise represents a movement from the Old to the New Law. In this movement Will meets biblical figures who are rushing towards Jerusalem to witness Christ's joust with the devil. These figures expound to Will central doctrines of the Trinity which require attention; but before we look to those ideas, it is important to say something about the mode of allegory Langland employs to place these figures, which is known as typological, or figural allegory.

The Old Law, as represented by the Old Testament, is both the cultural father of Christianity, and the precursor against which Christianity must define itself. This posed a profound textual problem for early Christians: how were they to read the Old Testament in such a way as to define themselves against it, and at the same time so as not to reject it? They responded in the way cultures most often do when faced with a textual body which is both precious and yet awkwardly at variance with a new order, by allegorising the text.[14] This habit of reading is already apparent, and explicit, in the letters of St Paul, where, for example, he argues that what is said about the two sons of Abraham has an allegorical significance (*'sunt per allegoriam dicta'*): one was born from a bondwoman (Hagar), the other from a free woman (Sarah); according to Paul, these women represent the two alliances, the Old and the New, whereby the 'children of Hagar represent the Jews, 'in bondage', while the Christians are the 'children' of promise' (Gal. 4.22–31). The Old Testament, then, is read as providing 'types', or 'figures', which foreshadow

---

14. Medieval commentators treated classical texts in the same way; it might be relevant to add the New Critical and Leavisite habit of 'ironising' texts as examples of a culture preserving and appropriating a textual corpus which is awkwardly at variance with a new order (irony is a branch of allegory).

the New Testament (thus the terms 'typological', or 'figural' allegory).

This fundamental habit of allegorising the Old Testament dominated Christian habits of biblical interpretation until at least the fifteenth century. Exegetes formalised the basic reading stance exemplified by St Paul by defining four levels of interpreting an Old Testament text. These are, in order: (i) the *literal* level, according to which the reader learns what really did happen as historical reality. It will be clear from the example just cited from Paul, that the matter for the allegory is not fictional, and that Abraham and his sons had a historical reality. One weakness of much allegorisation is that it evacuates the literal level of the text of any historical reality – once the text has been allegorised, then the allegorical meaning simply replaces the literal level of the text, which can be dismissed. Figural allegory avoids this weakness, since the historical level of the text remains intact; (ii) the *allegorical* level, whereby the Old Testament event looks forward to an event under the New Dispensation (the period after Christ), by which it will be fulfilled. Thus Abraham's son Isaac, born of Sarah, looks forward to, and is a 'type, or 'figure' for the children of the New Law (i.e. Christians); (iii) the *moral*, or topological level, according to which the reader draws moral lessons from his allegorical reading of the biblical text; and (iv) the *anagogical* level, by which events in the Old Law look forward to the soul's future in heaven.[15] With regard to the text of Galatians 4.22–31, for example, a Lollard preacher prefaces his interpretation by saying this:

> And so men seyn comunly that hooly writ hath foure wittis: the furste wit is of story, or euene as the wordis schulden toknen; the seconude wit is allegoric, that figureth thing that men schulden trowe, as thes two sonys of Abraham figuren thes two thingis [i.e. Jews and Christians]; the thridde wit is tropologic, that bitokneth wit of vertwis; the fourthe wit is anagogic, that bytokneth thing to hope in blis. Paul swith here the seconude wit . . .[16]
>
> *wittis*: senses; *trowe*: believe; *swith*: follows.

15. For the historical development of biblical exegesis, see Smalley (1964); for the application of this practice to European literature, see Auerbach (1959). Burrow (1982, Ch. 4) offers a lucid account of this kind of allegory in English writing, and distinguishes it from other kinds of allegory.

16. Cited from Hudson (1983, 556–7); letter forms have been modernised.

Despite its often arbitrary impositions of similarities between the Old and the New Testaments in practice, one can see why this system of reading proved so durable and satisfying: in theory it interprets the text of the Old Testament within an entirely coherent historical and moral frame, and joins the world of historical reality to the unchanging world of spirit without prejudice to either. In particular, the entire world of the Old Testament is felt to be imbued with a profound dynamism, since it mysteriously prefigures the Christian epoch, and calls forth the New Law for its fulfilment.

How is this system of thought (which is, after all, essentially a habit of reading) exploited by a creative poet such as Langland? It will be remembered that Anima tells Will that he can only know Christ through Piers – 'Petrus, id est, Christus' (XV. 212). This remark would seem to be the solution to a riddle, whereas in fact it stands as a riddle. It seems to suggest that Piers is being used as an Old Testament figure for Christ: just as the reader of the Old Testament finds Christ through mysterious 'figures', so too should Will find Christ through the 'figure' of Piers. The connection 'id est' supports this suggestion: when Christian exegetes made a connection between the Old and the New Testament, they characteristically joined the two with a shorthand method of simply using a form of the verb 'to be', normally 'is'; instead of saying 'figures forth', which would be more accurate, exegetes often made an equation – id est ('that is') (in the way 'i.e.' is still used as a shorthand to join ideas which are in some way equivalents). This exegetical habit can also be seen already in St Paul, who says, with regard to the water-giving rock struck by Moses in the desert, that 'that Rock was Christ' (I Cor. 10.4).

Not only does this last citation from Paul demonstrate the grammatical point about the connective used to join the Old and New Testament ideas, but its Latin form ('petra autem erat Christus') also provides a suggestive source for the allegoresis 'Petrus, id est, Christus'. Piers, it could be argued, represents an Old Testament figure in the world of Langland's own poem (as indeed he seems to in his helplessness before the Devil in the inner-dream), and it is through the figure of Piers that Will will find Christ. This seems to be in Will's own mind as he wakes from the inner-dream – he is in an Old Testament landscape (as is made clear in the first meeting), and it is Piers whom he seeks (XVI. 167–71).

Will does not meet Piers, but an Old Testament figure, Abraham. Or that is what Will calls him; in the actual naming scene, however, it is clear that Abraham stands for more than his historical self. Will asks the figure whence he comes, and where he is going, to which he replies:

> 'I am Feith,' quod that freke, 'it falleth noght me to lye,
> And of Abrahames hous an heraud of armes.
> I seke after a segge that I seigh ones,
> A ful bold bacheler – I knew hym by his blasen.'
>
> (XVI. 176–9)

freke: man; *falleth*: befits; *heraud*: herald; *segge*: man; *bacheler*: young knight.

The 'ful bold bacheler' after whom Abraham seeks is clearly Christ: the image of Christ as a knight who will joust against the Devil has been established in the inner-dream (XVI. 95), and will be the controlling image of the narrative up to the end of Passus XVIII. Abraham is not only looking for the knight Christ, but actively announcing him: a herald of arms is one who announces an imminent joust (cf. Chaucer's *Knight's Tale*, 2533). These images are intelligible in the light of the theory of figural allegory I have just described: the Old Testament figure seeks out and announces the New Testament, and thereby his historical reality (while not questioned) is transformed: he becomes Faith. Langland is not original in making the allegoresis Abraham *id est* Faith, and in fact he gives us the clue to one seminal text behind the association of Abraham with the model life under the Old Law: he says that he met Abraham on a mid-Lenten Sunday (l. 172). Each Sunday of the Church Year has a particular range of biblical texts designated to be read; one category of text is the Epistle, drawn from the letters of the New Testament. The epistle for Mid-Lent Sunday (the fourth Sunday in Lent) is Galatians 4.22–31, the text I cited earlier, in which the son of Abraham born of a free woman is interpreted as the 'child of promise', or as Christians being born from the New Covenant. In the preceding chapter of Galatians, Paul declares that 'those who have faith are the children of Abraham' (Gal. 3.7).

This Pauline allegorisation of the children of Abraham as the

'children of promise', or Christians, also allows us to understand
the figural force of Abraham's statements that God

> . . . bihighte to me and to myn issue bothe
> Lond and lordshipe and lif withouten ende,
>
> (XVI. 239–40)

where the 'issue' of Abraham should be understood figuratively
as all Christians (cf. e.g. Gal. 3.29). For the moment though,
Abraham cannot claim the heritage promised to him by God; in
his historical being he is under the constraints of the strict justice
of Truthe, and the encounter with Abraham ends with this
emphasis on his legal powerlessness. Will asks Abraham what he
has in his lap (an image developed from Luke 16.23). Describing the
souls there, Abraham says that it is a 'precious present'.

> '. . . ac the pouke it hath attached,
> And me therwith,' quod that wye, 'may no wed us quyte,
> Ne no buryn be oure borgh, ne brynge us fram his daunger;
> Out of the poukes pondfold no maynprise may us fecche
> Til he come that I carpe of: Crist is his name
> That shal delivere us som day out of the develes power,
> And bettre wed for us [wa]ge than we ben alle worthi'.
>
> (XVI. 261–7)

Here the idea of Old Testament justice is given very specific
anchoring in the legal language of fourteenth-century England:
Abraham and his Old Testament souls are 'attached', meaning
'under arrest' (MED sense 1(b); Alford *GLD*), in the 'daunger',
or 'possession' of the Devil (MED s.v. 1(a) and (c)); no 'maynprise' or 'wed' can release them, where both these terms refer to
the idea of bail, a payment which allows a prisoner to be
provisionally released from prison (cf. the legal terms used in
Passus IV. 87–90, and 179 and my earlier discussion, pp. 58–9);
Abraham prophesies that Christ will Himself offer this bail, that
He will 'wage' – i.e. stand as a guarantee (Alford *GLD*; cf.
punning use of this term IV. 96–100), or 'borgh' – a surety
(cf. IV. 89) (MED sense 2a(a); Alford *GLD*).

In I Corinthians 13.13 Paul says that three things abide: 'faith,
hope, charity, these three; but the greatest of these is charity'. The
first figure Will meets in his search for charity is Faith; it is clear
that Langland is working within the Pauline scheme of virtues

(known as the theological virtues), since the next figure he meets is Hope. Like Abraham/Faith, this virtue, too, has a historical, Old Testament referent, and he, too, is described in terms of legal powerlessness. Hope describes himself as a 'spie' (a scout, spying out territory before a battle (OED, 'spy', sense 2)), who is seeking a knight that gave him 'a maundement', or 'writ' on the mount of Sinai; the historical referent is clearly Moses, who marks the moment in Old Testament history when the Law from God is formally received (Exodus 31.18): a 'maundement' is 'a sealed writ, decree, directive' (Alford *GLD*); Moses's letter is an open letter (a 'letter patent'), and should be sealed. But from Moses's description of this law, it is clear that it is not yet fully operative, since when Will asks whether or not the letter is sealed, Moses/Hope replies in this way:

'Nay,' he seide, 'I seke hym that hath the seel to kepe –
And that is cros and Cristendom, and Crist theron to honge.
And whan it is asseled so, I woot wel the sothe –
That Luciferis lordshipe laste shal no lenger!'

(XVII. 5–8)

So Moses's legal document, the Old Law, is not effective until it is sealed by Christ; until then, Moses, like Abraham, is in the Devil's 'daunger'. The image of the seal of 'cros and Cristendom, and Crist theron to honge' is striking, since it momentarily fulfils the idea of a legal seal, which normally hung from the document; the recognition that this 'hanging' is of Christ on the cross takes the reader by surprise, though, since it overbears the idea of a paper document altogether, in the way the New Law overbears the legalism of the Old. And the 'law' itself which Moses bears on his 'patente, a pece of hard roche' (l. 10), itself expresses a Christian interpretation of the Old Law, since the words Will is privileged to see are not literally the Mosaic Law, but instead a summary of the words of Christ when asked to define the most important commandment of the law: '*Dilige Deum et proximum tuum*' ('Love God and thy neighbour'), with their attendant gloss: '*In hiis duobus mandatis tota lex pendet et prophete*' ('in these two commandments hang all the law and the prophets' (Matt. 22.36–40; cf. Luke 10.27). This, according to Christ, is the essence of the Old Law (and thus can stand for the Old Law on Moses's rock), yet in so far as it also surpasses the legalism of Mosaic Law through love, it is not effective until Christ comes to seal it.

Faith, Hope, and Charity: this is the cluster of concepts shaping this series of encounters, and we necessarily expect now to meet Charity, or Christ, the 'knight' whom Faith and Hope are seeking to release them. Instead of a direct encounter with Christ, as we might expect, Will suddenly finds himself participating in a version of the Parable of the Good Samaritan. This parable in Luke is recounted by Jesus in a meeting with a 'doctor of the law': the doctor says that to inherit eternal life you must love God and your neighbour ('*proximum tuum*'); Jesus agrees, but the doctor goes on to ask 'who is my neighbour?' (Luke 10.25–29), at which point Jesus tells the parable. So the parable, in its Gospel context, answers to Moses's 'maundement': 'Love God and thy neighbour'. It is true that the Samaritan is not an Old Testament figure, but the parable was, nevertheless, traditionally interpreted as an allegory for the impotence of the Old Law to help the man wounded (with sin) as opposed to the power of the New Law of Love, where the Samaritan represents Christ. The parable is given this interpretation traditionally, and we find it, for example, in a Lollard sermon; the priest and the Levite are interpreted as 'patriarkys bothe byfore the lawe and in the tyme that God yaf lawe', and as 'prophetys and othur seyntys that weren bynethe the furste seyntis' respectively; the Samaritan, 'that was Iesu' (Hudson 1983, 273).[17]

All figural allegory plays with the idea of equations which are not, in fact, wholly equations: 'the Old Testament figure, *id est* Christ', where the 'i.e.' really means something like 'stands for and calls forth the future' Christ. The Old Testament figure is, and is not Christ – he will only become Christ in time. It is this play of near equivalents which Langland creates in his poem: the Samaritan is, but is not Christ. He will only become Christ in the time of the poem, as it were, since Langland shows the Samaritan acting like Christ, but at the same time moving towards Jerusalem to witness Christ (unlike, incidentally, the parable Samaritan, who is coming from Jerusalem).

The Samaritan acts like Christ in the way he pauses to help, and to cure the wounded man, sending him to '*Lex Christi*, a graunge' (l. 73), whereas Faith and Hope play the parts of the

17. See St Jacques (1969), for associations of Abraham with the priest of the parable, made by liturgical commentators (Gal. 3.16–22 was the epistle for Trinity Sunday, when Luke 10.23–9 was the Gospel text).

priest and the Levite (Moses was, in fact, the first of the tribe of Levi), who avoid the wounded traveller. In his gloss on his actions, the Samaritan apparently identifies himself with Christ; with regard to the brigand who attacked the traveller, he says that

> . . . he seigh me that am Samaritan suwen Feith and his felawe
> On my capul that highte *Caro* – of mankynde I took it –
> He was unhardy, that harlot, and hidde hym *in Inferno*.
>
> (XVII. 108–10)
>
> *suwen*: follow; *capul*: horse; *caro*: flesh.

But it is clear that temporally the Samaritan is on the verge of, but still waiting for, the Christian dispensation; he goes immediately on to prophesy:

> Ac er this day thre daies, I dar undertaken
> That he worth fettred, that feloun, faste with cheynes,
> And nevere eft greve gome that gooth this ilke gate:
> O Mors ero mors tua &c.
>
> (XVII. 111–13a)
>
> *worth*: will be; *gome*: man; *ilke gate*: same way; *O Mors . . ..* O death, I will be thy death.

And in his account of why Faith and Hope failed, the Samaritan uses a deliberately obscure language about the Christian sacraments of baptism, penance, and the Eucharist; the language defamiliarises these common ideas by offering a pre-Christian account of them, evoking a strange, even barbaric rite of the kind found in romances of the period.[18] He says that Faith and Hope should be excused, since no medicine can help the man wounded with sin,

> Withouten the blood of a barn born of a mayde.
> And be he bathed in that blood, baptised as it were,
> And thanne plastred with penaunce and passion of that baby,
> He sholde stonde and steppe – ac stalworthe worth he nevere
> Til he have eten al the barn and his blood ydronke.
>
> (XVII. 95–9)
>
> *stalworthe*: sturdy; *barn*: child.

In Passus XVI–XVII, then, Langland elaborates the action of the inner-dream, by having Will experience the historical move-

---

18. For example, *Amis and Amiloun*, ed. Leach (1937), ll. 2197–208. This scene operates in similar ways, since the healing blood of the murdered children has sacramental resonances which emerge later.

ment from the Old to the New Testament, from the Old Law
to the law of charity. In previous visions Will had argued the
question of justice from an intellectual and moral point of view;
here the real force of that central question is recovered from a
historical point of view, as Will observes the impotence of good
men of the Old Law before the rights of the Devil. Langland
capitalises on a habit of biblical interpretation (figural allegory) to
create a dynamic representation of biblical history in his own
poem. And in so doing, we can see how differently the Bible is
being 'read' in this part of the poem: Holy Church, for example,
uses biblical texts in Passus I as illustrations of didactic moral
points; Will uses them in the third vision as counters in an intellectual, theological argument; Patience, in the fourth vision, uses
especially Gospel texts in an inspiring, paradoxical way; and here,
in the fifth vision, biblical time itself informs the narrative, as Old
Testament figures are seen from a New Testament perspective,
standing for and calling forth the Christian epoch of charity. The
Bible is now being 'read' by Will, as it were, in an inward,
sophisticated and dynamic way.

In this kind of reading we can see, in fact, a progression characteristic of medieval education. In programmes of biblical reading,
we read that students, having mastered the secular arts which aid
biblical reading (as Will does under Study in Passus X), move on
to study of the Bible. Whereas the literal, historical study of the
Bible is for beginners, such schemes posit the allegorical reading
as to be undertaken by advanced students. And in allegorical
understanding, students proceed according to a different order of
reading: whereas they should read according to the order of
history in literal study of the biblical text, they should follow
what Hugh of St Victor calls the 'order of cognition' in allegorical
reading. That is to say that allegorical reading should proceed
from those things which are more clearly known (i.e. the New
Testament) to those which are more obscure (i.e. the figures of
the Old Testament). This is the way Hugh puts it:

. . . thus the New Testament, in which the manifest truth is declared,
is in this [allegorical] reading to be placed before the Old, where the
same truth is announced, mysteriously adumbrated in figures. The
same truth is in both, but there [in the Old Testament] hidden, here [in
the New] manifest; there promised, here achieved (*Didascalicon*, VI. vi)
(Taylor 1961).

This (despite being what would have been a conservative scheme of theological instruction in Langland's period) is, it seems to me, the basic educational scheme in which Langland's figural allegory can be located. So the passage from the Old to the New Testament in the poem is not only historical and moral, but also educational and psychological, following as it does the 'order of cognition'. Will seeks out Christ not only 'figuratyfly' (C. XVI. 294), but also, as he says about himself, 'as myself in a mirour' (XV. 162).

Themes of Passus XVI–XVII: The Trinity

In this discussion of charity in the fifth vision, we have so far considered the narrative genre of Passus XVII (from the end of the inner-dream) to the end of Passus XVII. Of course this genre, like any genre, has inherent thematic force. But I would like to conclude the discussion of charity by turning briefly to the explicit theme of the encounters between Will and Faith, Hope and the Samaritan. By Faith, Will is instructed in the doctrine of the Trinity (XVI. 181–246) (surely a matter of faith); by Hope, with the doctrine of 'Love God and thy neighbour' (XVII. 9–20) (appropriate to Hope, who leads 'forth with love' (XVII. 119)). Will wants to know which of these doctrines to believe (XVII. 25–48; 126–32), and the Samaritan answers his questions (XVII. 133–295).

These are clearly not simple questions, and belong to the upper reaches of theological instruction. With regard to the first, the Trinity, Anima himself begins his satire on the Church by criticising friars and 'maistres' who

> . . . moeven materes unmesurable to tellen of the Trinite,
> That oftetymes the lewed peple of hir bileve doute.
>
> (XV. 71–2)
>
> *moeven*: raise; *unmesurable*: too difficult; *that*: such that; *lewed*: ignorant.

And as regards the second, the doctrine of loving one's neighbour, Will recognises that this involves the idea of loving one's enemy, of loving 'as wel lorels as lele' (XVII. 46). It is precisely this notion of loving one's enemy that Study had said was characteristic of Theology, and was what made Theology unintelligible to her as the mistress of lower, secular disciplines (X. 182–206).

The doctrine of the Trinity, as expounded in Passus XVI. 181–246, seems to me, quite frankly, 'unmesurable' to Abraham (or perhaps, in this case, to Langland). Abraham is given this speech about the Trinity not only because the doctrine is a matter of faith, but also because the historical Abraham's meeting with three angels, as recounted in Genesis 18.1–15, was interpreted by Christian exegetes as a meeting with the three persons of the Trinity. Abraham's speech about the doctrinal aspects of the Trinity falls basically into three parts: (i) a definition of the Trinity (ll. 181–90); (ii) a description of the Trinity's action in history (ll. 191–201); and (iii) a comparison of the Trinity with the three grades of the Tree of Charity – marriage, widowhood and virginity (ll. 202–24). Part (i) (ll. 181–90) is clear enough. Part (ii) (ll. 191–201) seems confused, since the 'issue', or 'children of charity', which spring from the Church, are described as 'Patriarkes and prophetes and apostles', whereas the mother (Holy Church) is described as 'Christ and Cristendom and alle Cristene' (l. 199). The apparent inconsistencies here (e.g. Old Testament figures being children of Christ) might be resolved by recourse to Paul's allegorical interpretation of Abraham's two wives, one representing the Old, the other the New Alliance (Gal. 4.22–31, the epistle for the 'mid-Lenten Sunday' on which Will meets Abraham). According to Paul's interpretation, Christians, 'like Issac' (Gal. 4.28), are the 'children of promise'. According to this reading, then, Old Testament figures, like Christians, can be seen as 'children' of the New Alliance. But part (iii) of this speech (the comparison of the Trinity with the three grades of the Tree of Charity) seems plainly confused. In the development of the analogy Abraham likens the Father to the creative state of matrimony; the Son (suggestively) to the widow; but when he comes to the Spirit, he likens it to a child, thus switching to an altogether different trinitarian analogy suggested (but rejected) by Augustine, according to which the Trinity may be likened to a man, his wife and their offspring, three persons but all sharing a common humanity (Schmidt 1987a, 347). This is simply inconsistent; despite many examples of inadequacy by different speakers in the poem, I do not find any of straightforward confusion of this kind, and therefore put the confusion at Langland's door. It may be significant that the analogy with the grades on the Tree of Charity is omitted from the C-Text (C. XVIII. 199–239).

The images the Samaritan uses to give some idea of the Trinity are, on the contrary, clear and illuminating. The Samaritan's task is to answer Will's question about what he should believe – Faith's doctrine about the Trinity, or (what seems less acceptable to Will!) Hope's doctrine about loving one's enemies. The Samaritan opens by saying that Will should believe both (ll. 133–6); in the body of his answer, the Samaritan focuses on the Trinity, by giving the notion human sense through two extended images; ultimately, however, it is clear that the discussion of the Trinity is also a discussion of loving one's enemies, and that the one subject (charity) is inseparable from the other (the Trinity).

The two images through which the Samaritan gives human sense to the notion of the Trinity are those of a hand and a wax taper. Both images are worked towards the same end, as providing examples of tripartite structures (fist, fingers, palm; wax, wick, flame) which are nevertheless unified and interrelated in their operation. Different ideas grow from these images (e.g. the creative power of the hand), but the Samaritan focuses particularly on their moral implications, where hurting the palm (the Spirit) incapacitates the whole hand, and 'blowing' with 'unkyndenesse' entirely quenches the flame of the Spirit. The candle image is used not only for its negative force, of quenching the flame, but also for its positive moral force, where the glowing of the wick will not 'gynne to glowe and to blase', until 'lele love ligge on hym and blowe' (ll. 225–7). When this happens, the 'might' of the Trinity (i.e. God's justice) melts into mercy, just as, says the Samaritan, icicles melt through the sun's heat 'in a mynut while to myst and to watre' (ll. 230–1).

CONCLUSION

This focus on the 'blowing' of mercy, which itself produces God's mercy, clearly brings the question of the Trinity into direct relation with the question of loving one's neighbours. As such, it also brings the Samaritan back to the central ideas to which the poem has been moving in the fourth and fifth visions – that 'the Fader [will] foryyve folk of mylde hertes/That rufully repenten and restitucion make' (ll. 237–8). I began this chapter by citing the confident affirmations made by the Samaritan concerning this central question, and by asking what was new about them in the context of the fifth vision. We are now in a position to answer this in summary form: Anima, embodying the whole soul, treats two questions in this vision – the Church on the one hand, and charity on the other. His treatment of the Church answers to Haukyn's state, betrayed as he is by the institution of the Church. Anima (as an embodiment of the reasoning, judging aspect of the soul) engages in a far-reaching satire of the institution as a whole, calling for its reformation. As an embodiment of the deepest, and most religious aspect of the soul – 'lele love', Anima also introduces Will to the theme of charity. This theme is treated from a historical, a moral and a psychological perspective from Passus XVI to the end of Passus XVII. At the end of the vision, then, Langland is ready to develop these two themes – those of charity and the Church. In Passus XVIII he brings the theme of charity to its intellectual and emotional fulfilment; in the last two passus, he returns to the reformation of the institution of the Church.

Chapter 7

Visions Six, Seven, and Eight: Passus XVIII–XX

PASSUS XVIII: Will falls asleep in Lent; his vision begins on Palm Sunday, as *Christ* (as yet unnamed), comes riding into Jerusalem, hailed by Faith (ll. 1–17a). Faith explains to Will that Christ will fight against Death, disguised in the arms of Piers Plowman (ll. 18–35a). Will witnesses the events leading immediately up to the crucifixion, and the crucifixion itself (ll. 36–70); he also witnesses the 'duel' of Christ and *Longinus* (ll. 71–91). Faith declares the victory of Christ, and the future loss of liberty for the Jews (ll. 92–109a). Will descends to Hell, and now witnesses a meeting between two sisters *Mercy* and *Truth*, who argue about whether or not men can be released from Hell; their argument is carried on by *Peace* and *Righteousness* (ll. 110–228). *Book* (the Bible) prophesies the resurrection of Christ and the releasing of Christ's 'kin' from Hell (ll. 229–59). Christ comes to the gates of Hell and commands the Devil to open them; the devils debate whether or not Christ has a right to mankind (ll. 260–314a); Christ breaks down the gates of Hell with His breath, and catches up those whom He loves; He illumines the basis in law by which He releases mankind (ll. 315–409a). Peace and Truth, Mercy and Righteousness embrace in celebration (ll. 410–25a). Will is woken by Easter bells, and calls his wife and daughter to come to church (ll. 426–34).

PASSUS XIX: Will writes what he has dreamed, and goes to church, where he falls asleep (ll. 1–5). He has a vision of Piers, who comes before the congregation, looking like

the wounded Christ (ll. 6–8). Will asks Conscience about
the identity of this figure Piers/Christ; Conscience
explains that it is Christ, who comes in the arms of Piers;
this provokes Will to ask why Jesus is called Christ;
Conscience answers this by defining Christ's role as
knight, king and conqueror. This discussion involves
Conscience in a recounting of the life of Christ, including
the resurrection and the delegation of power to Piers
(ll. 9–199). Will now witnesses a Pentecostal scene, where
the Holy Spirit descends on Piers and his companions,
distributing the gifts of grace (here different occupational
crafts) to them; these gifts include a plough for Piers to
sow the Word of God, and the Barn of Holy Church, or
Unity, in which to store the spiritual harvest (ll. 200–336).
As soon as Piers begins to plough, *Pride* and his followers
attack, in response to which Conscience advises Christians to withdraw into the Barn, where they should rule
themselves in penitential justice and obedience to the
cardinal virtues (ll. 337–93). There is opposition to
Conscience's advice about the Cardinal Virtues from a
brewer, and a speech by a *Vicar* about the difficulty of
finding anyone who practises these virtues (ll. 394–461).
The passus ends with a lord and a king exploiting the
virtues of Prudence, Fortitude and Justice to their own
ends, and the departure of the Vicar (ll. 462–85).

PASSUS XX: Will wanders in an unhappy mood, until he
meets *Need*; Need argues that Will should take what he
needs for his survival, and praises the state of indigence
(ll. 1–50). Will falls asleep, and dreams that he sees the
coming of Antichrist, who is followed by friars
(ll. 51–73). Conscience counsels the 'fools' of Christ to
retreat into the Barn of Unity and await the vengeance
of *Kynde* (ll. 74–9). Kynde attacks with pestilence
(ll. 80–105), until Conscience prays Kynde to cease his
attack; but the respite serves to restore the energies of
Fortune and her followers, who prepare to attack
Conscience (ll. 106–13). Lechery and Covetousness
attack, followed by Life, Pride, and Sloth, the offspring
of Life and Fortune (ll. 114–64). Conscience calls on Old

Age, who frightens Life, and assails Will himself
(ll. 165–98). Will asks Kynde how he might be avenged
on Old Age, and is advised to retreat into the Barn of
Unity, and to leave all other crafts except the craft of love
(ll. 199–211). Will retreats into the barn, which is under
heavy attack; Conscience calls on Clergy to save him, and
in response the friars offer their services; at first
Conscience rejects their offer, but ultimately allows them
to enter, on condition that they have suitable physical
provision, that they leave the study of logic, and that they
do not multiply uncontrollably (ll. 212–72). The friars,
under the instructions of Envy, do precisely what they
have been forbidden to do by Conscience, while the
attack on Holy Church continues (ll. 273–304). Conscience
calls the doctor Confession to cure the wounded through
penitence, but Contrition calls for a gentler doctor, *Friar
Flatterer*; at first Conscience refuses entry, but then re-
lents; Friar Flatterer gains entry, and causes Contrition to
stop being contrite (ll. 305–73). The attack on Holy
Church is renewed, but Contrition is unable to offer any
defence; Conscience declares that he will become a pilgrim, to seek Piers Plowman. The poem ends with Conscience calling for grace, and Will waking (ll. 374–87).

INTRODUCTION

As we have seen, the fifth vision is primarily concerned to understand the basis of God's mercy by searching out the source of
charity in the soul. For Langland, however, the idea of charity
is not only psychological and moral, but also historical. It is for
this reason that Will moves through Old Testament time in his
search for charity, meeting Abraham, Moses, and the *figura* of the
Samaritan. We also observed that for Langland the question of
charity is inseparable from institutional questions concerning the
Church: whereas the loving aspect of the integrated soul, Anima,
is concerned with charity as the source of the self, the reasoning,
judging part of Anima is concerned with the institution, the
Church, from which individual charity springs – since, as he says,
'holynesse and honeste out of Holy Chirche spredeth' (XV. 92).
    These topics controlled the subject matter and discourses of the

fifth vision: whereas Anima, through ecclesiology, attacked the Church in Passus XV, in Passus XVI and XVII Langland exploits a typological allegory in Will's movement through Old Testament time towards Christ. The same themes govern the remaining three visions of the poem: here Will's inner movement towards an understanding of charity culminates in his vision of Christ in the sixth vision (Passus XVIII), whereas the last two visions of the poem (Passus XIX and XX) treat a reformed, renewed Church.

In these last three visions, we can, moreover, see the connections developed between the inner idea of charity and the outer idea of the Church as an institution: it is precisely the victory of Christ's charity that allows for the establishment of the Church as an institution. And beyond this, we can see how the victorious Christ's delegation of power to the renewed Church answers to what I have described as the poem's central problematic, concerning the possibility of salvation in the face of God's 'truthe', or justice. For in Passus XIX Conscience describes the power Christ delegated to Piers to grant men pardon; after this act, Conscience says about Christ that

> Anoon after an heigh up into hevene
> He wente, and wonyeth there, and wol come at the laste,
> And rewarde hym right wel that *reddit quod debet* –
> Paieth parfitly, as pure truthe wolde.
> And what persone paieth it nought, punysshen he thenketh,
> And demen hem at domesday, bothe quyke and dede –
> The goode to the Godhede and to greet joye,
> And wikkede to wonye in wo withouten ende.
>   (XIX. 192–9)
> *wonyeth*: dwells; *reddit quod debet*: pays what he owes (i.e. 'makes satisfaction');
> *demen*; judge; *domesday*: judgement day; *quyke*: the living.

Superficially, this description of Christ as judge sounds exactly like the judgemental picture of God given both by Holy Church in Passus I (ll. 128–33) and by the Pardon in Passus VII. The last two lines cited here, for example, recall the austere wording of the pardon itself: (translated by the priest) '"Do wel . . . and God shal have thi soule",/ And "Do yvel . . . and hope thow noon oother/ That after thi deeth day the devel shal have thi soule!"' (VII. 112–14). The resemblance, however, provokes us to recognise that there is an essential difference in the definition of justice,

or 'truthe' here. Whereas the 'pardon' of Passus VII was sent from
an absolute 'Truthe', here in Passus XIX Christ is said to promise
salvation to those who 'pay perfectly'; here there is an allowance
made for those who fail to meet the standards of absolute 'truthe',
but who nevertheless repay, through repentance, the 'debts' they
have incurred through sin. So 'pure truthe' here is not absolute,
in so far as it allows for failure, and is prepared to forgive men,
'in covenaunt that thei come and kneweliche to paye' (l. 187) –
absolute truth has, that is, been tempered by a provisional pact;
it is only at the end of time that absolute 'truthe' will reassert
itself, to 'demen . . . bothe quyke and dede' (l. 197).

As I understand the poem, this is its central theological affirmation, and one that Will has been moving towards since his
point of conversion in the inner-dream of Passus XI. But how is
it possible for Langland to affirm that 'pure truthe' should be
prepared to forgive, even if only provisionally? Certainly the
poem often stresses the possibility of God's mercy from its
turning point of Passus XI, but Langland has not yet clarified how
mercy is possible without violating 'truthe'. These two profound
qualities, justice and charity, are almost inevitably at odds with
each other, as Langland shows with complete clarity in Passus IV,
where the King refuses to pardon Mede mercifully, since to do
so would be to perpetuate injustice. So far, that is, it is not clear
how the powerful can be charitable without at the same time
being unjust. This is the root question which needs to be
answered before the nature of God's pardon can be understood,
and it is, in fact, the question which the action of Christ in Passus
XVIII is designed to resolve. Once it has been resolved, then the
way is clear for renewed sense of what the Church's function is:
if forgiveness is possible, then an institution is necessary to
dispense it; and it is this topic which Langland broaches in the last
two visions, in his imaginative and daring representation of a
renewed, apostolic Church.

THE SIXTH VISION: PASSUS XVIII

In the inner-dream of Passus XVI, Christ is born into the poem,
as it were, as 'a justices sone', who must fight to possess the
fruit of Piers – he 'sholde . . . juste therfore, bi juggement of armes'
(XVI. 92–6). The pun on 'justices'/'juste' here suggests an iden-

tification of knightly action (i.e. jousting) with just action (Quilligan 1978, 103–4). In Passus XVIII this pun generates the basic narrative images and generic frame of the action, since Christ is consistently pictured as a knight acting in the manner of a romance hero, who at the same time is acting in accordance with justice. Langland takes two scriptural sources, the account of the crucifixion in the canonical gospels, and the apocryphal *Gospel of Nicodemus*, and sets them into the context of his own poem and his own period by making Christ a medieval knight, who fights to recover the fruit of the peasant Piers. In fact there are two fights in the passus, one a 'joust' with the knight Longinus while Christ is on the Cross, and the other a legal debate with the Devil in Hell. The first of these fights serves to define the new sovereignty which will be enjoyed by the Church, the second to define the precise basis in divine law on which that spiritual sovereignty will be based. I will consider the first fight on the Cross before looking at the legal debate with the Devil.

Christ as Noble Jouster

Throughout the later medieval period there were basically two doctrines of the Atonement (the doctrine according to which Christ's crucifixion achieves an 'at-one-ment' between God and man, after the separation caused by original sin). In the early Middle Ages, up to the eleventh century, the dominant theory was that the Devil had rights to man through man's original sin, but forfeited those rights when he unjustly laid claim to Christ (who tricked the Devil through his disguise as a man). In the eleventh century Anselm of Canterbury (1033–1109) developed a new theory, in his tract *Cur Deus Homo* (*Why [did] God [become] Man?*); according to Anselm's doctrine, man had fallen further than he was himself able to make reparations for; God could have simply forgiven man through His power, but as a way of demonstrating His love for mankind, and as a way of satisfying the demands of justice, He became a man Himself, satisfying God through the crucifixion (Southern 1963, Ch. 3).

These two doctrines had profound implications for cultural and artistic history: in the first theory ('the Devil's rights' theory), the main litigants are the Devil and Christ, since Christ is coming to satisfy law pertaining between God and the Devil over possession of mankind; Christ in this scheme is presented artistically as a victorious king meeting the Devil's rights. In Anselm's theory (the 'satisfaction' theory), the main legal actants are instead man and God, since it is God *qua* man who is satisfying God's justice. The Devil here is a mere gaoler, with no rights of legal possession. Christ is accordingly represented artistically as a suffering human. It is from springs such as this theory that the larger movement of late medieval popular piety, with its affective stress on the wounded Christ, derives.

The 'satisfaction' theory is the dominant theory in the later Middle Ages; given its accent on Christ's love for man, one literary tradition which develops from it is that of Christ the lover knight, who comes to free His lady (i.e. the soul), despite her unfaithfulness to Him. In the sequence which leads up to the joust on the Cross in Passus XVIII, Langland draws on some features of this tradition; there is no evocation of the soul as an unfaithful lady, but Langland does foreground the pathetic elements of Christ as a suffering knight.[1]

When Christ first appears in Passus XVIII, He both fulfils and paradoxically inverts the image of the victorious knight by which He has been heralded in the fifth vision:

> Oon semblable to the Samaritan, and somdeel to Piers the
>   Plowman,
> Barefoot on an asse bak bootles cam prikye,
> Withouten spores other spere; spakliche he loked,
> As is the kynde of a knyght that cometh to be dubbed,
> To geten hym gilte spores on galoches ycouped.
>   (XVIII. 10–14)
>
> *semblable*: similar; *somdeel*: somewhat; *prikye*: riding; *spores*: spurs; *spakliche*:
> lively; *kynde*: nature; *galoches ycouped*: slashed shoes.

Some aspects of this description conform to the idea of Christ as a young knight: He comes for His first adventure, in which He will be rewarded both with the order of knighthood and its accoutrements, such as the new knight's spurs. Other aspects of the description are at odds with this image of the aristocratic, knightly figure on the verge of his first victory, however: Christ is seen through the lens of the humble, patient 'figures' that have

---

1. See Waldron (1986) for a review and balanced account of scholarship on the topos of the Christ-knight.

preceded Him in the time of the poem, the Samaritan and the peasant Piers. He is not riding a horse, as we would expect a knight to do, but (following the Bible) an ass (Matt.21); and when we reflect on the spurs and 'galoches ycouped', we realise that they refer to the nails of the Cross, and to Christ's slashed feet.

Like many romance heroes, Christ comes to the fight disguised. But the disguises He bears seem to preclude His victory, since they expose rather than protect Him. He comes bearing the 'armes' not of a noble, but of a peasant (where 'armes' might mean both heraldic and military arms): Faith explains to Will that

> . . . Jesus of his gentries wol juste in Piers armes,
> In his helm and in his haubergeon – *humana natura*.
> That Crist be noght biknowe here for *consummatus Deus*,
> In Piers paltok the Plowman this prikiere shal ryde;
> For no dynt shal hym dere as *in deitate Patris*.
>
> (XVIII. 22–6)

> *gentries*: nobility; *haubergeon*: coat of mail; *humana natura*: human nature; *biknowe*: acknowledged; *consummatus Deus*: perfect God; *paltok*: under tunic; *prikiere*: horseman; *dynt*: blow; *dere*: injure; *in deitate Patris*: in the divinity of the Father.

The weapons that Christ bears are, then, paradoxically no weapons; instead of a literal knightly coat of mail ('haubergeon') or its under tunic ('paltok'), Christ wears the 'coat' of the flesh.

So the initial picture of Christ here is a pathetic, moving one of Christ's exposed humanity, in keeping with the 'satisfaction' theory of the Atonement. But whereas many works which exploit this image of the noble, suffering knight Christ do no more than evoke pathos through it, Langland exploits the image for its doctrinal and institutional implications.

The pathos is in part achieved through the social force of the images: like some romance heroes (e.g. Malory's Gareth), the knightly, noble Christ comes disguised as a peasant. But the full, doctrinal force of these paradoxical inversions is made clear after the first fight of the passus, that of Christ with the knight Longinus from line 78. Only the blind Longinus dares to touch Christ (Langland is following a legend which developed from John 19.34 (Peebles 1911)), and this act is pictured as a joust between the 'blynde bacheler' and the knight Christ. Longinus is cured of his blindness by the blood from Christ's pierced side, in response to which he acknowledges his defeat as a 'recreaunt knyght', in the manner of romance combatants (though in acknowledging himself to be 'recreaunt', he is, of course, acknowledging that he is 'creaunt', or faithful (Fr. *creant*, believing)). This victory immediately suggests the idea of '*Patientes vincunt.*' ('the patient/suffering are victorious') which has been associated with charity in the poem from Passus XIII forwards. But more generally, the image of the knightly Christ, victorious in His disguise as a peasant, is taken by Langland to signal a new spiritual order, and a new hierarchy of spiritual nobility. Faith addresses the Jews after Christ's victorious joust on the Cross against Longinus by declaring that their spiritual lordship has now ended:

> And youre fraunchyse, that fre was, fallen is in thraldom,
> And ye, cherles, and youre children, cheve shulle ye nevere,
> Ne have lordshipe in londe, ne no lond tilye . . .
>
> (XVIII. 103–5)
>
> *fraunchyse*: freedom; *thraldom*: servitude; *cherles*: bondmen; *cheve*: prosper.

Faith is recalling the biblical text with which Abraham was first associated – Galatians 4.21–31, in which Paul describes Christians as the children of the free woman Sarah, or the New Covenant. By implication, the Jews lose the spiritual nobility and freedom they had enjoyed until the crucifixion of Christ, and with it the 'londe and lordship and lif withouten ende' promised to the 'issue' of Abraham (XVI. 239–40) (Simpson 1985, 475).[2] By coming disguised in the 'paltok' of the peasant Piers, the noble Christ has ennobled all humans who acknowledged Him, and conversely left in thrall those who do not. This view of the Jews did, in fact, correspond to the status of Jews in England (before their expulsion in 1290), where they were regarded as 'serfs of the King's chamber' (Roth 1941, 96).

So in this first joust, Langland draws on some of the topoi derived from the 'satisfaction' theory of the Atonement, but he exploits them not so much for their pathetic force, but rather for their institutional implications – through Christ's 'patient' victory Christendom is established as the domain of the (spiritually) free and noble.

---

2. It should also be mentioned that Langland is working within a common icon-ographical scheme here, whereby the Synagogue is represented as blind-folded and losing sovereignty, as opposed to Ecclesia, who gains sovereignty at the moment of the crucifixion (Mâle 1961, 188–90).

Christ as Kingly Justice

In so far as Christ is represented as suffering, we can say that
Langland exploits some of the topoi derived from the 'satisfaction'
theory in the first encounter of the passus; in Christ's second
encounter, with the Devil, He comes instead as a king: as He is
about to enter Hell, Christ addresses the lords of Hell in this way:

> Prynces of this place, unpynneth and unlouketh!
> For here cometh with crowne that kyng is of glorie.
>
> (XVIII. 263–4)[3]
>
> *unlouketh*: unlock.

These lines suggest rather the 'Devil's rights' theory of the Atonement, in so far as Christ is represented as a king, and Christ
acknowledges the devils as figures of power ('princes') rather than
as mere gaolers. The very fact that Christ should be represented
in Hell confronting the Devil implies the 'Devil's rights' theory,
since according to this theory the Atonement is essentially a legal
settlement between God and the Devil.

And when Lucifer first speaks, it is clear that Langland is
working within this doctrinal tradition; Lucifer's first position is
one of legal assurance – he recognises that Christ cannot be
beaten, but insists that if Christ were to liberate souls from the
prison of Hell, then He would be acting out of pure force, against
the letter of the law, according to which the Devil has rights to
sinful man:

> If he reve me of my right, he robbeth me by maistrie;
> For by right and by reson the renkes that ben here
> Body and soule beth myne, bothe goode and ille.
> For hymself seide, that sire is of hevene,
> That if Adam ete the appul, alle sholde deye.
>
> (XVIII. 276–80)
>
> *reve me*: deprive me; *maistrie*: sheer force; *renkes*: men; *beth*: are.

Clearly, issues central to the whole poem are being raised here,
since, according to Lucifer's argument, Christ could not act out
of charity towards imprisoned mankind unless He were to break
the law. According to this persuasive argument, mankind is
permanently and inescapably bound in prison.

---

3. For a discussion of Langland's Christ and contemporary legal practice, see
   Baldwin (1981a, Ch. 4; 1981b).

Lucifer's argument is not without real force. This is proven by the fact that a figure called 'Truthe' agrees. Christ's legal battle with the Devil is framed by an exchange between four female figures, paired as Mercy and Truth, Peace and Righteousness. These figures, found in other literary works of the period (Traver 1907), personify a biblical citation from Psalm 84.11, 'Mercy and truth are met together; righteousness and peace have kissed each other'. When they first meet, however, they are not in harmony as the citation would suggest, but rather in total disagreement. Mercy and Truth appear from l. 113; whereas Mercy declares that 'man shal fro merknesse be drawe' (l. 136), Truth dismisses this as nonsense; uncontentiously, she declares that she as 'truthe' knows 'the sothe': 'For that is ones in helle, out cometh it nevere' (l. 148). As we have seen, 'Truthe' is the fundamental standard of God's justice, which, in the pardon of Passus VII, unconditionally damns men who fail to meet its standards; here the figure Truth clearly takes up the same uncompromising position. Not only this, but she is supported by her companion and semantic cognate 'Rightwisnesse', who is said to have existed first (l. 165); Righteousness uses legal formulae to insist against Peace that mankind shall be perpetually damned: 'I, Rightwisnesse, recorde thus with Truthe/ That hir peyne be perpetuel and no preiere hem helpe' (ll. 198–9).

Lucifer's case, then, that his claim to mankind is a just one, seems to be sustained by these figures of rational, legal authority. Langland certainly gives the 'Devil's rights' theory of the Atonement a strong case in this way, and thereby insists on the legal constraints within which the Atonement must take place. But in fact the theory of the 'Devil's rights' is refuted: even before Christ has actually entered Hell, Satan (as distinct from Lucifer (Pearsall 1978, 331)) questions Lucifer's claim that he holds mankind by right. Whereas Lucifer says that he is 'iseised' of mankind, using a legal term which denotes full legal possession (MED sense 2a (a), and 2b; Alford GLD), Satan argues instead that this 'seisin' is inoperative, since Lucifer tricked Eve through treason – 'it is noght graithly geten, ther gile is the roote!' (l. 291). And when Christ does come in triumph, His triumph is essentially a legal one, not one of sheer strength, nor of pure guile (Baldwin 1981a, Ch. 4). He, too, argues that Lucifer has gained possession of mankind through guileful treason, and that He, Christ, has simply

repaid him in kind according to the 'tooth for a tooth' principle
of the Old Law:

> Thow, Lucifer, in liknesse of a luther addere
> Getest bi gile tho that God lovede;
> And I, in liknesse of a leode, that Lord am of hevene,
> Graciousliche thi gile have quyt – go gile ayein gile!
>
> (XVIII. 355–8)
>
> *luther*: evil; *leode*: human; *quyt*: repaid.

So in this respect, it is clear that Langland is not himself
promoting the 'Devil's rights' theory, since Christ proves that
Lucifer does not have legal possession of mankind; he does, nevertheless, shape his narrative around this theory, precisely as a way
of refuting it, and as a way of insisting on the legal aspect of the
Atonement. But if Christ Himself refutes this theory, then how
can it be that Truth and Righteousness support it? Does Christ
disagree with these figures of apparently unimpeachable authority? No: just because the Devil does not have a 'trewe title'
(l. 293) does not necessarily mean that mankind will be released
from Hell, or that man does not deserve to be there. It simply
means that the Devil's status is reduced from owner to that of
gaoler. Once Christ has proved Lucifer's treason against Himself,
it remains true that mankind's sin against God must be repaid.
It is for this reason that Truth and Righteousness insisted that
mankind would not, and could not be released from Hell.

So even if Christ proves that Lucifer has infringed the law and
thereby lost his rights, it remains equally true that mankind has
also infringed God's law. If man is to be released from the prison
of Hell by Christ's charity, then this must be done without at the
same time breaking the law of Truthe. It is at this point that Langland has recourse to the 'satisfaction' theory of the Atonement,
whereby Christ pays the price, that mankind is unable to, for
original sin. Earlier in Passus XVI Abraham had prophesied that
Christ would offer Himself as a 'maynprise', or bail for mankind,
'and bettre wed for us [wa]ge than we ben alle worthi'
(XVI. 267). It is true that the idea of ransom does feature in the
'Devil's rights' theory, but Christ cannot be ransoming mankind
from the Devil here, since He has already proved that the Devil
does not own mankind. If Christ offers Himself as a 'maynprise',
this is to satisfy God's justice, not the Devil's. This is the 'satis-

faction' theory, and it is precisely this idea that Christ invokes when he first addresses the Devil:

> . . . Lo! here my soule to amendes
> For alle synfulle soules, to save tho that ben worthi.
> Myne thei ben and of me – I may the bet hem cleyme.
>
> (XVIII. 328–30)

The fact, then, that the souls of men belong to Christ merely improves Christ's claim; the essential legal act here is of redemption (Latin *re-emere*, 'to buy back'); Christ has made 'amendes' to God for man's sin against God; as such God's law is not infringed, but fulfilled through Christ's act of charity. Christ has not released man unconditionally – He has instead offered a bail, a temporary release from prison; man can only make this permanent by himself attempting to pay God back for sins whose debt he is able to pay.

Truth and Righteousness are wrong, then, but not about the past; why they are unable to see forward to Christ's act of mercy which at once transcends and fulfils the law is because they represent, as we have seen in Chapter 4, essentially rational principles which are unable to see beyond reason to the way in which an irrational love can satisfy and transcend reason. It is only at the end of the vision that the citation from the Psalms is enacted – Truth and Righteousness embrace Mercy and Peace:

> 'Trewes!' quod Truthe; 'thow tellest us sooth, by Jesus!
> Clippe we in covenaunt, and ech of us kisse oother,'
>
> (XVIII. 418–19)
>
> *trewes*: truce; *clippe*: let us embrace.

where the homophony on 'truce' and 'truthe' reveals the redefinition of 'truthe' as a more flexible, non–absolute kind of judgement – a 'sooth, by Jesus', as it were.

THE SEVENTH VISION: PASSUS XIX

In Passus XVIII, then, the central theoretical problem of the poem has been solved. In the inner-dream of Passus XI, Will had had an inkling of the solution to the problem of Dowel – he had realised the possibility of God's willingness to enter freely into a convenant with man, whereby man would be given a provisional chance to repay God for debts of sin into which he inevitably falls.

This initial perception is developed in psychological, moral, and finally historical terms in the following passus, right up to Passus XVIII, where Will perceives the legal and historical basis of God's covenant, established in Christ's debate with the Devil. Once this fundamental legal question has been solved, then the poem can turn its attention to the institution, the Church, which must 'capitalise' on God's redemption, by dispensing the sacraments, especially that of penance. This is, in fact, the subject of the following two passus, Visions Seven and Eight, and the subject to which I shall now turn. Before I look directly to those passus, it is necessary, however, to say something about Langland's use of biblical texts and the liturgy in the last four visions of the poem.

Will's Biblical 'Reading' and the Liturgy

As I argued in the last chapter, it is clear that Will enters into a new relationship with scriptural texts from the fifth vision forwards. Under the influence of what I described as Patience's 'New Testament poetics' in the fourth vision, Will returns to the Old Testament in the fifth vision, and sees it from a New Testament perspective, 'reading' Old Testament figures as dynamically pointing forward to the New Dispensation.

In Passus XVIII Will moves forward in biblical time (and in the order of the Bible), when the poem draws its source material from Gospel (both canonical and apocryphal) accounts of the crucifixion and the Harrowing of Hell. The distinction between Will experiencing these events and his 'reading' them is difficult to establish; at XVIII. 397a Will cites the Pauline text that a man 'heard unspeakable words, which it is not lawful for a man to utter' (2 Cor. 12.4). This refers to Paul's description of his own vision of heaven, his 'visions and revelations of the Lord' (2 Cor. 12.1), but whereas Paul uses the third person about himself – 'audivit' ('he heard') – Will uses the first person 'audivi' ('I heard'); this is a daring appropriation of a scriptural text, where Will implicitly identifies himself with St Paul,[4] and certainly claims

---

4. There are interesting comparisons to be made with Chaucer's *House of Fame* here. Chaucer's 'Geffrey' also implicitly compares himself to Paul (l. 981), but declines a journey to the heavens, it being beyond his powers to sustain the experience. He also declines to describe Hell in Book I, referring the reader to Virgil, Claudian and Dante (ll. 447–50).

personal experience of these events. But the source material of his visions is nevertheless textual; Will seems himself to point to the balance between seeing and reading as he descends to Hell: 'And there I saugh soothly, *secundum scripturas* [according to the Scriptures] . . .', he says (l. 112).

And in the seventh and eighth visions, the movement through biblical time and scriptural order continues: the seventh vision (Passus XIX) draws especially on the Acts of the Apostles and the Pauline Epistles to describe the apostolic life in its ideal form, whereas the last vision (Passus XX) presents a vision of the approaching end of time, in the apocalyptic coming of Antichrist. The sources for this passus are (as I shall argue later) especially the New Testament references to the signs of the last days, rather than the Book of Revelations itself (the last book of the Bible), but the poem can nevertheless be said to imitate biblical time, and the model of scriptural order in these visions also.

This more intimate experience of the scriptural text suggests that Will has moved into a much more individual relationship with Scripture than was implied in, for example, his first meeting with Holy Church, where the institution of the Church used scriptural texts for their dogmatic and moralising potential. This is certainly true, but it should nevertheless be noticed that Will's experience of the scriptural text is still mediated by the institution of the Church, through its liturgy (i.e. its forms of worship, including the biblical texts appointed to be read on given days of worship). Will first meets Abraham in Passus XVI on a 'myd-Lenten Sonday' (l. 172); this reference to a date in the Church Year begins a movement which carries right through to the vision of Pentecost in Passus XIX: at the beginning of Passus XVIII Will says that he slept 'til *ramis palmarum*' (Palm Sunday), and the events of that passus, and many of its Latin citations, are drawn from the liturgy of Palm Sunday leading through to Easter Sunday: the passus begins with Will saying that he dreamed of 'gerlis and of *Gloria, laus*' (l. 7) (an image drawn from the Palm Sunday liturgy, when children and the choir respond with '*Gloria laus*' to the verses chanted by the clergy and adults), and it ends with Will being woken by the bells of Easter morning (l. 428). And in Passus XIX, Will witnesses the coming of the Holy Spirit 'to Piers and to hise felawes' (l. 202). This is a representation of the coming of the Holy Spirit to Peter and the Apostles on the day of Pentecost as recounted in Acts 2.1–4, and as celebrated in the Christian liturgy on the feast of Pentecost, seven weeks after Easter. Will, with 'manye hundred', sings the hymn '*Veni Creator Spiritus*' ('Come Holy Ghost, Creator come'), which is a Pentecost vespers hymn.[5]

This liturgical frame to the action suggests that Will is implicitly acknowledging the fundamental institutional forms of the Church through which the events of Christian history are commemorated in an annual cycle. It is this form, in fact, which makes sense of Will both 'seeing' and 'reading' his visions, since it is through the liturgy that he can see and 're-present' ('make present again') the events of salvation history preserved in Scripture. Not only this, but the pattern of Will's waking moments here suggests that he is being drawn back into the institution. Will has been outside and wandering at the beginning of each vision up to and including the sixth, at Passus XVIII; the fourth and particularly the fifth visions are introduced by waking moments where Will is presented as an entirely marginal, almost crazed figure. At the end of the sixth vision, however, Will wakes into a domestic world of his wife and daughter (l. 429), and at the beginning of the seventh vision, he is pictured as participating in the ritual life of the Church:

> Thus I awaked and wroot what I hadde ydremed,
> And dighte me derely, and dide me to chirche,
> To here holly the masse and to be housled after.
>
> (XIX. 1–3)
>
> *dighte*: dressed; *derely*: well; *dide me*: took myself; *to be housled*: to receive Holy Communion.

In Passus XII Will had posited an apparent opposition between writing and going to church: if only someone would tell him what Dowel was, he would stop writing, and go to church (XII. 25–8). Here, instead, Will's writing and church going seem to be part of a continuum. The image of Will going off to church suggests an acquiescent figure, accepting the institution of the Church in the way in which he had in Passus I, even if from a more inward understanding of what that acceptance means. This

---

5. For a critical review of scholarship on Langland's use of liturgical texts, see Adams (1976).

might be true of Will, but Langland's purposes are larger than to plot Will's development; Langland, it seems to me, is concerned to examine the institutions which nourish the individual, and his attitude towards the Church in these last two passus is anything but acquiescent. Langland's own writing as a poet is not about to be absorbed into, and enclosed by a vision of a reintegrated Church. It is instead the motive of these last two passus radically to reform Church and society, through both passionate utopianism and satire. It is to this renewed vision of the Church, as presented in the seventh vision (Passus XIX), that I should now like to turn.

The apostolic Church and its crafts

Langland identifies Piers and his 'felawes' with the first Apostles to whom the Holy Ghost descended at the first Pentecost after the crucifixion; this suggests that Langland is concerned to recover the primal quality of the institution of the Church, though transposed to the contemporary Christendom of Piers Plowman. This is true, but, as we shall see, Langland also attempts to reimagine the whole of society as springing from, and contributing to, this renewed Church. Before this apostolic society is imagined, however, Conscience first defines the divine political order on which it is based. I shall briefly discuss this before turning to the way in which the apostolic ethos is imagined.

As we have seen in the discussion of Passus XVIII, Christ is pictured as a knightly, and eventually as a kingly conqueror, and Langland draws on the topoi of aristocratic romance in his presentation of Christ as a jouster. In Passus XIX these images are given a kind of exegesis from within the poem itself. Will has a vision of the transformed Eucharist, which he sees as a bloody Piers, but 'right lik in alle lymes to Oure Lord Jesu' (l. 8); Conscience tells him that Will sees the 'armes' of Piers, but that the figure itself is 'Crist with his cros, conquerour of Cristene' (l. 14). At this point another naming sequence occurs – Will wants to know why Conscience calls Jesus 'Christ', as opposed to 'Jesus'. Conscience replies by elaborating the idea of Christ as a noble warrior, both knight and king, whose crowning achievement is victory; to be called knight is 'fair', and to be called king 'fairer',

Ac to be conquerour called, that cometh of special grace,
And of hardynesse of herte and of hendenesse –
To make lordes of laddes, of lond that he wynneth,
And fre men foule thralles, that folwen noght hise lawes.

(XIX. 30–3)

hardynesse: courage; *hendenesse*: courtesy; *laddes*: men of low birth.

For Conscience the name 'Christ' means 'conquerour' (l. 62), and
it is on this aspect of His name that Conscience wants to focus.
Just as Faith had declared the new hierarchy of spiritual nobility
and thralldom after the 'joust' with Longinus, so too here does
Conscience focus on the new institutional order which the Atonement brings in its train. After the victory of Christ, Christians
become 'frankeleyns', and 'gentil men with Jesu', as opposed to
the Jews, who become 'lowe cherles' (ll. 34–41). Christ is
pictured, in fact, as operating in the way fourteenth-century kings
were expected to, and did act in war. In Passus III Mede had
presented the standard military practice whereby conquering
kings ennobled their commanders (Simpson 1985, 473); if the king
had fought in France and not accepted a treaty,

He sholde have be lord of that lond in lengthe and in brede,
And also kyng of that kith his kyn for to helpe –
The leeste brol of his blood a barones piere!

(III. 203–5)

brol: brat.

Whereas Mede's king is pictured as ennobling his earthly kin,
Christ ennobles His spiritual kin, who acknowledge Him as their
king.

In his account of the life of Christ (ll. 69–199), Conscience
focuses on the movement from Christ's personal name 'Jesus' to
His naming as 'Christ', or conqueror, at the resurrection (l. 152).
What clearly interests Conscience is the new 'political' order
established by Christ in His status as victor over the territory of
man's spirit. What Conscience sees as Christ's best act, or
'Dobest', . is not even the resurrection, but rather the act of
granting Piers power to pardon men for their sins – not the
victory itself, so much as the order which flows from it:

And whan this dede was doon, Dobest he [thou]ghte,
And yaf Piers power, and pardon he grauntede:
To alle maner men, mercy and foryifnesse;

[To] hym, myghte men to assoille of alle manere synnes,
In covenaunt that thei come and kneweliche to paye
To Piers pardon the Plowman – *Redde quod debes.*

(XIX. 183–8)

assoille: absolve; *to paye*: satisfactorily; *redde quod debes*: repay what you owe.

This description of the delegation of power under the new political order established by Christ's victory has startling implications when set into the context of the poem. In the Prologue, it was said that 'the Kyng and Knyghthod and Clergie' decided that the Commons should arrange for the production of food; the Commons, in turn, devise 'craftes' from their natural understanding, and 'for profit of al the peple plowmen ordeyned' (ll. 116–19). This standard and strictly hierarchical arrangement is transformed in Passus VI on Piers's half acre, where it is the humble Piers who leads the ploughing, and directs the knight. But even there, Piers remains a ploughman, and also accepts his social inferiority to the knight, in asking the knight to protect both himself and the Church (VI. 24–8). In Passus XIX, these relationships change dramatically: Piers is still called a ploughman, but he has become a pope; the knight and king Christ directly delegates power to the ploughman Piers to become the Head of the Church on Earth. Piers is said to have power to 'bynde and unbynde bothe here and ellis' (l. 190). This is a reference to Christ's delegation of power to the Apostle Peter in the Gospels: '. . . thou art Peter, and upon this rock I will build my church . . . And I will give unto thee the keys of the kingdom of heaven: and whatsoever thou shalt bind on earth shall be bound in heaven: and whatsoever thou shalt loose on earth shall be loosed in heaven' (Matt. 16.18–19). In the Latin of verse 18, Christ's words to Peter create a pun, which reveals the full sense of the name 'Piers': '*Tu es Petrus, et super hanc petram aedificabo ecclesiam meam*'. The medieval Church saw this as the basis of papal power; here Langland takes it up and applies it to a ploughman. So instead of Piers working for knighthood and the Church, Langland revitalises these feudal relationships by making Piers the head of the Church, working for the king Christ.

So the very foundation of the Church as it is imagined by Langland poses a radical rebuke to the hierarchy of the contemporary Church, given that its head is an unclerical figure of a ploughman.

Piers is seen to be more truly a pope than, for example, the papal figure of avarice as described by Anima in Passus XV, who

> . . . hath the keyes now and kepeth for his kynnesmen
> And for his seketoures and his servaunts, and som for
>   hir children.
>
> (XV. 247–8)
>
> *seketoures*: executors.

And it is from this moment in the poem, when the bases of Piers's power have been defined, that Langland daringly imagines a renewed apostolic Church, and, along with it, a renewed society of work, or 'craft', by connecting Piers with the Apostle Peter in the narrative of the poem. The Holy Spirit descends on Piers and his 'felawes', endowing them with the gift of tongues. And Langland pictures the Holy Spirit (or Grace) dividing the gifts of grace, drawing in part from St Paul's description of the different gifts of grace given by the Spirit to those charged with the apostolic mission of evangelisation (I Cor. 12.1–11). Grace promises to give 'tresor,/ And wepne to fighte with' (ll. 226–7), at which point he distributes different crafts among Christians. Most immediately Langland is representing (and transforming) a contemporary military practice here, according to which victorious military commanders distributed the spoils of war after the victory (Simpson 1985, 473); just as 'valiant conquerors that be past and goon departed largely theyre conquests and proyes to theyre men of armes' (according to a contemporary manual of chivalry) (Byles 1932, 77), so too does the Holy Spirit distribute the gifts, or grace of Christ's military victory to Christ's followers. At the same time, the division of these gifts is based on a biblical model, the 'division of gifts' described by St Paul in the first letter to the Corinthians. But whereas St Paul is concerned to describe the gifts of evangelisation (i.e. wisdom, knowledge, faith, healing, miracles, prophecy, the gift of languages and so on (I Cor. 12.8–10)), Langland's Grace extends this range of gifts by distributing the 'craftes' of a whole society; his gifts are clerical, commercial, manual, martial, and contemplative skills (ll. 230–52).

Langland, then, returns to the locus of the field, on which societies have been established in both the Prologue and in Passus

VI already. After the failure of the ploughing in Passus VI, and after the rejection of earthly food by Patience for the Active Man Haukyn, the poem finally returns to the agricultural space of the field, and reimagines the 'craftes' of labour as the product of an apostolic spirit, springing from the newly formed Church. Labour, or works, can now find a place in the scheme of salvation, since Christ has instituted an order in which salvation does not depend wholly on grace; instead, to achieve salvation, Christians must 'do well' through both works and through penance. And once labour can find a place in the economy of salvation, so too can Langland reimagine the social relations through which that labour is performed.

In this new society, relationships are modelled hierarchically, but the spirit which informs the crafts deflates any hierarchical or coercive force which might normally pertain to a feudal structure. Grace asks the commonwealth of crafts to let Conscience be their king, and Craft their steward; Piers is to be the 'procuratour and . . . reve,/ And registrer to receyve *redde quod debes*' (ll. 260–1). In this manorial hierarchy, however, individual conscience is the guiding principle, and the spirit which informs it is brotherly rather than coercive. For Christ not only establishes new political relationships through His kingship, but He also, through the incarnation and crucifixion, establishes new familial relationships. The fullest expression to this idea is given much earlier in the poem, by Trajan in Passus XI. Trajan says that it is better that some be rich and some poor in society,

> For alle are we Cristes creatures, and of his cofres riche,
> And bretheren as of oo blood, as wel beggeres as erles.
> For at Calvarie of Cristes blood Cristendom gan sprynge,
> And blody bretheren we bicome there, of o body ywonne . . .

(XI. 198–201)

In Passus XIX, when Grace has finished his distribution, he acknowledges that some 'craftes' are more attractive than others, but that the division has been arbitrary, and that the resultant structure is brotherly:

> 'Though some be clenner than some, ye se wel,' quod Grace,
> 'That he that useth the faireste craft, to the fouleste I kouthe have
>   put hym.

Thynketh [that alle craftes,' quod Grace], 'cometh of my yifte;
Loketh that noon lakke oother, but loveth alle as bretheren.'

(XIX. 253–6)

clenner: more refined; *useth*: practises; *lakke*: find fault with.

It is true that Piers is a spiritual ploughman here, preparing to
work with his team of the evangelists, whose ploughing is
harrowed by patristic interpretations of the Bible (ll. 264–75a).
And the 'hous' that he builds with Grace's help is designed to
store spiritual harvest, built as it is with the body of Christ, and
modelled as it is from St Paul's description of the 'edifying of the
body of Christ' (Ephesians 4.12) – the 'hous' is called 'Unite –
Holy Chirche on Englissh' (l. 330) (cf. Ephesians 4.3). But the
fruits of this ploughing are not purely spiritual, and Langland is
not turning his back on the fundamental questions of social hierarchy and labour that he had confronted in Passus VI. We have
already seen that the crafts distributed by Grace equip some of
their recipients for action in the world (including the skill 'to tilie,
to dyche and to thecche' (l. 239)); but beyond this we might
notice that the seeds sown by Piers are those of the cardinal
virtues (Prudence, Temperance, Fortitude, and Justice) – those
virtues which inform practical action. Prudence, for example,
teaches men who intend to watch over a pot to buy a long ladle,
if they want to 'save the fatte above' (ll. 281–2)! In representing
Piers sowing the seeds of the cardinal 'vertues', Langland is
punning on the biological sense of 'vertue', as the 'life-giving
power of a plant' (cf. l. 152), but the fruit of these 'virtuous'
seeds is practical action informed by knowledge of the Scriptures.

In considering Langland's reimagination of the society of the
field, we might also be able to see how his vision of society has
changed in profound ways from the society of the Prologue, or
of Passus VI. Given the emphasis on brotherly relations in the
division of 'craftes', we could see Langland's renewed vision of
society as modelled on urban, horizontal structures, despite the
manorial and hierarchical images which are also employed. The
word 'craft' in Middle English has a wide range of senses, many
of which are exploited by Langland. Sense 7, as listed by MED,
is 'an organization of craftsmen, a guild'. It is from this sense that
the word 'crafty' derives in, for example, III. 225: 'Alle kyn crafty
men craven mede for hir prentices'. Guilds were groupings of

merchants or artisans, designed to protect the interests of the group within the town or city; they also served as mutual and religious societies, with the emphasis on horizontal ties of loyalty ('brotherhede' and 'fraternite' are frequently used as synonyms for 'guild', or 'craft'). Trade guilds had existed from at least the twelfth century, but there is no real evidence of collective action by guilds before the end of the thirteenth century.[6] Langland's representation of a brotherly, harmonious world of 'craftes' may be answering to tensions between guilds in London at the time the B-Text was being written. Merchant guilds sought to restrain the power of artisanal trades in London, as in other cities and towns of late medieval England; the merchants had been successful in excluding industrial guilds, until 1381 to 1383, when a man from outside this group, John of Northampton, was elected mayor. He pursued a policy of keeping the price of food down, and of excluding merchants from power. His idealistic reforms met with powerful opposition from both the merchants and the King, and he lost the election of 1383; in 1384 he was accused of fomenting rebellion and condemned to death. This was afterwards mitigated to life imprisonment, and in fact he was released in 1387 (Chambers and Daunt 1931, 18–22).[7] These events are of course just after the composition of the B-Text, but they are the product of long-standing tensions characteristic of London and provincial town centres throughout the fourteenth century, and the roots of this particular confrontation go as far back as 1364 (Thrupp 1948, 75–80). The 'craftes' distributed by Grace certainly include both commercial and artisanal skills: some are taught 'with sellynge and [by] buggynge hir bilyve to wynne' (l. 236), while others 'to compace craftily, and colours to make' (l. 242). Other occupations are also included, which do not technically constitute guilds (e.g. priests, ploughmen), but the bourgeois model of the 'crafte', or guild is invoked as a model of brotherly love; whereas the guilds

6. See Platt (1979) for craft guilds, and Chambers and Daunt (1931), section II for the articles of some London guilds.
7. For a contemporary account of the story concerning John of Northampton, see *The Westminster Chronicle*, eds. Hector and Harvey (1982, 58–64). It may be relevant to note that Thomas Usk, who seems to have been impressed by Langland's poem (Skeat 1897, 483), was one of the figures most intimately involved in the guild strife of the 1380s, changing sides and eventually suffering execution (Chambers and Daunt 1931, 20–2).

of Langland's London are in fierce rivalry, Grace commands that no 'crafte' 'lakke oother, but loveth alle as bretheren' (l. 256).

In summary, Langland seeks to address fundamental issues of spiritual life in the world through his representation of a renewed Church, which re-creates the conditions of the primitive apostolic Church. Langland's solution to the problems of active life in the world are radical: only through a completely reimagined Church, with an unclerical figure at its head, can the problems of spiritual life in the world be broached. Langland can now return to the world of labour in the world, and reimagines labour relations as brotherly and horizontal in spirit.

The basis of this reimagined society is Piers as pope. In arriving at this radical position, Langland resembles the contemporary dissident movement, the Lollards, in many respects. Like the Lollards, Langland's ecclesiology is modelled on that of the equality, humility, poverty, and evangelism of the first Apostles (Leff 1967, 527, 530). In, for example, a Lollard tract, *Epistola Sathanae ad Cleros (The Epistle of Satan to Clerics)*, the Lollard writer ironically speaks through the *persona* of Satan, saying that Christ deceived 'us' (i.e. Satan and clerics), by appearing as a man:

> For he lyved in great pouerte and penance withowt worldly lordschipe and worldly covrtlynes, and also chese to his apostles and disciples ryght poor men, and if any were riche he made them poore both in sperett and in worldly good. So he tawght them to lyve in mekenes and pouerte, and preastis and clarkis that wolde be his successouris and his disciples euermore aftur he tawght them to kepe that rule . . . And so long as Crist lyvyd amongst the Iues, he reprovyd the byschopis and the princis of preastis and the scribes and pharesies . . . for thei were all gyven to auaryce and to lordschipe'.[8]

And when the unclerical figure Piers is made pope, this parallels certain statements by Wyclif and his followers. Wyclif declared that only God could elect a pope, not the tradition of the Church, and that, given the mere outward show of the priesthood, whose power to absolve depended entirely on God anyway, the distinction between priest and layman was unimportant; even a layman could be pope, in Wyclif's view (Leff 1967, 520, 526, 531, 533, 580; Hudson 1988, 327–34). The radicalism both of Langland and

---

8. Cited from Hudson (1978, 89). Letter forms have been modernised.

Wyclif takes especial force also in the immediate context of the writing of the B-Text between 1377 and 1379, and of Wyclif's *De Potestate Pape*, written in 1379 or 1380, since from 1378 there were rival popes (one in Rome, the other in Avignon), who declared war on each other in 1379.

If Langland's position shares some striking similarities with Wycliffite polemic in the image of the apostolic Church, it should be observed, however, that his position is also seriously at odds with the theoretical bases of Wyclif's doctrines. For Wyclif, there were two Churches, that of the elect, and that of the damned; both of these were absolute categories, determined by God's predestination of souls. But in so far as they are absolute, divinely appointed categories, it is impossible to know who belongs to the elect, and who to the damned. This had profound consequences for the existing order of the visible Church, since there remained no reason to accept its authority, and, moreover, no saving function it could perform, since God had already decided who was and was not saved (Leff 1967, 516–45; Hudson 1988, 314–27). The value of the sacraments was thus drastically reduced. As we have seen, such a view is totally at odds with the whole thrust of Langland's poem, which develops a covenantal theory of salvation (in opposition to a doctrine of predestination), and which sees in Christ's victory the opportunity for mankind to be saved through the sacraments, and in particular through the sacrament of penance, whereby men are to repay Piers, on behalf of God, what they owe, '*redde quod debes*'. Langland's radicalism, then, can be described as a 'conservative' radicalism, as it were, since in representing Piers as pope, he is seeking not to minimise the saving role of the Church, but to preserve and to underline it. And the aim of the successive attacks on the field, and on the 'hous' of Unity itself, is especially to destroy the power of the sacrament of penance. It is to the first of these attacks that I shall now turn.

The Retreat into the Barn of Unity

The moment Piers sets his hand to the plough, the common-wealth of crafts, and the apostolic Church at its centre are under attack: 'Now is Piers to the plow. Pride it aspide . . .' (l. 337). From this moment until the end of the poem, the institutional achievements of Christ's victory are under attack, and finally undone. The utopian vision based especially on the Pauline Epistles now gives way to an apocalyptic satire, drawn in inspiration from the descriptions of the last days in the New Testament. The utopianism and the satire are not at odds: the first attempts to rebuke the present Church by offering an image of re-presented perfection; the second by satirical analysis of present weaknesses.

The ultimate goal of Pride's attack is the 'berne' of Unity itself, but the immediate target is to 'breke' and 'bite atwo the mores' of the cardinal virtues sown in Piers's field (ll. 337–53). At the first onset of Pride, Conscience advises Christians to abandon the field and to retreat into the church (ll. 358–62). Conscience seems to make the same move away from the world that Patience had exhorted Haukyn to make – to retreat from the world of work, and to rely on spiritual food. For, having retreated into 'Piers berne the Plowman', he declares that he is not worried if Pride should come, since there is food enough ('the breed yblessed' of the Eucharist) for all those who have 'laboured lelly al this Lenten tyme' (l. 387). But in fact Conscience has not entirely abandoned the world of practical action, and of cardinal virtues, as this retreat might suggest. For he says that Christians can eat the 'breed yblessed' of the Eucharist, on condition that they have paid Piers 'redde quod debes' (l. 393). This repayment is taken to mean more than repayment through penitence to God here, and to include the idea of paying to each man what is due to him, or acting according to the virtue of Justice. For when a brewer refuses to be ruled by justice, Conscience rebukes him in this way:

> But thow lyve by loore of *Spiritus Iusticie*,
> The chief seed that Piers sew, ysaved worstow nevere.
>
> (XIX. 408–9)
>
> *worstow*: will you be.

To eat the bread of the Eucharist, then, requires that the spirit of justice (including, but broader than the justice of penance by which God is paid back) be observed.

But even if Conscience is still committed to the world of practical action through his commitment to the cardinal virtue of justice, Langland presents a world in which that commitment is undermined by ambiguities in the very definition of practical virtues. A 'lewed vicory' erupts into the action at this point

(l. 412), who sardonically declares that he has never seen any cardinal, unless one who came from the pope (l. 416); he delivers an extraordinarily direct attack on the pope,[9] and ends by pointing to the slipperiness in the very meaning of words denoting the cardinal virtues: prudence, for example, 'among the peple is gyle' (l. 458), by which he points to the semantic blurring of words denoting prudent foresight on the one hand, and worldly shrewdness on the other.[10] His speech is followed by a series of figures who enact the vicory's point: they knowingly corrupt the meaning of these virtues, by practising unjust action which bears a superficial similarity to, and is legitimated by, the cardinal virtues (ll. 462–79).

THE EIGHTH VISION: PASSUS XX

In a moving and comic moment in Passus XX, when Will himself has been rudely assaulted by Old Age, he turns to the figure Kynde (i.e. Nature, though with divine associations given Christ's 'blood brothership' with man), and asks to be avenged. Kynde counsels Will that to be avenged on Old Age, Will must go to the Barn of Unity, and hold himself there until he is fetched by Kynde. This suggests that the Christ-like nature of Kynde will provide a 'vengeance' against the onslaught of physical 'kynde'. But Kynde's advice goes further than this, and has implications for Will's activity in the world: Will should learn some 'craft' in

9. Views about Langland's view of the 'lewed vicory' differ: Adams (1978) sees him as perverting prudence 'through obfuscation', like the king who perverts justice, and the lord who perverts fortitude (p. 278); 'the vicar not only denounces guile, he exemplifies it, mixing half-truths with plain falsehood, and with advice repudiated by the rest of the poem' (n. 6, p. 278). This seems to me to misread the logic of the passage: the vicar denounces the way in which all the cardinal virtues are perverted, using prudence as an example (ll. 454–61). There follow two figures, the lord and the king, who knowingly pervert three of the cardinal virtues, i.e. intellect (an alternative for prudence), fortitude, and justice. At the beginning of Passus XX, Need shows how the fourth virtue, temperance, can be manipulated. As I see it, the whole speech of the vicory (ll. 412–61) is the voice of educated (he is clearly not literally 'lewed'), marginal satire, projected from a position not unlike what we may assume to be Langland's own position, and responding in ways not unlike Langland, even if he states his criticisms more explicitly. For a nuanced argument, see Schmidt (1987b, 119–22).
10. See Carruthers (1973, 157–73) for an account of the way in which language is generally subverted in the last two visions.

the barn, and in response to Will's question about what craft he should learn, the following encounter takes place:

'Lerne to love,' quod Kynde, 'and leef alle othere.'
'How shal I come to catel so, to clothe me and to feede?'
'And thow love lelly, lakke shal thee nevere
Weede ne worldly mete, while thi lif lasteth.'

(XX. 208–11)

catel: property; lelly: faithfully; mete: food.

Kynde's advice is uncompromising with regard to material realities: if Will learns the craft of love, then all other crafts, by which he might clothe and feed himself, will be rendered unnecessary – they should simply be ignored. Whereas Grace had established a commonwealth of actual, practical 'craftes' in Passus XIX, here Kynde transforms those practical activities into the craft of love, thus illuminating the learnt and skilful quality of love ('the craft so long to lerne', as Chaucer says in a different context),[11] while at the same time dismissing all worldly crafts. In so far as Kynde does dismiss worldly crafts, we might see this moment as a repetition of two other moments in the poem, when Piers rejects the field for the 'ploughing' of prayer in Passus VII, and when Patience offers Haukyn the essential 'liflode' of the word of God, which Haukyn is to eat when he is hungry or cold (Passus XIV). In all three instances active life in the world is rejected for a spiritual work or food.

The notion of poverty, then, is very close to the heart of Langland's concept of the apostolic Church, and one to which, as we have seen, he frequently recurs. Even if the commonwealth of crafts around the Barn of Unity fails, the essence of Unity can be preserved through the practice of the craft of love, at the expense of all other crafts. At the same time, it is clear that the fact of poverty without any means is at the source of the corruption of the Church as Langland sees it: for if Langland sees the essential role of the Church as being to administer the sacrament of penance, then he will see anything which threatens that sacrament as the greatest threat to the Church; and it is because friars have no means which causes them to threaten the sacrament of penance by 'selling' absolution, and by selling it cheaply. The point about the friars is put in Passus XX, by the figure of Need:

11. Parliament of Foules, l. 1.

And for thei are povere, paraventure, for patrymoyne hem failleth,
Thei wol flatere, to fare wel, folk that ben riche.

. . .

For lomere he lyeth, that liflode moot begge,
Than he that laboureth for liflode and leneth it beggeres.

(XX. 234–9)

paraventure: perhaps; *lomere*: oftener; *liflode*: sustenance; *moot*: must; *leneth*:
gives.

Near the centre, then, of Langland's poem, there is an unresolved
problem about the nature of poverty. The apostolic Church has
been established in Passus XIX, but if it is to succeed, it must be
poor, like the first Apostles, but at the same time not betray the
sacrament of penance through its indigence. It is unsurprising,
then, that Will should meet the figure Need at the beginning of
Passus XX, since the problem is 'staring him in the face', as it
were.[12] The problem of Need is treated in a theoretical way in
this waking episode, before it is set into an historical, apocalyptic
frame in the body of the passus.

Need

There are four cardinal virtues: Prudence, Fortitude, Justice, and
Temperance. The first three of these are exploited as a cover for
injustice at the end of Passus XIX: a lord says that he is prepared
to take from his tenant whatever his accountants tell him to, since
the accounts were made up with the spirit of Understanding (or
Prudence), and the rents will be collected by the spirit of Fortitude. This combination of corrupt accounting and brute force,
going under the name of intelligence and courage, is followed by
the declaration of a tyrannical king, who says that since he is the
law, then what he decides thus constitutes law (XIX. 468–79).
The spirit of Justice here becomes a cover for what is in fact an
unjust and tyrannical kingship.

It is only at the beginning of the next passus, and the next
vision, that the fourth of the cardinal virtues, Temperance, is
considered. Here Need, in a waking episode, accosts a hungry
Will, by encouraging him just to take what he needs to eat:

---

12. Two recent studies in particular outline the crisis faced by Franciscan ideal-
    isations of poverty in Langland's time: Aers (1983) and Pearsall (1988).

Coudestow noght excuse thee, as dide the kyng and othere –
That thow toke to thy bilyve, to clothes and to sustenaunce,
Was by techynge and by tellynge of *Spiritus Temperancie*,
And that thow nome na moore than nede thee taughte,
And nede ne hath no lawe, ne nevere shal falle in dette . . .

(XX. 6–10)[13]

that: (saying that) what; *bilyve*: livelihood; *nome*: took.

He goes on from here to argue that Temperance is superior to the
other virtues, and that Christ Himself 'was wilfulliche nedy'
(ll. 23–50). Need's first argument, cited here, might seem to
answer the problem of poverty at a stroke, since it plausibly
argues that man has a right to the necessities of life, and that the
poor man is released from the constraints of law in this respect:
stealing is no crime when starvation is the alternative. It is not
only plausible on moral grounds, but also on the basis of authorities from within the poem: Need's argument seems very close
to what Holy Church had said in Passus I, when she declared that
God had ordered the earth to help men 'Of wollene, of lynnen,
of liflode *at nede*/ In mesurable manere . . .' (l. 18–19) [my
italics]. Beyond this, Need's arguments seem to give a theoretical
support to those renunciations of worldly activity which punc-
tuate the poem.

On the other hand, the context of Need's speech might make
us wary: we should remember that his argument about
Temperance follows the deliberate misuse of the other three
cardinal virtues at the end of Passus XIX. Whereas the
powerful can manipulate intelligence, courage and justice, the
poor, and Will in particular, are being encouraged to manipulate
temperance; Need signals the connection – he encourages Will
to excuse himself, 'as dide the kyng and othere'. And we might
also be wary about Need's (proverbial) argument that 'need has
no law'. The central problematic of the entire poem has been
the inescapability of the law; in keeping with this, Conscience
describes the cardinal virtue of Justice as 'the chief seed that

13. Adams (1978), makes the point about Need's discussion of the fourth of the
cardinal virtues. I do not myself find his argument about the particular
exegetical source (Job 41.13 and its glosses) of the figure Need convincing.
The relation of Need in an apocalyptic context can be much more simply
explained by reference to standard, widely known anti-mendicant treatises
(which include, it should be said, the text from Proverbs (30.8–9), which is
also brought to light by Adams in the same article).

Piers sew', and insists that salvation is impossible without observance of justice (XIX. 408–9). In a poem so profoundly concerned with the need for the law to be met, the authority of Conscience's declaration cannot be underestimated. Need, on the contrary, makes a different hierarchy of the virtues: he says that there is 'no vertue bi fer to *Spiritus Temperancie*', neither Justice nor Courage (ll. 23–4). This is consistent with what he says about need having no law – if that is true, then justice is necessarily secondary. Whereas Christ's charity satisfied the law, Need would argue that the needy can simply ignore the law – Need will take the needy theif 'under maynprise', where Need exploits the legal term to point to its irrelevance (l. 17).

The argument is not taken any further here, and it is clearly a matter of great intellectual tension for Langland. It is also a matter of great institutional import, for the one apostolic movement which Langland sees in action around him, the friars, do uphold begging, or mendicancy. And it is precisely their lack of a fixed income which, in Langland's eyes, induces them to sell the sacrament of penance. It is to this historical, contemporary treatment of the problem that Langland now turns, in the body of the eighth vision.

The Attack on the Barn of Unity

In Passus XIX the attack on Unity had been made by the ahistorical figures of Pride and his followers; in Passus XX the attack is anchored in both history and contemporary reality in so far as the assailants are now Antichrist and his main followers, the friars. The attack of Antichrist is described from line 52, and the friars are the first mentioned among his followers (l. 58). The satire draws on specifically anti-fraternal currents of apocalyptic satire, but before we can understand this discourse, and why Langland should practise it here at the end of his poem, it is first necessary to understand something about apocalyptic traditions, and about how and why the friars became associated with the signs of the end of time.[14]

What traditions lie behind the figure of Antichrist? Unlike some world religions, Christianity is an intensely historical religion,

14. See Bloomfield (1962) for apocalyptic traditions relevant to *Piers Plowman*.

dividing as it does world history from creation to the end of time into distinct phases, with different possibilities for salvation. Whereas Langland has been concerned to move from the time before the law (Abraham), to the period of the law (Moses), to the period of the New Law (Christ) in Visions Five and Six, he moves to the present and the future in the seventh and eighth visions. And in the same way that the Bible itself ends with a vision of the end of time in the Book of Revelations, so too does Langland's poem. Both Old and New Testament texts conceived of this end as a terrible one, which would be heralded by the coming of the Devil in a deceptive shape, who would deceive and betray men through cunning, before the final end of time at the second coming of Christ and the last judgement (e.g. Dan. 9.27; Matt. 24; Mark 13; Luke 21; II Thess. 2.3–11; Rev. 20). In the Gospel of Luke, for example, Christ is asked what will be the signs of the last times, to which He begins to reply in this way: 'Take heed that ye be not deceived: for many shall come in my name, saying, I am Christ; and the time draweth near: go ye not therefore after them' (Luke 21.8). It is from scriptural texts such as these that the tradition of Antichrist developed (Emmerson 1981, Ch. 2).

This scriptural conception of the satanic deceiver is clearly behind Langland's presentation of the guileful Antichrist who appears in Passus XX. But why should Langland represent the friars as foremost among Antichrist's followers? The orders of friars (Franciscan, Dominican, Augustinian and Carmelite) were a relatively late medieval phenomenon; they developed out of, but in reaction against, burgeoning urban life. St Francis (c. 1182–1226), for example, was the son of a wealthy merchant from Assisi, but founded the order especially on ideals of apostolic poverty. He is said to have been inspired by hearing a passage from Christ's instructions to the Apostles concerning their comportment as evangelists (e.g. Luke 10.1–12); like the first Apostles, the Franciscans were to be sent forth in twos (as a pair appear at VIII. 8); they were, following Christ's words, not to carry money, nor bags, nor even sandals, and they were to be fed by whatever was given them in the houses where they were received. It is for this last reason that the friars were called 'mendicant' orders, from Latin *mendicare*, 'to beg'. The rapidity with which the mendicant orders spread throughout Latin Christendom suggests that they were clearly fulfilling a spiritual need which was not being met either by the regular clergy (monks and canons), or by the secular clergy – that clerical organisation based around the cathedral, with a bishop at its head.[15]

The impluse for the friars' institution as a movement, then, seems strangely close in spirit to the repeated movements in *Piers Plowman* to reject the world of practical concerns and to throw oneself on God's providence. Both are inspired by an ideal of apostolic poverty. This might make Langland's hostility to the friars puzzling, but it is comprehensible in the light of developments later in the thirteenth century. The friars aroused the hostility of the secular clergy, since they were taking over, or competing for, functions over which the secular clergy had previously enjoyed a monopoly. Friars were empowered both to preach and to dispense the sacrament of penance, and so could attract audiences which had previously been tended by the parish priest alone. One influential document expressing the hostility of the secular clergy to the friars is by a secular cleric, William of St Amour, *Concerning the Dangers of the Last Days* (1256), of which the basic polemical thrust is to associate the friars with the signs of the last times. In the light of some scriptural references to the last days, the very apostolic aims of the fraternal orders were turned against them; thus St Paul's warning against 'false apostles, deceitful workers, transforming themselves into the apostles of Christ' (II Cor. 11.13) became attached to the apocalyptic tradition, and was used as a way of making the friars appear like the precursors of Antichrist.[16]

This association of the friars with Antichrist was exploited by many fourteenth-century English anti-fraternal polemicists and satirists, especially by Bishop Richard Fitzralph in his tract *Defensio Curatorum* (*In Defence of Curates*) (1357) (Perry 1925), and, contemporary with Langland, by Wyclif and Lollard polemicists, who identify the pope with Antichrist. In the light of these anti-fraternal traditions, we can understand why Langland should

15. See Bolton (1983) for a general account of the fraternal movements, in the context of other reforming movements of the twelfth and early thirteenth centuries. See Bolton (1977) and Little (1978) for accounts of Franciscan poverty and its urban, mercantile context.

16. See Szittya (1977) for the exegetical traditions which associated the friars with the last days, and for the ways in which these traditions were used by English late medieval writers.

associate the friars with Antichrist, and with the last days. But in the light of the friars' apostolic ideals, we can also see why they should pose such an important question for Langland: if the fraternal orders are founded on ideals of apostolic poverty, and have yet become associated with Antichrist, what consequences does this have for Langland's own vision of the Church, which is also modelled on ideals of apostolic, voluntary poverty? It is no accident that the friars in particular should be singled out in Passus XX, for theirs is not merely one among many cases of clerical failing; it is, instead, an example of failing based on the very model of the Church which Langland most admires.

And the centre of this problem, for Langland, is an institutional one concerning the reasons why the friars must beg, and, therefore, why they must sell the sacrament of penance for their own profit. Despite wide differences in their view of the Church, both Fitzralph and Wyclif (in line with the basic traditions of antifraternal satire) join in condemning the idea of mendicancy. Fitzralph, for example, argues that the 'ordinary' (i.e. the secular priest) will hear confessions more responsibly, since he is not dependent for his livelihood on any profit he makes from the penitent:

> . . . for the parischon may skilfulliche deme that his ordynarie is a Juge lasse suspect & more skilful for to enjoy[n]e hym skilful penaunce & profitable for his synnes. For he schal nought suppose nother haue suspecioun, that his ordynarie hereth his schrifte for couetise of getyng & of wynnyng of bodilich help & socour.[17]

He goes on to point out that the friars 'by her fundacioun, thei beth ybounde to beggerie & to the heighest pouerte', and that, given this, the parishioner might well consider that the friar hears confession only out of the hope of profit, since his 'nede driueth to synne, by the which synne the nede myght be releued'. He cites Proverbs in a prayer to God to be relieved from beggary, lest, he says, he be 'conpelled by nede for to stele & forswere the name of my God' (p. 47; the biblical reference is Prov. 30.8–9). An argument such as this might make us even more wary about the advice of Need at the beginning of Passus XX. But to see what position the poem comes to with regard to this question, it is now necessary to turn back to the text.

17. Ed. Perry (1925, 46). Letter forms have been modernised.

Under the attack of Antichrist, the Barn of Unity is made vulnerable by the internal contradictions of its own ethos. Each time an act of mercy is 'courteously' made by Conscience towards the enemy, this merely serves to increase the enemy's power. This happens three times in the passus (ll. 106, 243, and 356), and I shall discuss each instance in turn.

Two of the signs of the last days, as described by Christ, are 'wars and commotions', and pestilences (Luke 21.9–11). Langland combines these signs in his representation of the attack of Antichrist, since disease is itself represented as making a military attack. Conscience, at the onset of Antichrist, appeals to Kynde to defend those 'fools' (cf. II Cor. 11.16–33) who take refuge in the Barn of Unity, in response to which Kynde 'cam out of the planetes,/ And sente forth his forreyours – feveres and fluxes' (ll. 80–1). In Middle English, an important sense of the word 'kynde' is 'Nature' (MED sense 8(a)); in Langland's poem the word has undergone a striking transformation, however, since the 'Kynde' of Passus XX is providential. It is true that certain writers contemporary with Langland do present Nature as a providential figure, acting in accord with divine principles; thus Chaucer, in his *Parlement of Foules*, describes Nature as 'the vicaire of the almyghty Lord' (l. 379). But this Chartrian view, which Chaucer inherits directly from Alain de Lille's *Complaint of Nature* (1160–70), nevertheless sees nature as a coherent, largely independent system, created by God but thereafter acting according to its own internal logic. Langland, on the other hand, sees nature as fundamentally transformed through salvation history; by Christ's becoming man's 'bloody brother' (cf. XI. 201), man's 'kynde' is profoundly transformed. When 'Kynde' comes in Passus XX, it is certainly a cosmic force, coming as it does 'out of the planetes', but it comes in response to a moral appeal (that of Conscience), and plays a part in salvation history. Kynde embraces man's spiritual nature, that is, in a way Hunger (called on by Piers in Passus VI) does not. For Langland, Kynde is, after the incarnation, 'grounded in God', in the words of one later alliterative poem, *Death and Liffe* (ed. Gollancz 1930, l. 289).[18]

After Kynde has attacked with pestilence, Conscience 'of his curteisie' (l. 106) prays to Kynde to cease, to give people a chance

---

18. White (1988, Ch. 3) also distinguished Langland's Kynde from the Chartrian conception of Nature.

to amend. In the same way that Piers's appeal to Hunger to cease in Passus VI is followed by a further rejection of solidarity with Piers, so too is Conscience's 'courteous' act of mercy followed by a surge of energy in the enemy camp. But whereas the failure of the ploughing in Passus VI was represented in satirical, social terms, here the renewed attack is registered as an apocalyptic event, in which the principles of physical nature fight for supremacy, and even for the right to claim the definition of 'health' for themselves. On the one hand the figure Life claims health for himself, at first not caring 'how Kynde slow' (l. 150), and relying on 'Physic' as soon as he is attacked with disease (l. 169). Whereas Christ Himself had been called 'Life' in Passus XVIII (ll. 29–35a), the figure Life in Passus XX is clearly a more restricted sense of the word, designating purely physical life, cut off from the divine roots of man's nature. On the other hand, it is the fuller sense of 'nature', Kynde, who advises Will to go into the Barn of Unity and learn the craft of love, in apparent disregard for the immediate necessities of his physical life (ll. 199–211).

So in the renewed attack on the barn, Kynde advises Will to leave all crafts except that of love. This seems to be a total rejection of any concern for worldly labour, and potentially to lead to the position proposed by Need at the beginning of the passus, that one need have no fear of begging. But Conscience now makes his second courteous act of mercy, and in this he definitely comes down against begging. Under attack after the respite of Kynde, Conscience calls for the Clergy to come and help him (as indeed Clergy had prophesied he would (XIII. 203–4)). The first clergy to respond to Conscience's cry are the friars, and from this point to the end of the poem, the models of the poetry are anti-fraternal, apocalyptic traditions.

When the friars first try to enter the Barn of Unity, Need suddenly reappears within the dream, and tries to persuade Conscience to bar entry to the friars. Since they lack 'patrymoyne', or a fixed living, says Need, they will flatter to sustain themselves.

> For lomere he lyeth, that liflode moot begge,
> Than he that laboureth for liflode and leneth it beggeres.
> And sithen freres forsoke the felicite of erthe,
> Lat hem be as beggeris, or lyve by aungeles foode!
>
> (XX. 238–41)

So Need's earlier argument, at the beginning of the passus, that there is nothing wrong with begging, must how be qualified: there is, in Need's view, nothing wrong with begging, but the beggar is at the same time less trustworty in principle than one who works for his sustenance. So Need might defend begging, but still want to keep the friars out of the institution of the Church – they can either beg, or live on 'aungeles foode'. This comment resembles the moments in the poem when earthly food is rejected for spiritual food, but here it is made sardonically, effectively saying that either the friars can beg, or starve. And in rejecting this advice, Conscience laughs, and instead 'curteisliche conforted' the friars and calls them into the barn. This second act of courtesy towards potential enemies is made out of mercy, but in making it, Conscience does, nevertheless, attempt to guard the Church against the threat to which the friars expose it. For one of the first points Conscience makes is that the friars will have 'breed and clothes/ And othere necessaries ynowe' (ll. 248–49). So Conscience recognises that Need is right about the beggar flattering more readily than the man works for his living, and accordingly wishes to change the very foundation of the fraternal orders in this respect, and in respect of their uncontrolled numbers (ll. 253–72).

For the second time, however, Conscience's act of mercy serves to provoke, rather than stem the threat to the barn. The friars are taught the doctrine of the community of property by Envy (ll. 273–6), which suggests that the current of the poem is now moving strongly against Need's opening declaration in favour of begging; or it suggests, at the very least, that the pro-beggary argument cannot serve as the basis of an *institution* (as indeed Need himself argues at ll. 234–41). This last point is dramatically enacted in the last movement of the poem, which focuses on the question of beggary in relation to the sacrament of penance.

Conscience's first act of courteous mercy is to all of Christendom under the pestilential attack of Kynde; his second is to the mendicant orders in particular, and his third is to a single friar, 'Frere Flaterere' (l. 356). The logic of these last two moments is to test the strength of the Church against the power of sin represented by Antichrist. The strength of the Church is tested by first defining the institutional danger of begging, and then to see how begging affects, and corrupts, the sacrament of penance – the sacrament which allows Christians to 'capitalise' on the

Atonement, by 'paying back' their spiritual debts to Piers the Plowman. In this last moment, the entry of 'Frere Flatterere', not only is the Church effectively rendered useless, but Conscience himself is weakened.

Just as Life earlier in the passus called for a doctor in his sickness, Conscience calls for a 'leche', or doctor, to heal those who are wounded under the attack of Antichrist. Unlike the doctor of 'phisik' who failed to heal Life, the doctor Conscience calls for is a spiritual doctor, who can 'shryve', or absolve sinners, to restore their spiritual 'kynde'. The confessor appointed by Conscience is too demanding for the wounded, and Contrition asks Conscience to call 'Frere Flaterere', since, he says, many a man is wounded through hypocrisy (l. 318). Contrition's suggestion is itself hypocritical, and Conscience at first resists it, saying that the secular clergy, or Piers Plowman, are perfectly adequate to act as 'leche'. Suddenly, however, Conscience himself changes his mind, and agrees that the friar be fetched. This is an astonishing moment, since the source of greatest spiritual strength, the individual conscience, is itself weakened. The implication of this must be that for Langland the individual conscience is sustained by the institution of the Church, and that individuals are in a profound sense constituted by the Church; as the Church is threatened, so too is the individual conscience. Conscience accepts a hypocrite; the line between accepting a hypocrite and being a hypocrite is very thin.

One of the signs of the last times mentioned by Paul in the Second Epistle to Timothy is the appearance of traitors who 'creep into houses, and lead captive silly women laden with sins' (3.6). William of St Amour identified these '*penetrantes domos*' with the friars, who will, William says, break into not only the houses of men, but also into the '*domus conscientiae*', the 'houses of the conscience'. In William's exegesis they do not enter the house of conscience through the door, for the 'door of the conscience is he who has the cure of souls' (cited from Szittya 1977, 305). This, clearly, is the anti-fraternal topos that Langland bases the last scene of his poem on: Peace, the porter of Unity (drawn from Eph. 4.3), attempts to bar the door to 'Sire *Penetrans-domos*', because, he says, the last of this kind 'salvede so oure wommen til some were with childe' (l. 348).

But there is one important difference here in Langland's account from that of William of St Amour; Langland's friar does enter through 'the yates' (l. 349), and Conscience comes to greet him, 'curteisly'. Whereas the legal principle Conscience had acted as an 'unerring lexicographer' in Passus III and IV, the individual conscience in Passus XX seems unable to distinguish the hypo-critical from the genuine, as Pride's followers had predicted (XIX. 347–51). For the third time, Conscience's courtesy, and, apparently, his weakened discretion, spur his enemy into action; and precisely in so far as penance is for Langland the essential sacrament of the Church, this particular failure of the individual conscience renders the entire Church useless. Contrition is effec-tively nullified, since 'for confort of his confessour contricion he lafte' (l. 372).

This is clearly a moment of catastrophic proportions: not only is the ideal, apostolic Church rendered useless, but the very constitution of selfhood, to which the whole poem from Passus VIII has been directed, is on the point of disintegration. Will's search for charity in his own soul had opened out into an historical conception of charity and selfhood, where the movement through the Old to the New Testament not only resolved the dialectic of justice and charity in the human soul, but also established the bases for the institution of the Church in the soul – it is Conscience, 'Goddes clerk and his notarie' (XV. 32), who is to be crowned king in Christendom (XIX. 258). Conscience the king is clearly a common principle of conscience for all Christians, rather than an individual conscience. And because the will has ceased to be wilful and individual, it is no longer the locus of the action, and has given way to the conscience, who is not special, or 'proper' to one individual.[19] The poem has led to an institution as much as to a psychological faculty in which that institution is to be grounded; at the end of the poem, both seem to be on the point of disintegration.[20]

19. This is not to say that Will the narrator has been wholly incorporated into the new psychological frame of the poem, such as to make him disappear from the action. It is true that the will *per se* is no longer the locus of the action, but Will the ageing narrator survives as an actant, in his encounters with Kynde and with Elde. See Lawton (1987) for the way in which the subject of *Piers Plowman* is not a stable continuum, but rather determined by the way in which different discourses in the poem present the will.

20. See Martin (1979, Ch. 6) for an account of the way in which personification itself seems to be on the point of disintegration in Passus XX.

The very last dreaming moment in the poem suggests at least the possibility for renewal in the psychological faculty, and possibly in the institution. Conscience is not destroyed, and leaves the Church on pilgrimage; but at the same moment as he leaves the Church, he also diagnoses its central institutional weakness, that friars are without any fixed source of income:

> 'By Christ!' quod Conscience tho, 'I wole bicome a pilgrym,
> And walken as wide as the world lasteth,
> To seken Piers the Plowman, that Pryde myghte destruye,
> And that freres hadde a fyndyng, that for nede flateren
> And countrepledeth me, Conscience . . .
>
> (XX. 381–5)
>
> *fyndyng*: living; *countrepledeth*: plead in opposition to.

In the same way that Conscience's pilgrimage away from the academic clerical ambience in Passus XIII was felt to be a movement of spiritual renewal, so too is this last moment felt to be a moment of spiritual energy. Conscience insists on the injustice of flattery provoked by need ('countrepledeth' is a legal term), and thereby rebuts the opening arguments of Need that 'need has no law', and that Temperance is superior to justice. Or at the very least he rebuts these arguments as the basis of an institution. But whereas Conscience's pilgrimage in Passus XIII had ultimately led to the founding of a renewed apostolic Church, Conscience's departure at the end of the poem is from that Church, in its failure. Langland has exhausted the discourses of both conservative and radical wings of the Church, and it is unclear to me what discourse the poem could possibly adopt, or what institutional form it could imagine. Whereas Kynde had advised Will to 'avenge' himself by retreating to the Barn of Unity, what form could the 'vengeance' Conscience now calls for take, since he is leaving the barn?:

> '. . . Now Kynde me avenge,
> And sende me hap and heele, til I have Piers the Plowman!'
> And siththe he gradde after Grace, til I gan awake.
>
> (XX. 385–87)
>
> *hap*: good chance; *heale*: good health; *siththe*: afterwards; *gradde*: called.

The world Conscience enters seems to be a purely individual one, where one's relationship with God is a matter of grace alone, since the institutional forms through which restitution can be made (by which man might merit salvation) have been destroyed.

In conclusion to this discussion of the eighth vision, then, we can say that Langland's concern with begging, with which he begins the vision, is central to his diagnosis of the Church's total failure: the Church's essential function is to dispense the sacrament of penance; because the friars need to flatter to gain their livelihood, they betray this sacrament. Langland's anti-fraternalism, then, is not restricted to particular corruptions within the fraternal orders, but is provoked by the recognition that the friars are destroying the entire Church. And in so far as they are doing this, their activity assumes apocalyptic proportions.

But Langland's attack on mendicancy as the basis of the Church has implications not only for the friars, but also for himself. As I argued earlier, one of the reasons Langland focuses on the friars is because they purport to represent an apostolic ideal of poverty which is very close to Langland's own. Despite arguments made in the poem that the early apostles worked (e.g. XV. 290–3), Langland gives much fuller imaginative representation to moments where work for food is rejected in favour of spiritual food (i.e. Piers in Passus VII, Haukyn in passus XIV, and Kynde in Passus XX). To be in the world seems necessarily to compromise 'truthe', and provokes Langland to reject the active life; at the same time, this rejection of the world, and reliance on alms seems to lead inevitably to the destruction of the Church. This is a dilemma of great moment, but from which there seems no escape.

CONCLUSION

In conclusion to this whole chapter, we can say that the final three visions of the poem take up and develop the intimately related themes of charity and the Church which Anima had raised in Passus XV: whereas Passus XVIII takes the theme of charity to its triumphant conclusion in Christ's charitable fulfilment of the law, the last two passus (Visions Seven and Eight) treat the Church as the institution which capitalises on the new political relations established between man and God by the Atonement. The covenant between man and God, whereby man can 'dowel' through penance, and 'pay back what he owes', allows Langland to return to the locus of work, the field, and reimagine both the Church and society. The vision of the Church is one of apostolic simplicity, with Piers as a pope at its head, and the society which flows from this Church is non-hierarchical and brotherly in spirit. Langland's poem imitates biblical time, and moves, accordingly, from a vision of Christ, to the establishment of the Church, to a vision of the last days, or Apocalypse. In Langland's apocalyptic vision, anti-fraternal satire assumes cataclysmic proportions, since the friars' need drives them to treat penance as a commodity. This, for Langland, creates unresolvable tensions, since his own vision of the apostolic Church is modelled on the very ideals of poverty characteristic of the fraternal orders. In this cataclysm, it is not only the institution which disintegrates, but also the self: given the intimacy of relation between institutions and individuals for Langland, it is inevitable that the disintegration of the Church should also entail the weakening of the individual conscience.

Conclusion

In one sense, *Piers Plowman* is a remarkably consistent poem, which never moves far from a central problematic, concerning the relations of justice and love. In Passus I Holy Church states this theme:

> 'Whan alle tresors arn tried,' quod she, 'Treuthe is the beste.
> I do it in *Deus caritas* to deme the sothe.'
>
> (I. 85–6)

The poem is consistent in its adherence to the problems raised by this statement: how can love *judge* that justice is the best treasure, when the predisposition of love will be to dissolve judgement, and to place mercy before justice? This is the basic thematic question of the poem, developed in the first two visions, with their affirmation of unremitting justice in the earthly and divine realms respectively; it is the theme of the third vision, in which Will makes a crucial recognition that God's law is not absolute, but statuted, thereby mercifully allowing room for failure; in the fourth vision this intellectual recognition is absorbed by the will, in the knowledge that penance is the means by which one meets the terms of God's covenant. And in Visions Five to Eight inclusive the poem explores the nature of charity, by defining how it can supervene justice, without violating the demands of justice. These visions also turn to the institution, the Church, which is responsible for dispensing the sacrament of penance, a sacrament made possible through God's mercy, and designed to allow man to meet the standards of His justice.

If the poem is consistent in its development of this theme, I have also tried to stress how this development is clear. I have tried, that is, to stress intelligibility and coherence of structure at all points. A conclusion, nevertheless, might be a fitting place to express at least some sympathy for 'Kytte' and 'Calote' (XVIII. 429): Langland isn't easy to live with, and there are many points where my exposition rightly incurs the charge that 'to generalise and, more, to rationalise the working of a creative mind as large, as subtle, and as obliquely allusive as that of Langland is clearly so hazardous as to constitute an impertinence' (Russell 1988, 234). This charge has seemed worth incurring in the interests of shedding at least some light where before there has been, for the poem's general readership, obscurity.

The relations of justice and love, then, constitute the basic theme of the poem. But Langland's presentation of this theme is not at all static, or a matter of simple declaration. On the contrary, the poem is dynamic, in so far as it calls attention to its own procedures, and changes its own procedures, in its exploration of the relations between justice and love. The *manner* of the search for charity becomes as much the subject of the poem as charity itself.

Many previous studies have worked from this basic observation about the poem's dynamism. On the whole, this dynamism has been formulated in personal terms, whereby the poem is seen as tracing Will's progress as a Christian. In this study I have tried to show how profoundly the poem is indeed embedded in a sense of personhood. From Passus VIII forward, the poem is shaped around the structure of the human soul as Langland understood that structure: in the third vision, Will, as the will, interrogates the rational part of his soul, and the educational institutions which train the reason; in the fourth vision the focus is on the will itself, guided by conscience and patience; in the fifth vision Will encounters the integrated soul, Anima, who contains both the rational and the affective powers of the soul. But Anima also contains more religious aspects of the soul's constitution, charity and conscience. It is Will's vision of the Tree of Charity in his soul which determines the action up to and including Passus XVIII, where Will seeks out charity in Christ; and it is Conscience who is the dominant presence of the last two visions. What generates this journey into the deepest aspects of the self is of course the search for an understanding of how justice and charity relate.

So Langland's psychology, or sense of selfhood, has been a recurrent theme of this book. But as soon as we formulate the poem's movement in this way, we recognise that Langland's conception of what it is to be a person is different from our own. One of these differences concerns the intimacy of relationship between the self and institutions in Langland's poem. In the first vision, for example, we can see how the institution of monarchical justice has psychological concepts (Reason and Conscience) at its base. Of course these are legal concepts in the political discourse of the first vision (rather than individual psychological faculties), but the fact that the same words are used both for aspects of the soul and for institutional concepts reveals the intimacy of relation between institutions and selfhood. Another example of this closeness of relation is the third vision, where Will questions educational institutions as much as the rational parts of the soul which are trained by those institutions. A final example, and perhaps the most telling, is the final vision, where the Conscience is almost identified with the institution of the Church: as the Church disintegrates, so too does Conscience fail.

Given this intimacy of relation, I have tried in this book to go beyond simply charting Will's development as a self, since that development necessarily embraces Langland's sense of corporate institutions. So I have taken serious account of monarchical, ecclesiastical, manorial and educational institutions. It could be argued that all these institutions can ultimately be reduced to questions of the Church as an institution: the presentation of monarchical justice in Passus IV is incomplete without the more profound reformation of the soul, which is ideally effected through the penitential systems of the Church; the manorial scenes presented in Passus VI and XIX are presented as the loci of penitential action; and the educational institutions Will encounters in the third and fourth visions are basically concerned with religious education. The Church embraces the action of the poem: Holy Church is the first institution Will meets in the poem, and the last two visions represent the construction and disintegration of the Church.

In my consideration of corporate institutions, and especially of the Church, I have tried to show that Langland's position with regard to the Church is not a static one, but one which can only be defined by tracing the process of the poem, whereby institutional attachments come under strain, and give way to others. Theological 'truthe' seems to be a unitary principle in Passus I,

automatically implying ecclesiastical and political allegiances of a
conservative kind; but as Langland follows through the logic of
his central question (concerning the relations of justice and love),
the reader discovers competing voices *within* the institution of
Holy Church. In its broadest terms, my argument has been that
the movement of the poem is from allegiance to feudal, authoritarian, vertically organised institutions (where the dominant
quality is 'truthe') to fundamentally non-hierarchical, brotherly,
horizontally organised institutions (where the dominant quality
is charity). The meaning of the poem lies less in the conservative
or the more dissenting positions (despite their interest and importance), than in the movement between them.

So in tracing the development of the poem's central concern
with the relations of justice and love, I have tried to give an
account not only of selfhood in *Piers Plowman*, but also of the
corporate institutions by which the self is shaped. The areas so
far considered in this conclusion require students of literature to
take quite serious account of theology, psychology, and institutional history. But for students of literature, perhaps the biggest
challenge offered by the poem is its poetic form. My own
students (and, no doubt, many other readers of the poem) have
often complained that the work is 'dogmatic'. My argument in
response to this complaint has been that the poetic form of the
work is correlative with its theological, psychological and institutional attachments. As Langland moves theologically from
consideration of God as Truthe to consideration of God as Kynde,
so too do the poetic forms of the poem change from being authoritarian to being more personal. As the poem moves
psychologically from the reason to the will, so too do the poetic
forms of the poem change from rational and analytical to being
affective and synthetic. The poem's form is determined by the
soul's form. And as Langland moves institutionally from a hierarchical to a 'brotherly' sense of institutions, so too do the
discourses of the poem change from being those whose authority
is centred outside the self, to those whose authority is centred in
the self. Holy Church's commitment to 'truthe' in Passus I
seemed to imply not only conservative institutional allegiances,
but also, concomitantly, authoritarian discourses. As the poem
proceeds, I have argued that Langland explores the premises of
such authoritarian discourses, and as those premises are found to

be inadequate, the poem adopts a range of discourses which, while never outside the institution 'Holy Church', are not authoritarian and closed.

Another way of putting the point about the formal changes in the poem is to say that the structure of the poem is unstable and self-consuming, undercutting itself as the inadequacy of its means of progressing is recognised. In fact the poem is full of tiny models of verbal subversion. Holy Church recommends that 'mesure is medicine' (I. 35), neatly using the model of 'medicine' to undercut it: if one is temperate, medicine will be unnecessary. This strategy, of which there are many examples, also characterises larger narrative units in the poem, such as that of using pilgrimage as a narrative model to subvert the normal practice of pilgrimage, in the second vision. And if we were looking to the poem to provide us with textual models of this procedure, we might go to the treatment of documents in the poem. Langland often uses documents as the model for his poetry: take, for example, the marriage charter of Mede and False in Passus II; the pardon Piers receives in Passus VII; the 'patente' of Patience in Passus XIV, and the writ carried by Moses in Passus XVII. I have treated each of these individually in the body of this book, but by putting them together, it is possible to see a common strategy applied to each: they are proposed as documents in order to undercut the premises of the document. Mede's marriage charter uses legal forms to subvert law; Piers's 'pardon' undermines the premises of a normal pardon; the 'patente' of Patience must be written on the parchment of 'pure pacience', which undercuts the purely legal, documentary status of the patent; and the writ of Moses will be sealed by Christ 'hanging' from the cross, which evokes, but overbears the idea of a seal hanging from a legal document. In their strategy, at least, these 'texts' are more like *Piers Plowman* than the texts which are promoted as models from within the poem – the pious stories of 'Tobye and of the twelve Apostles', for example, that Study recommends (X. 33).

If formal change is in part explicable in terms of changes in institutional attachment represented in the poem, this has implications for cultural history more generally: we can see the way in which the literary category of form bears historical significance within it. But formal change in the poem also has implications for literary history, and for the history of reading. A sub-theme

of this book has been that biblical texts are used in different ways
as the poem proceeds (cf. Barr 1986); without specifying each kind
of use, we might notice that Will changes in the poem from being
a passive receiver of biblical texts designed for moral instruction
at the beginning of the poem, to being an active 'reader',
especially from Passus VIII forwards. Holy Church uses scriptural
texts in an authoritarian and dogmatic way in Passus I, but when
in Passus XI Will comes face to face with the ultimate text of the
tradition to which Langland is committed, Scripture, the event
is not one of passive reading, submissively accepting a 'closed'
text; instead, Will responds to the text of Scripture in a personal
and liberating way. From this vision on in the poem, Will's
'reading' of scriptural texts is more inward and poetic, and
designed to appeal to the deeper reaches of the self. So despite the
initial commitment to habits of reading which are purely subservient, Langland represents a movement towards a more intuitive,
personal reading. In its testing and revaluation of textual authority, it could be said that *Piers Plowman* is much more like
Chaucer's *House of Fame* than it is like, for example, Chaucer's
Parson's Tale (setting aside the very different institutional and
textual traditions within which *Piers Plowman* and *The House of
Fame* are working). Again, the meaning of the poem lies not so
much in one kind of reading or another, but in the movement
between them.

Langland's culture might be foreign, or at best ancestral, to our
own; readers in a secular, liberal culture might find much in *Piers
Plowman* that they want to resist. But for anyone who agrees that
we know ourselves through cultural history (and not just the
cultural history of our own, immediate tradition), Langland's
poem affords an extraordinary occasion for self-knowledge.

Bibliography

The following abbreviations are used:

Alford   *A Companion to Piers Plowman*, edited by John A. Alford
                  (Berkeley: University of California Press, 1988).
Alford GLD   John A. Alford, *PP: A Glossary of Legal Diction*, PP
                  Studies, Vol. V (Cambridge: D. S. Brewer, 1988).
Blanch   *Style and Symbolism in PP*, edited by Robert J. Blanch
                  (Knoxville: University of Tennessee Press, 1969).
CHLMP   *The Cambridge History of Later Medieval Philosophy*, edited
                  by Norman Kretzmann, Anthony Kenny, and Jan
                  Pinborg (Cambridge: CUP, 1982).
EC   *Essays in Criticism*.
EETS   Early English Text Society.
ELH   *English Literary History*.
e. s.   extended series.
JEGP   *Journal of English and Germanic Philology*.
LSE   *Leeds Studies in English*.
MED   *Middle English Dictionary*, edited by Hans Kurath (Ann
                  Arbor: University of Michigan Press, 1956–).
MERELGR   *Medieval English and Religious and Ethical Literature: Essays
                  in Honour of G. H. Russell*, edited by Gregory Kratzmann
                  and James Simpson (Cambridge: D. S. Brewer, 1986).
MESGK   *Medieval English Studies presented to George Kane*, edited by
                  Edward Donald Kennedy, Ronald Waldron and Joseph S.
                  Wittig (Woodbridge, Suffolk: D. S. Brewer, 1988).
NM   *Neuphilologische Mitteilungen*.
n. s.   new series.
N & Q   *Notes and Queries*
o. s.   original series.
OED   *Oxford English Dictionary*, edited by James A. H. Murray,
                  Henry Bradley, W. A. Craigie, C. T. Onions (Oxford:
                  Clarendon Press, 1933).
PBA   *Proceedings of the British Academy*.

PL   *Patrilogia Latina*, edited by J.-P. Migne, 221 vols.
PP   *Piers Plowman*.
RES   *Review of English Studies*.
SP   *Studies in Philology*.
TRHS   *Transactions of the Royal Historical Society*.
Vasta   *Interpretations of PP*, edited by Edward Vasta (Notre
            Dame, Ind.: University of Notre Dame Press, 1968).
Wilkins   *Concilia Magnae Britanniae et Hiberniae*, edited by D.
            Wilkins, 4 vols. (London, 1737).
YLS   *The Yearbook of Langland Studies*.

The Works Cited list is the key to the author–date (or, in the case of editions, editor–date) reference system used in the text and footnotes. When more than one work appears by the same author and/or editor in the same year, the works are designated a, b, c, etc.

(1) *Editions*

Alfred, King of England:
Carnicelli (1969)   *King Alfred's Version of St. Augustine's 'Soliloquies'*,
    edited by Thomas A. Carnicelli (Cambridge, Mass.: Harvard
    University Press).

Amis and Amiloun:
Leach (1937)   *Amis and Amiloun*, edited by MacE. Leach, EETS o. s.,
    203 (London: OUP).

Aquinas, Thomas:
Gilby (1964)   *Summa Theologiae*, Vol. I, *Christian Theology*, edited by
    Thomas Gilby (London: Blackfriars).

Brown (1932)   *English Lyrics of the Thirteenth Century*, edited by Carleton
    Brown (Oxford: Clarendon Press).

Book of Privy Counselling:
Hodgson (1944)   *The Cloud of Unknowing and the Book of Privy Coun-
    selling*, edited by Phyllis Hodgson, EETS o.s., 218 (London: OUP).

Caxton, William:
Byles (1932)   *The Book of the Faytes of Armes and of Chyvalrye*, edited by
    A. T. D. Byles, EETS o.s., 189 (London: OUP).

Chambers and Daunt (1931)   *A Book of London English 1384–1425*, edited
    by R. W. Chambers and Marjorie Daunt (Oxford: Clarendon Press).

Chaucer, Geoffrey:
Benson (1988)   *The Riverside Chaucer*, third edition, General Editor Larry
    D. Benson (Oxford: OUP).

'Cleaness':
Andrew and Waldron (1978)   *The Poems of the 'Pearl' Manuscript: 'Pearl'*,
    'Cleaness', 'Patience', 'Sir Gawain and the Green Knight', edited by
    Malcolm Andrew and Ronald Waldron, York Medieval Texts,
    second series (London: Edward Arnold).

Cloud of Unknowing:
Hodgson (1944)   *The Cloud of Unknowing and the Book of Privy Coun-*
    selling, edited by Phyllis Hodgson, EETS o. s., 218 (London, OUP).

Conflict of Wit and Will:
Dickins (1937)   *The Conflict of Wit and Will*, edited by Bruce Dickens,
    Leeds School of English Language Monographs, 4 (Leeds: Leeds
    School of English Language).

Death and Liffe:
Gollancz (1930)   *Death and Liffe*, edited by Israel Gollancz (London: OUP).

Destruction of Troy:
Panton and Donaldson (1869)   *The Gest Hystoriale of the Destruction of*
    Troy, edited by George A. Panton and David Donaldson, EETS
    o.s., *39* (London: Trübner).

Durandus of St Pourçain:
Durandus (1556)   *In Sententias Theologicas Petri Lombardi Commentariorum*
    Libri Quatuor (Lyon).

Epistola Sathanae ad Cleros:
Hudson (1978)   *Epistola Sathanae ad Cleros*, in *Selections from English*
    Wycliffite Writings, edited by Anne Hudson (Cambridge: CUP),
    pp. 89–93.

Fitzralph, Richard:
Perry (1925)   *Defensio Curatorum*, edited by Aaron Jenkins Perry, in
    Dialogus inter Militem et Clericum, EETS o.s., 167 (London: OUP),
    pp. 39–93.

Gaytryge, John:
Perry (1867)   *Gaytryge's Sermon*, edited by George C. Perry, in *Religious*

Pieces in Prose and Verse, EETS o. s., 26 (London: Kegan Paul, Trench, Trübner), pp. 1–15.

Gower, John:
Macaulay (1900)   *The English Works of John Gower*, Vol. I, edited by G. C. Macaulay, EETS e. s., 81 (London: OUP).

Holcot, Robert:
Holcot (1494)   *Super Libros Sapientiae* (Hagenowe).

Hugh of St Victor:
Taylor (1961)   *The Didascalicon of Hugh of St Victor*, translated by Jerome Taylor (New York: Columbia University Press).

John de la Rochelle:
Michaud-Quantin (1964)   *Tractatus de Divisione Multiplici Potentiarum Animae*, edited by Pierre Michaud–Quantin, Textes Philosophiques du Moyen Age, XI (Paris: Vrin).

Langland, William:
Kane (1988a)   *The A-Version. Will's Visions of PP and Do-Well*, revised edition, edited by George Kane (London and Berkeley: Athlone Press and University of California Press).
Kane and Donaldson (1975)   *PP: The B-Version. Will's Vision's of PP, Do-Well, Do-Better and Do-Best*, edited by George Kane and E. Talbot Donaldson (London: Athlone Press).
Pearsall (1978)   *PP by William Langland, An Edition of the C-Text*, edited by Derek Pearsall, York Medieval Texts, second series (London: Edward Arnold).
Rigg and Brewer (1983)   *PP, The Z-version*, edited by A. G. Rigg and Charlotte Brewer, Studies and Texts, 59 (Toronto: Pontifical Institute of Mediaeval Studies).
Schmidt (1987a)   *The Vision of PP, A Complete Edition of the B-text*, edited by A. V. C. Schmidt (London: J. M. Dent).

Lay Folk's Catechism:
Simmons and Noloth (1901)   *The Lay Folks' Catechism*, edited by T. F. Simmons and H. F. Noloth, EETS o. s., 118 (London: Kegan Paul, Trench, Trübner).

Macrobius, Ambrosius Theodosius:
Stahl (1952)   *Commentary on the Dream of Scipio*, trans. William H. Stahl (New York: Columbia University Press).

Mum and the Sothsegger:
Day and Steele (1936): *Mum and the Sothsegger*, edited by Mabel Day and Robert Steele, EETS o. s., 199 (London: OUP).

Pearl:
Gordon (1953) *Pearl*, edited by E. V. Gordon (Oxford: Clarendon Press).

Pecock, Reginald:
Hitchcock (1921) *The Donet by Reginald Pecock*, edited by E. V. Hitchcock, EETS o. s., 156 (London: OUP).

Rotuli Parliamentorum:
Strachey (1767–77) *Rotuli Parliamentorum*, edited by J. Strachey (London), Vols. II and III.

Sir Gawain and the Green Knight:
Davis (1967) *Sir Gawain and the Green Knight*, edited by J. R. R. Tolkien and E. V. Gordon, second edition revised by Norman Davis (Oxford: Clarendon Press).

Statutes of the Realm:
The Statutes of the Realm   (London 1810, 1816), Vols. I and II.

Trevisa, John:
Babington (1865) *Polychronicon Ranulphi Higden, with the English Translations of John Trevisa*, edited by Churchill Babington (London: Longman, Green, Longman, Roberts, and Green).

Usk, Thomas:
Skeat (1897) *The Testament of Love*, in *Chaucerian and Other Pieces*, edited by W. W. Skeat (Oxford: Clarendon Press), pp. 1–145.

Wars of Alexander:
Skeat (1886) *The Wars of Alexander*, edited by W. W. Skeat, EETS e.s., 47 (London: Trubner).

Westminster Chronicle:
Hector and Harvey (1982) *The Westminster Chronicle*, 1381–94, edited by L. C. Hector and Barbara F. Harvey (Oxford: Clarendon Press).

Wycliffite Sermons:
Hudson (1983) *English Wycliffite Sermons*, edited by Anne Hudson, Vol. I (Oxford: Clarendon Press).

(2) *Secondary*

Adams (1976)   Robert Adams, 'Langland and the Liturgy Revisited', *SP*, **73**, 266–84.

  (1978)   'The Nature of Need in *PP* XX', *Traditio*, **34**, 273–302.

  (1983)   'Piers's Pardon and Langland's Semi–Pelagianism', *Traditio*, **39**, 367–418.

  (1985)   'The Reliability of the Rubrics in the B-Text of *PP*', *Medium Aevum*, **54**, 208–31.

  (1988a)   'Langland's Theology', in Alford, pp. 87–114.

  (1988b)   'Mede and Mercede: the Evolution of the Economics of Grace in the *PP* B and C Versions', in *MESGK*, pp. 217–32.

Aers (1975)   David Aers, *PP and Christian Allegory* (London: Edward Arnold).

  (1980)   *Chaucer, Langland and the Creative Imagination* (London: Routledge and Kegan Paul).

  (1983)   '*PP* and Problems in the Perception of Poverty', *LSE* n. s., **14**, 5–25.

Alford (1974)   John A. Alford, 'Haukyn's Coat: Some Observations on *PP* B. XIV. 22–7', *Medium Aevum*, **43**, 133–38.

  (1977)   'The Role of Quotations in *PP*', *Speculum*, **52**, 80–99.

  (1988)   'The Idea of Reason in *PP*', in *MESGK*, pp. 199–215.

Auerbach (1959) Erich Auerbach,'Figura', in *Scences from the Drama of European Literature* (New York: Meridian), pp. 11–76.

Baker (1980)   Denise Baker, 'From Plowing to Penitence: *PP* and Fourteenth Century Theology', *Speculum*, **55**, 715–25.

Baldwin (1981a) Anna P. Baldwin, *The Theme of Government in PP*, PP Studies, Vol. I (Cambridge: D. S. Brewer).

  (1981b)   'The Double Duel in *PP* B XVIII and C XXI', *Medium Aevum*, **50**, 64–78.

Baldwin (1913) J. F. Baldwin, *The King's Council in England during the Middle Ages* (Oxford: Clarendon Press).

Barnie (1974)   J. Barnie, *War in Medieval Society* (London: Weidenfeld and Nicolson).

Barr (1986)   Helen Barr, 'The Use of Latin Quotations in *PP* with Special Reference to Passus XVIII of the 'B' Text', *N & Q* n. s., **33**, 440–8.

Barratt (1982)   Alexandra Barratt, 'The Characters "Civil" and "Theology" in *PP*', *Traditio*, **38**, 352–64.

Bloomfield (1958)   Morton W. Bloomfield, '*PP* and the Three Grades of Chastity', *Anglia*, **76**, 227–53.

  (1962)   '*PP*' *as a Fourteenth Century Apocalypse* (New Brunswick: Rutgers University Press).

Boitani (1982)   Piero Boitani, *English Medieval Narrative in the Thirteenth and Fourteenth Centuries*, trans. Joan Krakover Hall (Cambridge: CUP).

Bolton (1977)   Brenda Bolton, '*Paupertas Christi*: Old Wealth and New Poverty in the Twelfth Century', in *Renaissance and Renewal in Christian History, Studies in Church History*, Vol. 14, pp. 95–103.

(1983)   *The Medieval Reformation* (London: Edward Arnold).

Bolton (1980)   J. L. Bolton, *The Medieval English Economy*, Everyman's University Library, Vol. 1274 (London: J. M. Dent).

Bowers (1986)   John M. Bowers, *The Crisis of Will in PP* (The Catholic University of America Press: Washington DC).

Bullock-Davies (1978)   Constance Bullock-Davies, *Menestrellorum multitudo: Minstrels at a Royal Feast* (Cardiff: University of Wales Press).

Burrow (1957)   J. A. Burrow, 'The Audience of *PP*', *Anglia*, **75**, 373–84.

(1965)   'The Action of Langland's Second Vision', *EC*, **15**, 247–68. Rpt. in Blanch, pp. 209–27.

(1982)   *Medieval Writers and their Work: Middle English Literature and its Background 1100–1500* (Oxford: OUP).

Carruthers (1973)   Mary Jean Carruthers, *The Search for St Truth: A Study of Meaning in PP* (Evanston, Illinois: Northwestern University Press).

Chenu (1969)   M.-D. Chenu, *La théologie comme science au xiiie siècle*, Bibliothèque Thomiste, Vol. 33 (Paris: Vrin).

Coleman (1981)   Janet Coleman, *PP and the 'Moderni'* (Rome: Letture di Pensiero e d'Arte).

Collins (1985)   Marie Collins, 'Will and the Penitents: *PP* B X. 420–35', *LSE* n. s., **16**, 290–308.

Cooper (1987)   Helen Cooper, 'Langland's and Chaucer's Prologues', *YLS*, **1**, 71–81.

Courtenay (1987)   William J. Courtenay, *Schools and Scholars in Fourteenth-Century England* (Princeton: Princeton University Press).

Davenport (1988)   W. A. Davenport, 'Patterns in Middle English Dialogues', in *MESGK*, pp. 127–45.

Davlin (1971)   Sister Mary Clemente Davlin, "Kynde Knowynge' as a Major Theme in *PP* B', *RES* n. s., **22** 1–19.

(1981)   "Kynde Knowyng' as a Middle English Equivalent for 'Wisdom' in *PP* B', *Medium Aevum*, **50**, 5–17.

Dillon (1981)   Janette Dillon, '*PP*: A Particular Example of Wordplay and its Structural Significance', *Medium Aevum*, **50**, 40–8.

Dod (1982)   Bernard G. Dod, 'Aristoteles Latinus', in *CHLMP*, pp. 45–79.

Donaldson (1949)   E. Talbot Donaldson, *PP: The C-Text and its Poet*,

Yale Studies in English, Vol. 113 (New Haven: Yale University Press).

Dove (1986)   Mary Dove, *The Perfect Age of Man's Life* (Cambridge: CUP).

Dronke (1981)   Peter Dronke, 'Arbor Caritatis', in *Medieval Studies for J. A. W. Bennett*, edited by P. L. Heyworth (Oxford: Clarendon Press), pp. 207–53.

Duggan (1987)   Hoyt N. Duggan, 'Notes Towards a Theory of Langland's Meter', *YLS*, 1, pp. 41–70.

Emmerson (1981)   Richard K. Emmerson, *Antichrist in the Middle Ages: A Study of Medieval Apocalyticism, Art and Literature* (Manchester: Manchester University Press).

Ferguson (1965)   A. B. Ferguson, *The Articulate Citizen and the English Renaissance* (Durham, NC: Duke University Press).

Fisher (1988)   John H. Fisher, '*PP* and the Chancery Tradition', in *MESGK*, pp. 267–78.

Fleming (1977)   John V. Fleming, *An Introduction to the Franciscan Literature of the Middle Ages* (Chicago: Franciscan Herald Press).

Foucault (1972)   Michel Foucault, *The Archaeology of Knowledge*, trans. A. M. Sheridan-Smith (London: Tavistock).

Frank (1951)   Robert Worth Frank Jr, 'The Pardon Scene in *PP*', *Speculum*, 26, 317–31.

(1953)   'The Art of Reading Medieval Personification Allegory', *ELH*, 20, 237–50. Rpt. in Vasta, pp. 217–31.

Gilbert (1980)   Beverly Brain Gilbert, ' "Civil" and the Notaries in *PP*', *Medium Aevum*, 50, 49–63.

Gilson (1955) Etienne Gilson, *A History of Christian Philosophy in the Middle Ages* (London: Sheed and Ward).

Godden (1984)   Malcolm Godden, 'Plowmen and Hermits in Langland's *PP*', *RES* n. s., 35, 129–63.

Goldsmith (1981)   Margaret E. Goldsmith, *The Figure of PP: The Image on the Coin, PP* Studies, Vol. II (Cambridge: D. S. Brewer).

Gradon (1980)   Pamela Gradon, 'Langland and the Ideology of Dissent', *PBA*, 66, pp. 179–205.

(1983)   '*Trajanus Redivivus*: Another Look at Trajan in *PP*', in *Middle English Studies presented to Norman Davis in Honour of His Seventieth Birthday*, edited by Douglas Gray and E. G. Stanley (Oxford: Clarendon Press), pp. 93–114.

Grant (1982)   Edward Grant, 'The Effect of the Condemnation of 1277', in *CHLMP*, pp. 537–9.

Gray (1986)   Nick Gray, 'The Clemency of Cobblers: a Reading of "Glutton's Confession" in *PP*', *LSE* n. s., 17, pp. 61–75.

Griffiths (1985) Lavinia Griffiths, *Personification in PP*, *PP* Studies, Vol. III (Cambridge: D. S. Brewer).

Harvey (1975) E. Ruth Harvey, *The Inward Wits, Psychological Theory in the Middle Ages and the Renaissance*, Warburg Institute Surveys, Vol. 6 (London: The Warburg Institute).

Hilton (1969) Rodney H. Hilton, *The Decline of Serfdom in Medieval England* (London: Macmillan).

(1975) *The English Peasantry in the Later Middle Ages* (Oxford: Clarendon Press).

Hudson (1982) Anne Hudson, 'Lollardy, The English Heresy?', *Studies in Church History*, **17**, 261–83. Rpt. in Anne Hudson, *Lollards and their Books* (London: Hambledon Press, 1985), pp. 141–63.

(1988) *The Premature Reformation – Wycliffite Texts and Lollard History* (Oxford: Clarendon Press).

Justice (1988) Steven Justice, 'The Genres of *PP*', *Viator*, **19**, 291–306.

Kane (1965) George Kane *PP: The Evidence for Authorship* (London: Athlone Press).

(1981) 'Music "Neither Unpleasant nor Monotonous"', in *Medieval Studies for J. A. W. Bennett*, edited by P. L. Heyworth (Oxford: Clarendon Press), pp. 43–63.

(1988b) 'The Text', in Alford, pp. 175–200.

Kaske (1963) Robert E. Kaske, '"Ex vi transicionis" and its Passage in *PP*', *JEGP*, **62**, 32–60.

Kaulbach (1985) Ernest N. Kaulbach, 'The "Vis Imaginativa" and the Reasoning Powers of Ymaginatif in the B-Text of *PP*', *JEGP*, **84**, 16–29.

Kean (1964) P.M. Kean, 'Love, Law and *Lewte* in *PP*', *RES* n. s., **15**, 241–61. Rpt. in Blanch, pp. 132–55.

Keen (1973) M. H. Keen, *England in the Middle Ages: A Political History* (London: Methuen).

Kellog (1972) Alfred L. Kellog and Louis A. Haselmayer, 'Chaucer's Satire of the Pardoner', in Alfred L. Kellog, *Chaucer, Langland, Arthur: Essays in Middle English Literature* (New Brunswick: Rutgers University Press), pp. 212–44.

Korolec (1982) J. B. Korolec, 'Free Will and Free Choice', in *CHLMP*, pp. 629–41.

Lawton (1982) David A. Lawton, 'Middle English Alliterative Poetry: An Introduction', in *Middle English Alliterative Poetry and its Literary Background*, edited by D. A. Lawton (Cambridge: D. S. Brewer), pp. 1–19.

(1987) 'The Subject of *PP*', *YLS*, **1**, 1–30.

(1988) 'Alliterative Style', in Alford, pp. 223–249.

Leclercq (1974) Jean Leclercq, *The Love of Learning and the Desire for God*, trans. Catherine Misrahi (London: SPCK).

Leff (1957) Gordon Leff, *Bradwardine and the Pelagians, A Study of his 'De Causa Dei' and its Opponents*, Cambridge Studies in Medieval Life and Thought n. s., Vol. 5 (Cambridge: CUP).

(1967) *Heresy in the Later Middle Ages*, 2 vols. (Manchester: Manchester University Press).

Lewis (1945) N. B. Lewis, 'The Organization of Indentured Retinues in Fourteenth Century England', *TRHS*, fourth series, **27**, pp. 29–39.

Little (1978) Lester K. Little, *Religious Poverty and the Profit Economy in Medieval Europe* (London: Paul Elek).

Lohr (1982) C. H. Lohr, 'The Medieval Interpretation of Aristotle', in *CHLMP*, pp. 80–98.

McFarlane (1944) K. B. McFarlane, 'Bastard Feudalism', *Bulletin of the Institute of Historical Research*, **20**, 161–80. Rpt. in K. B. McFarlane, *England in the Fifteenth Century: Collected Essays* (London: Hambledon, 1981), pp. 23–43.

(1973) *The Nobility of Later Medieval England The Ford Lectures for 1953 and Related Studies* (Oxford: Clarendon Press).

Mâle (1961) Emile Mâle, *The Gothic Image*, trans. from the 3rd edition by D. Nussey (London: Collins).

Mann (1973) Jill Mann, *Chaucer and Medieval Estates Satire*. (Cambridge: CUP).

(1979) 'Eating and Drinking in *PP*', *Essays and Studies*, **32**, 26–42.

Martin (1979) Priscilla Martin, *PP: the Field and the Tower* (London: Macmillan; New York: Harper and Row, Barnes and Noble).

Michaud–Quantin (1949) P. Michaud–Quantin, 'La Classification des puissances de l'ame au xiie siecle', *Revue du Moyen Age Latin*, **5**, 15–34.

Middleton (1972) Anne Middleton, 'Two Infinites: Grammatical Metaphor in *PP*', *ELH*, **39**, 169–88.

(1986) '*PP*', in *A Manual of the Writings in Middle English 1050–1500*, Vol. 7 (New Haven: The Connecticut Academy of Arts and Sciences (pp. 2211–34), 2419–48.

Miller (1983) Paul Miller, 'John Gower, Satiric Poet', in *Gower's Confessio Amantis: Responses and Reassessments*, edited by A. J. Minnis (Cambridge: D. S. Brewer), pp. 79–105.

Minnis (1979) A. J. Minnis, 'Literary Theory in Discussions of *Forma Tractandi* by Medieval Theologians', *New Literary History*, **11**, 133–45.

(1981) 'Langland's Imaginatif and Late-Medieval Theories of Imagination', *Comparative Criticism*, **3**, 71–103.

(1984) *Medieval Theory of Authorship: Scholastic Literary Attitudes in the Later Middle Ages* (London: Scolar Press).

Morris and Strayer (1947) *The English Government at Work, 1327–1336*, edited by W. A. Morris and J. R. Strayer, 2 vols. (Cambridge, Mass.: Mediaeval Academy of America).

Murtaugh (1978)   Daniel M. Murtaugh, *PP and the Image of God* (Gainesville: University Presses of Florida).

Oberman (1957)   Heiko A. Oberman, *Archbishop Bradwardine: a Fourteenth Century Augustinian* (Utrecht: Drukkerijen Uitgevers-Maatschappij).

(1963)   *The Harvest of Medieval Theology: Gabriel Biel and Late Medieval Nominalism* (Cambridge, Mass.: Harvard University Press).

Overstreet (1984)   Samuel Overstreet, '"Grammaticus Ludens": Theological Aspects of Langland's Grammatical Allegory', *Traditio*, **40**, 251–96.

Pearsall (1988)   Derek Pearsall, 'Poverty and Poor People in *PP*', in *MESGK*, pp. 167–85.

Peebles (1911)   R. J. Peebles, *The Legend of Longinus in Ecclesiastical Art and in English Literature* Bryn Mawr Monographs, Vol. 9 (Bryn Mawr).

Peter (1956)   John Peter, *Complaint and Satire in Early English Literature* (Oxford: Clarendon Press).

Platt (1979)   Colin Platt, *The English Mediaeval Town* (London: Granada).

Postan (1942)   M. M. Postan, 'Some Social Consequences of the Hundred Years War', *Economic History Review*, **12**, 1–12.

(1971)   'England', in *The Agrarian Life of the Middle Ages. The Cambridge Economic History of Europe*, Vol. 1, second edition, edited by M. M. Postan (Cambridge), pp. 549–632.

Potts (1982)   Timothy Potts, 'Conscience', in *CHLMP*, pp. 687–704.

Quilligan (1978)   Maureen Quilligan, 'Langland's Literal Allegory', *EC*, **28**, 95–111.

Roth (1941)   C. Roth, *A History of the Jews in England* (Oxford: Clarendon Press).

Russell (1988)   George Russell 'The Imperative of Revision in the C Version of *PP*', in *MESGK*, pp. 233–42.

St Jacques (1969)   Raymond C. St Jacques, 'The Liturgical Associations of Langland's Samaritan', *Traditio*, **25**, 217–30.

Samuels (1985)   M. L. Samuels, 'Langland's Dialect', *Medium Aevum*, **54**, 232–47.

Schmidt (1968)   A. V. C. Schmidt, 'A Note on Langland's Conception of 'Anima' and 'Inwit'', *N & Q* n. s., **15**, 363–4.

(1969)   'Langland and Scholastic Philosophy', *Medium Aevum*, **38**, 134–56.

(1986)   'The Inner Dreams in *PP*', *Medium Aevum*, **55**, 24–40.

(1987b)   *The Clerkly Maker: Langland's Poetic Art*, *PP* Studies, Vol. IV (Cambridge: D. S. Brewer).

Schweitzer (1974)   Edward C. Schweitzer, ' "Half a Laumpe Lyne in Latyne" and Patience's Riddle in *PP*', *JEGP*, **73**, 313–27.

Simpson (1985)   James Simpson, 'Spiritual and Earthly Nobility in *PP*', *NM*, **83**, 467–81.

(1986a)   'From Reason to Affective Knowledge: Modes of Thought and Poetic Form in *PP*', *Medium Aevum*, **55**, 1–23.

(1986b)   'The Transformation of Meaning: A Figure of Thought in *PP*', *RES* n. s., **37**, 161–83.

(1986c)   'The Role of *Scientia* in *PP*', in *MERELGR*, pp. 49–65.

(1986d)   ' "Et Vidit Deus Cogitationes Eorum": A Parallel Instance and Possible Source for Langland's Use of a Biblical Formula at *PP* B. XV. 202a', *N & Q* n. s., **33**, 9–13.

(1987)   'Spirituality and Economics in Passus 1–7 of the B-Text', *YLS*, **1**, 83–103.

Smalley (1960)   Beryl Smalley, *English Friars and Antiquity in the Early Fourteenth Century* (Oxford: Blackwell).

(1964)   *The Study of the Bible in the Middle Ages* (Notre Dame, Ind.: University of Notre Dame Press).

Southern (1963)   Richard Southern, *St Anselm and his Biographer: A Study of Monastic Life and Thought 1059–c. 1130* (Cambridge: CUP).

Spearing (1972)   A. C. Spearing, 'The Art of Preaching and *PP*', in *Criticism and Medieval Poetry*, second edition (New York: Edward Arnold), pp. 107–34.

(1976)   *Medieval Dream Poetry* (Cambridge: CUP).

Starkey (1981)   David Starkey, 'The Age of the Household: Politics, Society, and the Arts *c*. 1350–c. 1550', in *The Later Middle Ages*, edited by Stephen Medcalf (London: Methuen), pp. 225–90.

Stokes (1984)   Myra Stokes, *Justice and Mercy in PP* (London and Canberra: Croom Helm).

Sumption (1975)   Jonathan Sumption, *Pilgrimage: An Image of Mediaeval Religion* (London: Faber and Faber).

Szittya (1977)   Penn R. Szittya, 'The Anti-Fraternal Tradition in Middle English Literature', *Speculum*, **52**, 287–313.

Thrupp (1948)   Sylvia L. Thrupp, *The Merchant Class of Medieval London 1300–1500* (Chicago: University of Chicago Press).

Traver (1907)   Hope Traver, *The Four Daughters of God*, Bryn Mawr Monographs, Vol. 4 (Bryn Mawr).

Turville-Petre (1977)   Thorlac Turville-Petre, *The Alliterative Revival* (Cambridge: D. S. Brewer).

Waldron (1986)   R. A. Waldron, 'Langland's Originality: The Christ-Knight and the Harrowing of Hell', in *MERELGR*, pp. 66–81.

Wenzel (1988)   Siegfried Wenzel, 'Medieval Sermons', in Alford, pp. 155 –72.

White (1986)   Hugh White, 'Langland's Ymaginatif, Kynde and the

Benjamin Minor', *Medium Aevum*, **55**, 241–8.

(1988) *Nature and Salvation in PP*, PP Studies, Vol. VI (Cambridge: D. S. Brewer).

Wittig (1972) Joseph Wittig, '*PP* B, Passus IX–XII: Elements in the Design of the Inward Journey', *Traditio*, **28**, 211–80.

Yunck (1963) John A. Yunck, *The Lineage of Lady Meed: the Development of Mediaeval Venality Satire* (Notre Dame: University of Notre Dame Press).

(1988) 'Satire', in Alford, pp. 135–54.

Index